LEST WE FORGET

— STORIES OF CANADA AT WAR —

ILLUSTRATED EDITION
FROM *LEGION MAGAZINE*

PROSPERO
B·O·O·K·S

LIBRARY AND ARCHIVES CANADA CATALOGUING IN PUBLICATION

Lest We Forget: Stories of Canada at War/selected by Jane Dewar from the pages of *Legion Magazine.*

First ed. published Toronto: Lester & Orpen Dennys, 1986 under title: True Canadian War Stories.

ISBN 978-1-55267-708-7

1. World War, 1939–1945—Personal narratives, Canadian. 2. World War, 1914–1918—Personal narratives, Canadian. I. Dewar, Jane II. Title: True Canadian War Stories.
FC543.T78 2008   940.54'8171   C2008-903120-2

This collection produced for Prospero Books.

Key Porter Books Limited
Six Adelaide Street East, Tenth Floor
Toronto, Ontario
Canada M5C 1H6
www.keyporter.com

Cover design: Muse Publishing and Communications Inc.
Electronic formatting: Muse Publishing and Communications Inc.
www.musecommunications.ca

Front cover photograph: Jack H. Smith, Library and Archives Canada—PA-166370
Back cover photograph: Vancouver Public Archives, Photo 8516

Printed and bound in China.

08 09 10 11 12 5 4 3 2 1

CONTENTS

INTRODUCTION

Grand strategy is not the stuff of these stories. They are, for the most part, memories that light up the small corners of great events. Taken together, they give a sense of how two major wars and a so-called police action shaped the Canadian character and influenced our postwar development. And they come from a unique record of those years.

Legion Magazine has been gathering these experiences for sixty-eight years. Beginning life as *The Veteran*, the voice of The Great War Veterans Association, in 1917, it became *The Legionary* in 1926 when veterans' associations joined together to form The Canadian Legion of the British Empire Service League, and was reincarnated as *Legion Magazine* in 1969.

Choosing from abundance posed problems. We ended up with material that reflected the times, the conditions, and the people; a few stories can be appreciated now for what they revealed of the future. The style of the stories varies too, reflecting the time of publication. We regret what had to be left out.

Jane Dewar
Editor and General Manager
Legion Magazine
Ottawa, March 1986

PART I

∿

THE FIRST WORLD WAR

DEAR DAD
Gordon L. McIntosh

Niagara Camp, Sept. 24, 1915
Right after dinner we fell in and marched over for our first inoculation. They inject the serum with a hypodermic needle just below your collar bone, 500 germs the first dose, 1,000 the second and 1,500 the third and then a vaccination on top of that. I'm beginning to feel dopey combined with cold chills....

St. Martin's Plain, Shorncliffe, Kent, England, Oct. 28, 1915
We arrived here OK last Tuesday at noon, just about all in after being on baggage fatigue from 10:30 Monday morning until after 6 at night. It's no joke working down in the hold of an ocean liner moving heavy boxes of rifles and all the rest of the stores and equipment of 1,800 men. We didn't have our boots and puttees off from 4:30 Monday morning until Tuesday night.

St. Martin's Plain, Nov. 10, 1915
It was a beautiful night last night and we could distinctly hear the booming of the big guns at the front and every once in a while the whole southeastern sky would be lighted with the glare of battle. It's hard for one to realize that he is so near the actual seat of war but it makes one realize how close the actual fighting is when he sees the hospital ships come in, as Alan and I did last Sunday at Folkestone.

Folkestone, Dec. 22, 1915
A new order was issued last Saturday telling us that from Jan. 1st our pay will be $1.60 a day instead of $1.10 so we will be OK. So you will not need to send $5 per month to me. Thank you very much just the same, but you can probably put it to better use than I can. When we get to France we only draw a franc a day (20¢) but that will be plenty for me to get along on....

France, May 8, 1916
Such an enormous amount of heavy traffic would spoil the best road built, and it keeps a lot of men busy keeping them in shape. Large numbers of civilians are employed and I never saw such slow, lazy beggars in my life. When they're breaking stone it takes them about five minutes to decide where they'll hit it, and about as long to lift the hammer for the next blow.... The people, on the whole, treat the soldiers very well, but they certainly soak us for anything we buy. Right out here in the country we have to pay 4¢ apiece for eggs and bread is 15¢ a loaf.

What's left of Courcelette, France, in 1916.

France, May 14, 1916
If Sam Hughes could hear the opinions expressed of him by the fellows over here, I don't think he'd feel like coming over to review 'his' troops....It certainly isn't very encouraging to the fellows over here, who get the dirty end of the stick, to have our ministers and statesmen so damnably indifferent and inefficient.

* Selected by his son, Dave McIntosh

The suburbs of Lens, France, as seen from Hill 70 in 1917.

Belgium, July 16, 1916

After five days incessant shelling we have had a rest for the past two days, but we expect that Fritz will break loose again at any old time. It certainly is an awful strain to be under shellfire for such a length of time, and we get some idea of what the fellows in the trenches have to go through. Our nerves were worn to a raw edge, and we would jump if a door banged.

Belgium, July 27, 1916

The asphyxiating gas kills every living thing it touches, and rots sandbags in to a substance flimsier than thistledown, so you can imagine what it will do to one's lungs.

Belgium, Aug. 10, 1916

The news from all the fronts certainly is good and we are all feeling very cheerful and looking forward to a speedy victory....What do you think of me trying for a commission in the Royal Flying Corps?...The chief question is, is it worth while at this late date?

France, Sept. 11, 1916

We got caught on a narrow road and were held up until 800 horses passed us twice, going to and from a watering place.

Canadian Corps, Nov. 26, 1916

Today we had the afternoon off, so we went in to a nearby town for a bath. There are splendid baths there which are used by, and in fact were built for, the miners. It is a great big building, with hundreds of shower baths in it, and one can use all the hot water he wants. It is all built with tiled floors and there are lockers for clothes. It sure is fine, when one remembers how for months he has had to bath in a pailful of lukewarm water.

France, Nov. 27, 1916

It is some consolation to know that Roy was killed by a clean bullet wound and died instantly. He was not blown to atoms like lots of poor fellows, or mangled and suffering for a long time.

France, Dec. 14, 1916

The parcels have been coming to me in bunches these past few days. Got one from Elsie today, with a peach of a leather vest in it from Jean and Chris and her. If I'm not warm enough this winter, it's my own fault. Also got a parcel from the Beebe Camp-Fire Girls, containing tobacco, candy, etc.

France, Jan. 3, 1917
(on return from London and first leave in a year)

The number of loose women running around London is appalling. And they are practically living off the soldiers on leave. Some of them, a great many in fact, are nothing but mere children.... You asked me in a previous letter if the authorities issue rum to the men. Yes, they do, but in such small quantities there is not much danger of it hurting them. It is issued to the fellows in the trenches every morning at 'stand-down,' one large tablespoonful to each man. When a fellow has 'stood to' all night in a trench with the rain pouring down, or lain out in a shell-hole for hours at a stretch on 'listening post,' he needs something to stimulate him. I know of plenty of cases of men who never take a drink out of the trenches, but who take their rum issue every morning when they are in…. The cold weather causes us a lot of extra work as we have to drain the radiator on our lorry every night and fill it again in the morning and whenever we stop it has to be bundled up like an invalid.

France, Jan. 15, 1917

Am glad you received my cable and letter in time for Christmas Day. It certainly must have been very lonely for you all but we can look forward to Christmas, 1917. I'm sure we shall all be home then.

France, Feb. 4, 1917

'What will the U.S. do now?' is what we are all wondering over here and we are all eagerly awaiting developments. If the States does come in, the last refuge of the slackers in Canada, in case of conscription, will be gone, which will be one good thing it will accomplish…. My French is pretty good now, but there is still plenty of room for improvement. I certainly get plenty of opportunity to use it, and I can carry on a conversation fairly well now.

France, Oct. 4, 1917

P.S. Aunt Jean is very much incensed over the fact that I cannot get leave and I am afraid she will be writing the War Office about it.

France, Nov. 28, 1917

The war loan appeared on orders today and all the men are requested to invest what they can and, besides helping themselves, help the cause a little more. I suppose the five-year bonds would be the best for you to buy for me from my bank credit. Perhaps the war will last so long that I shall just get home in time to redeem them myself.

France, Jan. 23, 1918

I have made application for a commission as pilot in the Royal Flying Corps and my papers are in the orderly room now to be forwarded to headquarters…. If I get through all right, I shall be doing far more than I am at present to help along the cause which we all have so much at heart.

France, April 30, 1918

I was in a place yesterday which of late has been almost incessantly bombed and shelled by Fritz, and you cannot imagine what it is like to drive through a city, through street after street, and never meet a living soul and see nothing but gaping walls and roofless buildings. It gave me the creeps and, apart from the shells, high explosive and shrapnel, which were bursting on the outskirts of the town all the time we were there, I was mighty glad to go. It will take years of repair to make the place habitable once more…. We go up for our interview with the RAF officer on May 3rd and I hope he passes us all.

C Flight, 4 Sqdn., No. 1, RAF Cadet Wing, Hastings, June 28, 1918

We men who have served overseas have to be very particular as more is expected of us than of the chaps of 19 who have just joined up. Our belts and rifle slings have to be kept spotlessly white and all brass parts of our equipment, buttons etc. must positively dazzle one…. We expect to get our new RAF uniforms in a couple of weeks. The new uniform is blue, I believe.

Royal Air Force, Christ Church, Oxford, Sept. 11, 1918

The latest rumor around here is that our course at the school of armaments will last for nine weeks instead of three. Of course all this preliminary work is very necessary, but I would like to get down to the real work and I'm afraid Heinie will throw in the sponge before I get a chance to drop some nice large scenery removers on him.

Ardchoille, Airdrie, Scotland, Nov. 17, 1918

Here I am, still on leave, and wondering what is going to happen to me now that the war is over and I don't belong to anyone really. Have received no posting orders yet and yesterday a letter from the air force told me that my leave was extended indefinitely and I only wish I could pack up and beat it for home. I cannot tell you how I am looking forward to getting home again.

Royal Air Force, Yatesbury, Wilts, Jan. 4, 1919

From what we hear the chances of an early return are good, as cadets are being sent back as quickly as possible, so I may be home by the end of January after all.

Shorncliffe, Kent, March 17, 1919

Things are very gay in London just now and one cannot wonder at the people letting loose after the terrible four years of strain they have been through. Labor troubles certainly look bad, though, and if this railway and miners' strike comes off it will paralyse everything and still further delay our return home, of which there seems no immediate prospect. When I returned to camp I was received with the joyful news that we are all to receive our commissions, our clothing allowance and first-class passage home, so the air ministry has come to its senses at last…. Perhaps when they get the German mercantile marine at work we shall stand more chance of getting home before we are all old and grey. The fellows are all thoroughly fed up and about ripe for almost any kind of a disturbance…. Hoping that it won't be long before I shall be on my way home, I remain, as ever,

Your affectionate son,
Gordon ◡⌐

AN INCIDENT
James Frances

The second draft for overseas service was very much like the first, and, for that matter, it differed little from those that were to follow. It was the same heterogeneous collection of saints and sinners, rich and poor, the good, the bad, and the utterly indifferent, sharing the same characteristics as the others. Their common trait was a good physique, their common anxiety was to get over there, and their common fear was that all would be over before they could get there. And these characteristics held them together in spite of orderly-room sergeants, and inoculations, and physical jerks, and the thousand and one petty annoyances of army routine. They were a motley assortment, indeed. Smart looking ex-Imperials rubbed shoulders with the latest graduates from the awkward squad, who had but lately acquired the art of lifting one foot past the other with some semblance of measure. The hard-boiled marched and slept and ate with the tenderfoot, and managed somehow to keep from treading on his toes. The down-town business man meekly right-turned and formed-fours and galloped distractedly in open formation at the peremptory command of his erstwhile shipping clerk. A motley assortment, indeed. But no one had yet dreamt of Ypres, or Vimy Ridge, or of the Canadians entering Mons.

Nobody had paid much attention to McAllister before the arrival of the draft at Shorncliffe. The few whom the fortune of war had thrown in contact with him had given little thought to the matter and were generally content, when his queerness was mentioned, to pass it off with a joke or a suggestive tap on the forehead. To put it more plainly, the Platoon was of the opinion that poor Mac was mildly and harmlessly insane, and a subject of speculation to some of the more reflective minds was how he had managed to enlist, and why. Not that there was anything in his appearance to suggest that he had "put one over" on the medical examiner. He walked, talked, and acted outwardly as any sober and rational person would do, and if a strange light would shine at times in those candid blue eyes no one gave it more than a passing thought. For those were stirring days when the hardest and steadiest would suddenly find themselves the centre of an emotional vortex, when sensations hitherto unexperienced would seize upon the fabric of the nervous system and thrill its owner to an emotional standstill. There was no lack of stimuli, and McAllister, on account of his highly temperamental character, probably received more than his share. It was generally conceded, in any case, that there were lots on the effective much crazier than he. And Mac had shown himself a model soldier. He was a good man on parade, and he was always attentive, obedient, cheerful and willing. He was consequently esteemed by the officers and the non-coms, and he was liked by his comrades, but, curiously enough, he had no intimate friend or crony. While the rest of the gang were enjoying a few hours' leave after a hard day's training, or flitting around the various little distractions which the camp afforded, Mac could invariably be found in his cot, reading his Bible. And the din and racket occasioned by the bed-time preparations of half a hundred rough and tumble soldiers would always soften a little while Mac knelt down, on his bare knees, for a few minutes of silent prayer which preceded "Lights Out."

One of the few subjects which Mac liked to discuss was the probable cause of the war. "The Germans," he was once heard to say, "were a good people, but they have turned away from the Lord." An impious listener pleasantly inquired if it were McAllister's mission to bring the wanderers back to the fold, but Mac merely turned a compassionate eye in his direction and smiled rather sadly. He was clearly aggrieved that anyone could approach so serious a subject in so frivolous a spirit. We were not left long in doubt, however, as to the nature of his mission. To a few of the older and more serious-minded men

McAllister one evening suggested that plans be made for the launching of a stirring religious revival. The need for a movement of this kind was evidently urgent. He had little faith in the efficacy of the conventional agencies—religion sandwiched between cheerful songs and coffee and cakes was too easy-going altogether—and the time was at hand when the work of salvation must be taken up more earnestly. He had had a vision, he said, in which his own figure had appeared clothed in a Highland uniform, leading the Platoon in a victorious charge on the battlefield. His listeners, unfortunately, were not greatly impressed by his proposal, or perhaps they lacked the all-essential enthusiasm which Mac was vainly endeavoring to instil. In any case, nothing was done; the boys continued to frequent the Y.M.C.A. and the Methodist Mission, to roar out hymns and imbibe hot tea, and Mac reluctantly relapsed into his accustomed reserve. The rumors which had been associating the second overseas draft with a Highland battalion suddenly ceased and a few days later we were on our way to reinforce the —th.

We had been in the front line just three or four days when I was awakened, one morning, by the sound of a heated altercation going on directly in front of the dugout. The stentorian voice of the Company Sergeant-Major was insistently commanding someone to come down and to stay down, and each of the commands, as they issued from under the stubborn mustache of the C.S.M., was accompanied by a long and loud volley of hair-raising expletives. After the storm had somewhat subsided, I cautiously withdrew the gunny sack which served for a front door, and peered out anxiously into the bay. Against the parapet stood McAllister, flushed and obviously annoyed, grasping his rifle so tightly that the veins stood out in knotted lumps on his hands. Further along the section the C.S.M. could be heard raging away, the sound growing fainter in the distance. Grabbing my own rifle I trailed along in his wake and arrived at Company headquarters in time to hear him make his report. He had to complain, it appeared, of the conduct of Private McAllister, who insisted on standing on the firing step, with his head and shoulders showing above the parapet in full view of the enemy, after the danger of such a practice had been repeatedly pointed out to him. When remonstrated with, Private McAllister would only reply that a Higher Power than the Company Sergeant-Major was protecting him, and that no harm could touch him. The Company Commander's usual cheerful grin had disappeared completely by the time the C.S.M. had completed his narrative, and after some discussion it was agreed that Private McAllister should be sent to the rear as soon as the battalion was relieved, and would not be permitted in future to return to the line.

It happened the following morning. Mac was standing on the firing step in his usual position, and I was busily engaged scraping the mud off my legs with a Lee Enfield bayonet. I had just warned Mac of the danger to which he was exposed, but he had taken no heed. I was looking at him as he stood there, his hands in the pockets of his greatcoat, his rifle resting in the crook of his arm, waiting for him to speak. A few words left his lips when—CRACK!—the phrase was cut short, and poor McAllister fell forward on his knees, his jugular severed by a sniper's bullet. Shrieking for stretcher-bearers, I hastened to render whatever help I could, but Mac was already beyond the reach of all human aid.

We placed him on the low parados and covered him with sheet and blanket until the night would come when we could carry him out for burial. The smile of the old days was still on his lips, and the sightless eyes were staring, wide open, into eternity.... ॐ

EYES! EYES! EYES!
Will R. Bird

It was when the "Prairie Squirrels" were at Parvillers that Pete Mullins was sent down the line as a shell-shocked case, with every man in his platoon knowing that he had not been near a shell explosion. Yet none of them derided him, or said he was swinging the lead, for he was, for the time at least, as pitiful a physical wreck as one would care to see.

He kept hiding his face with his hands, and shuddering, and when they got him to bed at the hospital he lay for six days with his face to the wall. When they spoke to him or tried to get him to turn all he would say was "Eyes—eyes—eyes."

Ted Hiller was with Pete all that terrible day when he saw the eyes, and it was Ted who told me the story.

It was the morning after Parvillers was captured, he said, and Pete and I were out in a sort of fox hole we were using as a listening post. We figured that we were about half way across No Man's Land, but things were in such a jumble down there that we couldn't be sure. It was a jungle of old wire and trenches where the fighting the day before had been bloody and hard, and where our guns had smashed things completely.

The hole we were in was a pit like a well, deep enough for us to stand in, and big enough to let one sit down when he was on watch. There were big weeds and thistles all around the hole and we could look through them. I thought it was as good a place as any for the day, but old Pete was nervous. In the attack on the 8th Pete had been nearly shot by one of our own boys, who mistook him for a Fritz when he tried on one of their pot helmets, and the old man's nerves hadn't got over the shock. Our section was about thirty yards behind us, in a stretch of old trench, but Pete thought they should be nearer.

When it got real light I got up and did first sentry. I reached out and made little lanes through the weeds and we had a corking good field of observation. I watched the right for a while at first, and it was one grand mess of rotting sandbags and jumbled timbers and old trench revetting and broken brick. Old Pete got to his feet after a while and started to stare out on the left. Then he gasped and grabbed my arm. "Look—see," he gurgled.

To the left of our pit, seated in a hollow, was a Heinie. His steel lid lay at his feet and his face was a gray color that matched his tunic. He was sitting among a rubble of splintered plank, braced there as rigid as if something had taken his attention, but stone-dead!

There was a blood-clotted bandage lying beside him and we could see that he had been trying to dress an awful wound in his thigh. He must have died of shock as he sat there, or else a bullet had got him through the heart. His eyes gave me an uneasy feeling. They were dull and unobservant, but curiously disturbing, for they seemed to be focused full on us, as if he were watching us in a disinterested fashion. Pete insisted on changing sides with me at once. "I can't stand the look of that man's eyes," he whispered, and his whisper was shrill.

I'll own I found it a test myself. I couldn't seem to avoid them, and their dull, unwinking stare was enough to give anyone the creeps. I tried looking away beyond him and studying other things. I tried to pick out Heinie's new lines, to see a machine gun post, to watch for aeroplanes, anything I could think of, but in five minutes it would be as if I were simply forced to look at those wide-open, expressionless eyes.

Finally I made myself look at the wreckage of a machine gun emplacement. A big shell had made a direct hit and sandbags and timbers and steel rails were scattered in all directions. A sap had led to the post, and it was blocked completely. Where it entered the main trench the parapet had been blown away, and as I watched I saw a man raise his head. It was a Heinie, and I knew by the way he got up and looked around that he had no idea where we were.

I watched that place for over an hour and in that time saw eight or ten Germans. Then an officer came and got up and looked over our way. After that I couldn't see anyone except a sentry who had stayed in plain view. It was very quiet. Not a plane was over and none of our guns were firing in that sector. The war was away over on our flanks.

It began to get hot. There was no breeze at all and the sun was blistering hot, choking hot, in our burrow. Sweat scalded and blinded us. After a while the distant guns seemed to tone down until the quiet itself was irritating. Then flies, those big blue ones, began to buzz about the dead Heinie, and we noticed that there were dreadful smells. My stomach almost turned.

It seemed an eternity before noon. We had sneaked out to our pit before it was light and there was no hope of being relieved until it was dark again. We had only a little water with us and it had got so warm and brackish that we couldn't drink it. The German sentry at the saphead got himself a plank seat and sat on it as he watched our way. I had my field glasses and focused them on him. He was staring in a vacant way, and was dirty and not shaved and very tired looking.

All at once Pete grabbed me again. "Eyes!" he hissed, in a way that made me jump. "Just eyes."

I squeezed over beside him and he pointed at the debris near us, where crossed rails, tangled in a V, seemed to cover an opening of sorts, possibly a small crater. There was a narrow, dark opening down beneath them. "There were eyes in that hole," he whimpered. "I seen them."

I watched and watched, and the minutes dragged by. I was fighting flies all the time and I was acutely aware of the dead German. I was cussing all smells and was properly fed up with everything—when I saw them. My scalp seemed to crawl and I fairly froze. Two eyes had certainly appeared in the gap under the rails, and they had simply glared into mine. I felt as if I had had a look at some weird underground monster. One instant was all I saw them, then they vanished.

It was all so utterly unreal that I leaned back and wiped the sweat from my forehead and eyebrows, and then I looked again. For a long time I couldn't see a thing but that black, narrow space under the wreckage—then the eyes were there. They seemed to leap into the place, and I couldn't make out a face to fit them into. They stayed longer that second time and I flinched from them in spite of myself. I never saw such a mixture of fear and hatred and madness in eyes of any kind as in those faceless orbs under the rails.

My first impulse was to take a shot at them, and then I realized that it would be suicide to do so. Old Heinie could snipe us if we tried to leave our hole, and if we fired a shot he would know where we were. Then I wondered if the eyes belonged to a German scout who had made himself a listening post under the debris. No man could possibly have wormed down between the steel rails which were crossed, and I was certain that the eyes did not belong to any sane person. All at once a Heinie machine gun opened up and its bullets were cracking and snapping over us for five or ten minutes. Pete was sure that Fritz had discovered us, and he begged me to throw a Mills bomb into the hole when the eyes returned.

I talked to him and quieted him but he kept whimpering every once in a while and pushing against me so that I could feel him shaking. That place was enough to try any one's nerves, but he got my goat and I talked to him rough till he stopped his whimper. I had the safety of my rifle released all the time, and a couple of Mills bombs ready to throw. A bunch of aeroplanes droned over us, but there was no other sound. The machine gun had stopped firing as suddenly as it commenced. The sun got fair overhead and the heat in that hole was suffocating. Flies had come in clouds and they were all over the dead Heinie, at his wound, in his ears, clustering in his hair and around those eyes that watched us. A rat appeared and went over to him and nosed the bloody bandage, but those dull, unintelligent

eyes looked at me all the time. I had to shift over to the other side of the pit.

The eyes were there in the dark hole again! They appeared as if my glance had called him. For a full minute they looked straight into mine and I felt as if I were being mesmerized, then there was nothing but the void between the rails. I wondered if the sun was playing tricks with us. There were heat waves dancing all over the wreckage. I watched a long time, but could only see the black gap, and was feeling quite relieved—when they popped up again.

An hour went by. I had been looking at my watch every twenty minutes since morning. Sometimes those eyes were there, sometimes they weren't, until at last I felt that I would get as bad as Pete. He wouldn't try to look over at all but stayed huddled down in the hole, making funny little noises like a hurt thing.

The Heinie sentry stayed on his plank and stared in his stolid way. He must have been tortured by the heat, but he never moved other than to scratch himself regularly. I ducked down beside Pete and tried to eat my ration of bread and cheese, but had such a nausea that I couldn't swallow a bit. Pete wouldn't try to. He just moaned and wanted to know how much longer we would be there. I stood up, and those livid eyes under the rail seemed to almost jump at me. It gave me such a queer sensation that I had to squat down again. When I rose up they were still there, and more malignant than ever. I prodded Pete. "You get up and take a turn," I said, as savagely as I could. "I'm tired of looking all the time."

He got up—looked—and ducked, white-faced and trembling, and I had to clap my hand over his mouth to keep him from crying out. He had looked out his own side, at the dead German. "He's moved—he's moved," he gulped through my fingers.

The sweat on my skin turned cold and goose flesh was all over me. Pete was telling the truth. That Fritz had moved. He had shifted so that his hand had dropped down, black and curled like a hen's foot, and his tunic collar was tight under his chin as his head tipped forward. He seemed nearer to us.

I tried to soothe myself, for I was getting mighty shaky. There was some explanation, surely. It was only three o'clock. Five hours to go before we could expect a relief. I squatted down again. "You've got to look over part of the time," I growled. "It's too hot for one man to keep his head up all the time, and if we don't watch the Heinies are liable to sneak over on us."

He muttered about something, but got up. Then he shot down again, gasping. He sobbed with fear and he caught me around the knees. I grabbed a bomb and jumped up. A pair of small, beady, blood-red eyes were peering through the weeds not a foot from mine. It was a rat! Ugh! I spit at him. Those eyes were cruel, foul glitters.

Pete whimpered and clung to me and wouldn't listen to anything I said to him. Our long day of fighting, and the killing, had shaken his nerves badly. We had taken the ground we were on on the previous day and it had not been a picnic. The eyes under the rails drew mine every time I looked over. They had a sort of fascination, there was something uncanny about them. I squirmed around Pete and looked over on the left, at the dead man. One long look and I was almost as bad as Pete. I pulled him to his feet. "Look over there," I said. "I'm going to beat it before something else happens. That Heinie's moved again."

Pete stood and shuddered and licked his lips. "He moved, he moved, he moved," he whispered in a sing-song, and then he began to blab about eyes.

The German had moved. One leg, the unwounded one, was almost doubled now. Not a shot had been fired since noon, and there had been nothing to move him. I stared around, felt dizzy. The sun blazed down unmercifully, and I felt that all around us there were eyes and eyes and eyes, staring, glaring, beady eyes, dull, unmoving eyes, eyes without faces; eyes…eyes…eyes.

Then I yelled, and Pete caught at me like a wild man. Flies had swarmed all over the dead man's nose and as I looked I had seen his eyes close!

Pete caught at me again, but I fought him back and jumped out of the pit. I never thought of the German sentry at all. I jumped a shell hole and hopped over old wire and slid into the trench where our section was— and was lucky not to get shot. Our chaps had been half asleep and they had all seized their rifles. Then Pete came tearing in, and he ripped his puttees off his legs on the wire.

I told our chaps what I had seen and then we had to take charge of Pete. He got to shaking so that he couldn't stop and we had to send him back to the transport lines. He got worse all the way back.

Our corporal was hard to scare and my story made him curious. Not a shot had been fired at Pete or me and so he crawled out through the wire and put up his tin hat. Nothing happened and so he went on till he reached our pit. He looked over and couldn't see the sentry I had told him about. So he signalled us to join him.

Half an hour later we had worked around till our platoon was in the trench where we had seen the Germans. They had beat it. We looked at the dead man. His eyes were closed, and they wouldn't believe me when I said they had been open. Then I showed them the gap under the rails—and eyes looked up at us!

"Who the hell are you?" yelled the corporal. "Speak up, or I'll heave a bomb down there."

He would have, too, but just then our officer came and took charge of things. We told him about the eyes, and he set us to work pulling away the wreckage. After we got the top stuff away we found that there was only room enough for a man's head to show in the hole. We pried the rails apart—and there was our German!

He was a pitiful figure. Evidently he was one of the German machine-gun crew and had been buried by the shell that wrecked the post. He was so badly shell-shocked that he had lost his voice, and his mind was affected. He would only glare at us. Our stretcher-bearers doped him and they took him away.

Then one of our chaps crawled into the cavity and explored. He found a timbered passage that led under the refuse on which the dead Heinie was lying. The shell-shocked man had tried to force his way out there and his efforts had moved the corpse. As the dead man's head tipped forward the stiff collar of his tunic had pushed up the skin of his face and closed his eyes. The corporal pushed his head back and they opened! Ugh!

You know these advance advertisements they throw on the screen at the movies, how the eyes sometimes appear first? Well, I didn't go to the pictures for three years after I came home for fear I'd see them.

Pete was never sent back to the battalion. ↶

BUSINESS IS BUSINESS
Gregory Clark

"What we need," said Marrigat, "is a stick of dynamite about twenty feet long."

"Or," said Sir John Hawkins, "a derrick and one of these 'ere 'ooks."

"A keg of stumping powder," added Beaubien.

"Well, why not make a stick of dynamite twenty feet long?" asked Brown. "Take a piece of one-inch pipe, and fill her full of ammonal and put a fuse to her—bingo."

Marrigat got up and said:

"Come on. That's done already."

These four, Marrigat's gang, had been notified to stand by for a raid, an identification raid. The major had discovered Marrigat's gang in the midst of his company at Vimy, where these four inseparables, who marched abreast, bunked together, ate together, played together, and shared all, had performed at least half a dozen miracles: outflanked a pair of machine guns, cut the main cable of the enemy telephone system, catapulted red ground flares an enormous distance so that the enemy guns, thinking this to be the new British line, shelled short and destroyed their own last line of defence; and that four volunteering as crew to a Stokes gun sergeant induced him to fire air-bursts at a low-flying aeroplane that was trying to solve the riddle of the ground flares. It was those air bursts, fuses cut down to three seconds, that took the major over to the gun and to the discovery of Marrigat's gang in the innocent midst of his own command.

"Who the blazes?" demanded the major, kneeling on the rim of the large shell hole where the Stokes was uplifting its stovepipe snout.

"Whuff!" coughed the Stokes, as Marrigat himself leaned smartly away from the gun. A whiskey-bottle shell leaped soaring into the sky; the German machine, hastening now, roared over, and the short-fused shell, dangerously short, burst with a grey smash to one side of the banking Hun.

Marrigat, watching, turned a happy face to the major.

"What's the idea?" said the major, in his party manner. "Are you aware that you are likely to get your bloody head blown off? Get back to your platoon. Are you the sergeant of this gun?"

"Yessir. I lost my crew. These men came and offered to run it, if I would show them."

Marrigat said:

"The Hun has went home."

All looked, and the machine was speeding away into the east.

"Well," said the major, "Marrigat, you stay here with these three and serve the gun until the sergeant gets his own relief for you. But don't tinker with fuses, you hear? Stokes guns are not Archies."

The major was slightly elated as he scuttered back to the trench where his company lay. "I've got to use those boys."

That was how Marrigat's gang was discovered. Vimy won Marrigat and Sir John Hawkins the military medal. A raid five weeks later placed the same decoration on the tunics of Beaubien and Brown.

They were excused duty, in and out of the line. They were designated as raiders. The time they had on their hands was left to them to think up new ways of distressing the enemy.

"A little raid," said the major, "an identification raid. Brigade wants only one identification, still in good condition, if possible, still able to speak. Now, let me know to-night what you would like to do. Take a look at the lay of the land. Have a talk with the scouts."

With the scout sergeant they made a tour of No Man's Land at dark, and found a place where the wire was only twenty feet across, good and thick, matted. And beyond the wire they heard a German with a bad cold.

Beaubien, when they got in, said:

"Now, if he has got a bad cough, likely the whole platoon has got a bad cold, eh?"

"In effect, yes," said Sir John.

"That's where we go in, then," said Beaubien.

Here Marrigat said:

"What we need is a stick of dynamite, twenty feet long."

So, with Brownie's suggestion of a pipe full of ammonal, the Mills bomb explosive, and a very pretty one, the four went back to a ruined village to find a piece of pipe.

They had not long to look. In the best house in the village they found a length of inch pipe about thirty feet long, and they carried it back to the support trench, where bomb stores were.

With an enormous pull-through and emery paper, they wiped the rusty pipe clean, poured it full of explosive, bored a small hole in a lead plug for the fuse and plugged her tight.

With this strange weapon they crawled out, at nine o'clock, dark, sliding it with them as they crawled. It took them an hour and a half to insert the awkward length of pipe under the matted, tangled barbed wire. It met obstructions time after time, but at last they thrust it home—all the way.

Uncoiling the fuse, they withdrew forty feet, and sent Brown back to tell the major to get ready for a bang.

Brown came back and whispered, "O.K."

Sir John Hawkins, the derrick worker, accustomed to mines and quarries, fired the fuse with the major's cigaret butt that Brown had brought out from the trench, reversed, in his mouth.

The instantaneous fuse hissed, and forty feet away a huge flame and roar leaped up. Marrigat and his gang lay with eyes tight shut, face to the ground. While the debris was still falling the four scrambled up, charged the spot of the explosion, and found as they had expected, a large lane torn in the belt of tangled barbed wire.

Marrigat in front, pistol in hand, slid into the splendidly planked German trench. Brown behind him had a large iron nut slid on to the handle of his trenching tool. This made a little club called a whiffer. Sir John and Beaubien followed, carrying nose bags full of Mills bombs.

Their ears, dulled by the explosion, could still make out the clatter of near-by machine guns in the night. Their job was immediately lighted by a cloud of German flares, shot aloft from right and left. In the vivid boarded trench, scattered full of dirt and torn wire, they stood waiting for an identification to show himself.

"Not more than twenty steps either way," shouted Marrigat. "Beaubien, this way." And he went left, making a grotesque shadow in the livid trench. Brown with his whiffer, and Sir John on his heels, with bombing arm laid back, ready to throw beyond, went right.

"One, two, three, four," counted Brownie, and paused at a bend. Around the bend came a German bayonet, thick and broad, and gleaming in the light of the constant flares. Slowly it came. Brownie and Sir John pressed themselves against the side of the trench. The bayonet, with infinite caution, came around, followed by the muzzle of a rifle. Brownie, his whiffer in his left hand, suddenly seized the muzzle and gave a great heave. The rifle exploded down the trench and a large German, with a vast shout, fell on his face at their feet. At the same instant Sir John lobbed a bomb lightly over the bend, where it fell, amid a furious thudding of feet, and exploded. Brown with his foot tipped the German's deep helmet forward and off, and cracked him neatly and lightly with the whiffer on the back of the head.

Lengthening each time, Sir John had rapidly thrown three more bombs, when, with a rush, Marrigat and Beaubien came from behind. Brown and these two took the German by the armpits and dragged him back to where the lane in the wire was. Sir John, his long arm flailing, began to lob his bombs in both directions.

Then Marrigat removed from his side pockets two bombs that looked like black tins of salmon. With a match he lit them and threw one to the left and one to the right. Dense clouds of white smoke rose up and spread before them. The lane screened against the green calcium glare of the flares, the party, a leg and an arm apiece, hauled their identification up out of the trench, and through the lane.

The white smoke billowed and eddied around them, choking them. But they reached a deep hole and lay in it.

For fifteen minutes the flares leaped and lobbed, the machine guns raved, back and forward. From the Canadian trench not a sound. The German field guns that had opened up died away. In a moment of darkness, Marrigat's gang and the identification scrambled up and on. Flare! Down they dropped at the tell-tale pop. In three minutes the major and ten men found them, took their burden from them and scuttled into the trench.

"Very neat," said the major. "Is he all right?"

"I just tapped him," said Brown.

"Just a little tap." He bent down and felt the German's head. "Yep! It's swelling. He's all right."

They poured cold water on the German's head and wrists, patted his wrists as if he had fainted, pillowed his head on Marrigat's lap.

He stirred, raised a hand to his brow.

They heaved him to his feet and led and pushed him, in dumb bewilderment, down towards the major's dugout. In the candle-lit chamber they sat him down on a bench, and the four stood smiling at him, while the major took the phone and told headquarters they had got a feldwebel for an identification. "Two seven seventh Bavarian," said he.

Rum was handed around. The German got his first. The four, in turn, held their granite cup of rum up to him.

"Good luck," said Marrigat.

"The war's over," toasted tall Sir John.

"Hoch der Kaiser," said Beaubien.

"Gesundheit!" greeted Brown, who had cracked him.

The four saluted the major; he, helmetless, smiled upon them. Up into the chill night they went, back down the trenches to the dugout and the soiled cribbage board. ॐ

WHAT PRICE LIBERTY?
Will R. Bird

Spring in the Ypres Salient! Its green was spread over the fields and hedges, and its urge was in the blood of the men who were billeted in St. Julien. They thrilled to the adventure of the trenches, organized spy hunts, prowled in the early dusk, eager to be doing something zestful. They were members of two platoons of No. 3 Company of the 13th Royal Highlanders of Canada, and it was irksome to be so restrained beside the headquarters staff; they wished to be with their fellows in the firing line.

A piano was being pounded by some ardent musician and lusty voices roared a chorus. Private Lorne A. Higgs and a comrade were strolling under a few trees near the houses, looking at the new graves there.

"Suppose," said the other chap, "the Germans had you cornered, would you surrender?"

"No," said Higgs, "I'd give them all I had as long as I lasted. They'll never take me prisoner."

The next day, April 22nd, was bright and peaceful. Higgs and his chum had found field glasses and they gazed at the trenches forward. These seemed to have flimsy defences, and only the shell holes in the green sod made it a war scene. Hedges lined the fields and here and there were clumps of trees while small brooks were silvery channels in the sunlight. One such divided two companies of the battalion.

The morning passed peacefully and the afternoon was waning when suddenly the German guns crashed in a terrible chorus and a deluge of shells fell on the ditch-like trench just ahead of supports. For two hours the shells rained down and sods and debris were hurtled high as black smoke mushroomed into a murky screen.

The men in St. Julien had stood to arms and there was eager comment. What did the Germans intend doing? Was it an attack? Then it came. A runner dodged into the village. "Gas!" he shouted. Gas! Gas? Using gas…why…surely not…gas?

The world became a chaos. There were orders and counter-orders, and soon night had come. All around the Salient seemed an arc of shell fire and machine guns rattled like mad things. Wounded men were streaming across the fields. Gasping, frothing Turcos had struggled to the hedge near St. Julien and were lying there, their rifles ready.

At dark Higgs was one of a party rushing up towards Poelcappelle, and they were to take position near some farmhouse. No one seemed certain of direction. A house loomed before them. Crack-crack-crack! A storm of rifle shots. The house was filled with the enemy!

The 13th men tumbled into the ditch, got into a field, fixed bayonets. Hand-to-hand fighting seemed inevitable, but the Germans stayed in the building. A moment, and the party rushed on. A guide had met them. Then they were in a line of sorts. Some bits of trench remained, little better than a ditch. Dead men were strewed around, wounded men, and rifles. They occupied shell holes, any cover. Daylight brought renewed shelling, sniping, fighting, but all day they clung to their trench. By the time night had fallen they were but half their strength of the morning, and many of those remaining had wounds.

Fall back! The order was whispered along, and soon they were back at a new angle, and enduring more shell fire. Morning brought ghastly revelations. Dead men were in sight in all directions, and few living survived. They seemed alone, in front. Fall back! The order was called hoarsely, and back they straggled, a few at a time, fighting, holding the enemy from an overwhelming rush. They stopped beside a brook and found shelter behind willows. The firing was terrific. They had had no rest, no respite. Ears were deafened by explosions. They felt that further endurance was impossible.

Fall back to right of St. Julien. Once more Higgs escaped the rain of bullets and reached a shell hole, a link along a sort of trench line. In it were members of the 10th Battalion, men of the 14th, and the officer

Canadian soldiers cover their eyes and help guide each other following a gas attack. The scene is part of the miniseries *Far From Home: Canada and the Great War.*

commanding was Major Ormond, of the 10th.

Suddenly a square of white appeared from the hedge in front. The Germans were behind it, and each man ceased fire as he saw the white emblem slowly hoisted and waved. What did it mean? Was it the Germans who occupied that trench back of the hedge? Or was it the French?

The white square was moved from side to side, insistent, demanding attention. "Someone should go see what they want." No one knew who spoke first but in a moment all were suggesting an advance. Then Corporal Wauchope, of the 10th Battalion, announced that he would go out if someone would volunteer to go with him. He looked at Higgs.

"All right," said Higgs, "I'll go."

"Then leave your rifle and equipment. They wouldn't let us go over with them."

"But what do they want? What's the use of going?" Higgs didn't like the look of things.

"We'll soon find out," urged Wauchope. "I speak German. Hurry up, before they take that white sign down."

It was about one hundred yards to the hedge, and Higgs halted as he saw a row of gray field caps behind it. No soldier was coming to meet them, there had been no movement.

"Let's go back," he said. "There's something wrong about this."

"Alt!" It was a harsh voice that bellowed a string of gutturals from the hedge, and Wauchope gulped.

"We've got to go in," he said. "They've got us covered and they've a machine gun at that. He says they'll shoot us like dogs unless we go on to the hedge."

There had come a short lull in the shelling and all at once they seemed to be exposed to all the German army. Higgs saw rifle muzzles poking through the hedge everywhere, dozens of them, scores of them. Then he discovered that he was walking towards them, alongside Wauchope.

It seemed a nightmare, a mad dream. The world was full of buzzing noises, of round, bronzed faces that stared at him, ugly faces that leered, rifle muzzles that threatened. He was conscious of a weakness in his knees, of warm perspiration, of a terrible desire to leap on someone and have it over with, to be killed. Wauchope said nothing, but had his hand on Higgs' elbow, guiding him, hurrying him.

The trench was just back of the hedge. Higgs saw a red face in front of him, felt a hot heavy hand on his. Then he was in the trench, among gray men. They jostled against him, feeling for weapons, pushing him along. In a moment he was in low ground, had left the trench and was being hurried along a path.

Wauchope was apart from him. The Canadian lines seemed a thousand miles away. A German with a revolver ready in his hands took place behind Higgs, another kept pace with him. They came to a wounded Canadian lying in the torn earth, and he called for water. Higgs had none, but he paused. The fellow was a 16th man.

"On." The German's revolver prodded him, and there was grim menace in the action. Life was cheap to the German.

British shells were screaming overhead and some dropped very near. The Germans flung themselves down, ran, ducked, dodged and showed great nervousness. But their prisoners were stoical. Not a man flinched, and they sneered at their escort.

A brick house was reached. It was a dressing station, and wounded Germans stood on the sheltered side. They glowered at Higgs, spoke among themselves. He was halted and pushed into a corner. A burly man with fixed bayonet stood guard over him. Higgs wanted a drink. He was hot and thirsty, and it was all so unreal. An hour before he had been with his mates.

More prisoners were brought in. They did not talk but stood as if in a stupor, dazed by swift happenings. Fifteen were grouped in the house, then they were marched to Roullers. Suddenly Higgs reacted to the situation. He realized all that had happened, and thought of papers he carried, a sketch of their positions he had made. As he marched he shredded them to bits, and his escort did not detect what he was doing.

They were ushered into a church, and other prisoners were there. German sentries closed about them, stripped off their badges, and searched for souvenirs. Some were handled roughly. An officer came and superintended a systematic search, but found nothing of importance. They spent the night in the upper part of a convent. Then they were loaded into box cars.

It seemed an endless journey. They were cramped together, thirsty, hungry, weary, disgusted with their luck. A guard told them they were being taken to Giessen, Germany, but no one cared. It was hot, and they opened the car doors. Presently they were passing through a village. Onlookers, men, women and children, shouted at sight of them. Thud! A clod of earth crashed against the car side. Then came a fusillade of stones, sticks and clods. They pushed the doors shut.

Among the crowded ones were many wounded men and during the long 31-hour trip no attention was given to them. They lay and suffered and their comrades were powerless to help them in any way. Once they stopped, and were given food and water, barely enough for one meal.

Giessen proved a big city, on rising ground. The prisoners were divided into companies, ten in all, and each company was in four barracks. These were enclosed by an eight-foot wall with wire on top. At the corner of the camp field-guns were mounted on ten-foot platforms, and sentries paced on the roads between the barracks. Every precaution was taken. There seemed no chance of escape.

The entire camp was surrounded by a high board fence and in one corner was a large bath house. There the prisoners had one bath per week, and a powder was sifted into the water making a solution powerful enough to remove all hair from the body. They stood around naked while the guards baked their clothing in a dry heat oven for two hours. This was done to kill all vermin.

Camp routine did not vary. Reveille was at six o'clock, breakfast at six thirty, roll call at seven forty-five. From eight till ten the men were doing physical drill, and dinner was served at eleven thirty. From three until five more drill was given, mainly physical exercises, and roll call was at six thirty. Supper was served at seven and eight o'clock meant lights out. Three lights were left burning in each barracks.

The food was poor, consisting mainly of soups, and often prisoners fainted during the drill hours. All nationalities had been placed together in order to lessen the chances of an organized riot, but Higgs met several Canadians and made friends with a Sergeant

Hammond, and Ptes. Fraser Davidson and Merton Kittredge. It was the 4th of July before the first parcels arrived from England, and they were manna to the starved men. These had been supplied by the Red Cross, and each prisoner had assigned ten shillings per month to the organization. The men were paraded to the hut where the parcels were stored and there each received his own, after it was examined carefully. Notwithstanding all precautions, however, many maps got through, hidden in tinned meats, and more than one received a compass in a loaf of bread. Kittredge was one of the lucky ones.

The prisoners had to learn the "goose step," and to salute the officers. Some rebelled, but it was better to make a pretence of obeying. The instructors soon made it known that the Canadians were the poorest parade ground men in uniform.

Giessen was a headquarters camp and working parties were sent from it in all directions, to factories, mines and farms. Some of these refused to work, especially those sent to cement factories and the salt mines. A passive resistance was begun and the men had to be brought back to camp. There they were placed in punishment barracks and all mail and parcels kept from them. Each day they were forced to dig ditches, and then to fill them again.

Some of the working parties were placed on tasks that released German soldiers for the front, and these parties promptly refused to work. Some of the prisoners were beaten, but this procedure only stiffened the resistance. Then the guards took one man at a time from the sight of the others and after a time a shot was heard. The remaining sentries stated that the unfortunates were being shot, and tried to make the others go to work. But it was all a sham. Afterwards the ones supposed to have been shot were returned to the company.

In July Higgs was sent with a party to work in a copper mine in the south of Germany, not far from the Rhine. They at once began the game of passive resistance, and would put their shovels in the ore cars, and have them smashed as the ore was dumped. Others placed lumps on the rails and caused wrecks. The civilian miners carried revolvers, but they did not threaten to use them. Instead, they seemed disgusted in having such helpers. At night the prisoners were billeted in houses.

There was a yard in the rear where the prisoners were allowed to exercise, and this enclosure was strongly wired. After two days in the place there came a terrific thunderstorm, and every man, guards and all tumbled inside for shelter—except Higgs. He had figured on such a move, and now he worked eagerly to get through the wire. No one looked out during the downpour and finally he had squirmed through. He was not missed until roll call and then the Germans searched persistently under all the beds.

All the while that he had been a prisoner Higgs had been determined to escape. He had been captured by trickery. The Germans had told him that the white square was really a signal to their artillery, denoting their position, but he felt it was a clever subterfuge. And he burned whenever he thought of how tamely he had been taken, without a chance of fighting. Yes, he would escape, no matter how difficult it might seem.

The wire was strong and he tore his hands as he struggled with it. The rain beat down in torrents, poured down, and lightning played in great flashes. Then he was through—outside! He ran and ran and ran, wildly and blindly. His overall uniform became sodden, soaked through, and tired him. At last a clump of bushes in a hollow was reached, and there Higgs hid, shaking with nervous excitement, soaked to the skin, watching for pursuers. None appeared, and so he lay where he was until dark, shivering as he chilled.

After trying to estimate direction Higgs left his covert and entered a valley. There were hills on either side that would make hard climbing if he were chased, but he remained on the low ground as the darkness there was like a pit, and after a time reached a river, and followed a road that led along its banks. All night he travelled, taking no risks, peering into all shadows, listening at intervals. But he met no person, heard no one, and as dawn came he hid in the thick tangled vines of a vineyard.

Just before reaching the vineyard he had crossed a vegetable garden, and as he lay in his new refuge he ate half-grown carrots. All day he lay there, and saw peasants working in their fields, and, in the afternoon, two men working in the garden he had crossed.

At long last it was dark again, and Higgs emerged from the vines. He was cold, and cramped with lying still, and very hungry. He did not know where he was, but hoped that the river he had followed led towards Switzerland.

The moon came up and shed brilliant light over everything. It made easier travelling, but Higgs was now in an area of vineyards and as he went along a hard path he removed his boots. Sound seemed to carry in the still air. He was in the centre of the district and hurrying along when all at once his heart seemed to stop beating. He halted, froze rigid. Fifteen paces away stood a German sentry leaning on his rifle!

The man did not stir. He was dozing, with his eyes closed. Higgs had not made a sound as he padded along. A split second he stood, then darted behind a large tree. The sentry moved, stretched, looked around, took a few steps back and forth, then stood again. For fifteen minutes Higgs hugged the tree and watched. The bright moonlight was like day, and the long shadows on the grass would reveal him at once. At last the sentry began to doze again. His head sagged and, like a cat, Higgs stole to the nearest vineyard.

He got among the vines. His heart was palpitating and he was wet with perspiration. He tried to listen, and imagined footsteps. The shadows were grotesque, seemed crouching men. He ran and dodged wildly, and at last had to stop and force himself to believe that he was not being chased. He had wasted precious time in his dodging about. On he went, watching, listening, from field to field, skirting farms, using occasional paths, and daylight came before it seemed that he had gone a mile. But he was in luck. Another extensive vineyard was close by, and he once more gained a refuge behind thick vines. But it was a long day, a terrible day. He was colder, so tired he could not sleep, and was more hungry than he had ever been before.

As soon as it was dark he got away from the vines and headed along the river. A sort of desperation had seized him. He must get on, cover territory, or he would get sick before he had gotten anywhere. He crossed a road, then turned and went along it, walking swiftly.

For an hour he travelled, making good time, then a black blur in the gloom proved to be a big truck. The driver was just mounting to his seat, had been stopped to examine a tire, and as he got into the cab Higgs, driven by some wild impulse, climbed in at the rear. Bales of goods made a fairly comfortable seat and before he could realize what a chance he had taken he was being whirled through the night.

It was restful to lean back among the bales, but he tingled all over. Where was the truck going? Where would it stop? It was useless to think of jumping from the rear. The driver seemed in a hurry and they roared along at fifty miles an hour. Long strings of lights streamed past and often they met or passed small strings of traffic. Then, before Higgs could do a thing toward escaping from the truck, they entered a city!

It was a great wide avenue they entered and the lights made bare every corner. On, on they went, branching into other streets, into main thoroughfares. Higgs cowered from view, his mind a chaos of emotions. Why had he taken such a chance? It was agonizing to think how reckless he had been.

They passed a large building and a clock announced the time, nine thirty p.m. Then they slowed, turned a corner and went up a rather narrow street. In its darkest part the truck stopped. The driver jumped down, ran to a gate and opened it. He then drove through it in low gear and as they crossed the sidewalk Higgs dropped from the rear. A moment more and he had walked to a lane and was hurrying along it.

His position seemed more desperate than before. He was now in a large city, his clothing crumpled from dampness, torn by contact with bushes. He was dirty and unshaved, and could not speak German. Surely the first man who met him would shout, and seize him.

The alley ended in three footways. Should he go back or trust to one of the passages? It seemed dangerous to do either. At last footsteps sounded, and he entered the right passage. After going along it a distance he saw an open door, and at the same time discovered that he was reaching another narrow street. Hurrying by, odors caught at his nostrils. Food, hot food! Coffee!

He stopped, listening. There was no sound of anyone near. He stepped nearer, peered in. It was a kitchen. A kettle steamed softly on a stove, a big gray cat was curled in a chair. On a table were dishes just used. Three persons had had a meal, and had gone, probably, to the front of the house. They had left a plate of bread, two sausages, a pot of coffee.

Hunger will drive a man to any extreme. Higgs stepped into the kitchen, intending to grasp the bread and sausage and run. Instead, he stood there, wolfing the food, and poured himself two cups of strong hot coffee. It was more than manna, it nerved him, made him a new man. He ate and ate, all the sausage and most of the bread, then stuffed the last two slices into his pocket, and stole away.

The narrow street was not well-lighted. He walked hurriedly along it, and at the first turn met two men. At sight of them he almost stopped. His knees seemed to lose all strength. Somehow he kept on. They were husky fellows, roughly dressed. A moment, and they were beside him.

"Good night," grunted one in German language. Higgs understood it. "Goot nacht," he returned, doing his best to sound guttural.

They passed on, never giving him a second look, and three women appeared. They spoke, and Higgs answered with another "Goot nacht."

Midnight found him still in narrow streets. A dozen times he had been sure he was caught. He was weary, and so sleepy he could scarcely keep going. The hot coffee and food had caused it. Time and again he had exchanged greetings with passersby, but no one took a second look at his bedraggled person. Then, as he thought he was reaching the outskirts of the city, he saw a file of men approaching, German soldiers!

For one wild instant he thought of flight, but it was useless. They would see him immediately he started. Only one other thing remained. He stepped into the nearest doorway and tried the latch. It yielded noiselessly. He pushed the door inward and softly entered. There was no light, no sound. Outside, on the pavement, the German patrol marched past, tramping heavily. The echo of their steps died away, and he swiftly opened the door and departed. His heart seemed in his mouth until he was away from the spot, but no one shouted after him. Luck was with him.

It was almost dawn when he left the city behind. Three times he had met lone travellers, and none had spoken to him, and once he had sighted another patrol, but so distant that he had easily hidden in an alley. Gradually the houses thinned, and at last he was in the country. But he could not find open ground. The houses were too close together.

Desperately he hurried. Soon it would be light. He was in a village before realizing it, and a dog barked at him. He perspired as he hurried, his footsteps seemed to wake every echo. Houses, gardens, shops, he passed them in frantic haste, panting, hurrying, all but running, and the village simply extended into a second one. Lights appeared in two houses. Then, as he was considering hiding in a shed, he saw wide fields on the left. A little longer and he was crossing them. Beyond was a vineyard, and there he hid, and was asleep before the sun had risen.

Higgs slept all day, then ate his two slices of bread. A garden was near and his first move was to crawl into it and get more carrots as provisions. Then he went on. It was his fourth night of freedom and he thought that, considering his ride in the truck, he must be a long distance from the prison camp, and he began to wonder what lay on the other side of the river he had followed. Then he came to another stream, another river, a very large one.

A village barred his way, and he kept to the river bank. It was quite light as the moon was high, and he soon saw that he would certainly be seen if he kept on. A wharf jutted out into the stream, and beside it was a small boat. In a moment he had reached it, eager to use it.

But the boat was fastened to the wharf by a chain, locked there. He searched the vicinity, and saw that there were no other boats. He went to the high ground, and saw several people grouped near where he must pass. Desperately he went back to the wharf, and searched until he found a bar. With it he tried to force the lock.

Higgs was so intent on his efforts that he never saw a movement or heard a footstep. Nothing happened until two thick strong arms were around him, gripping him like a grizzly. It all happened in the fraction of a moment. The arms seized him and he flung down to the planks, throwing all his weight and strength into his first struggle. The civilian who had caught him was hurled down and crashed beneath him, but did not relax his grip until Higgs had squirmed into position to use his elbow, and by that time a second man had leaped into the fray. Twice Higgs almost got to his feet. He is a well-built man, and was fighting like a cornered animal. In the end, condition told. He had

starved three days, had only one meal in that time, and the odds were against him. They pinioned him to the wharf and shouted wildly for help.

It came. A dozen persons came running, and there were excited cries. Three police officers came puffing and grunting. Higgs was dragged to his feet, held firmly between two huskies, and marched to a lock-up.

A sentry paraded outside his door. The cell was cold and damp and dark, but he huddled on the floor and tried to sleep. Morning brought him a bowl of soup, and a lady who talked perfect English. "Tell me all," she said, "or they will shoot you for a spy. It's your only chance."

Higgs tried to argue with her. She was certainly an English woman. It was useless. "I'll have you shot if you don't tell me all," she said coldly, and meant it. So he described his getaway, and an escort came to take him back to Giessen.

His guards placed him in a second-class carriage and in it were several soldiers. They were wearing side arms and at the sight of Higgs they began to jabber and talk excitedly. One of them, a burly fellow who had been drinking, drew his bayonet. He came over and made thrusts at Higgs, coming within an inch of his neck. The guards whispered between themselves, and seemed apprehensive, yet powerless to prevent such actions. The thrusts got nearer, and the steel ripped his overalls. Some of the other soldiers spoke roughly to the big fellow. He had worked himself into a passion. He glared at Higgs, towering over him, then turned and went back to his seat. At the next station he and his comrades left, and the guards tried to explain to Higgs how near death he had been.

At Giessen they placed him in a wooden cell for two days and then an interpreter came and went with him to a court martial. Higgs told the same story that he had given the woman, and was sentenced to 18 days in the stone barracks, the punishment block. For three days he lived on bread and water and on the fourth day he was given camp rations, usually potato or

Soldiers huddle inside a muddy trench in France, in 1915.

cabbage soup, and a raw herring. This system was used throughout his punishment. He had no blankets, and the place was damp. His cell was six feet long and six feet wide and metal had been placed over the air hole, so that he was in utter darkness. On every fourth day the covering was removed, and on the fourth night a blanket was provided. Its use only tended to make the prisoner feel the cold more keenly on the succeeding night, but it was never refused.

When the first raw herrings were issued at camp, he had his sent back to be cooked, and never saw it again. After that he ate them raw. The warden came into his cell on the fourth day with a bar with which to open the metal covering and see that his cell was in order. Higgs did not spring to attention and the man shouted fiercely and made to hit him with the bar. It was a narrow escape.

Two loaves of bread and a jug of water was his allowance for three days, and the bread was made of potatoes, often containing the half of a potato in the centre. The loaf was six inches across and two inches thick. No matter how careful he was, Higgs always had eaten the two loaves in two days, and on the third day had nothing. Then he would get down in the dark and wet his finger and feel for the crumbs that were on the

floor. A Russian who was imprisoned in the next cell wore high-topped leather boots, and when released he had eaten the leather down to the ankles.

After the cells Higgs was taken back to the Camp and fitted with a uniform marked with red rings. These were painted on the shoulders and knees and signified that he had attempted to escape. He was not allowed to go with others for his parcels and was closely watched.

The Red Cross parcels contained, besides food, blue uniforms, boots, shirts, etc., and the Germans ordered that red strips be inserted in the side of the trouser legs. The work was done by Belgian tailors and Higgs and others bribed them to sew the red cloth on the outside instead of cutting out a strip of blue cloth. Then, in event of escape, the red tell-tale could easily be torn away.

In January, 1916, Higgs was sent to Lichenhorst Camp in Hanover, and there they had a canteen provided at which they could purchase beer and some few canned goods, mostly fish. Their work was cutting heather and baling it with crude hand machines. They also dug ditches and Higgs managed to get his uniform so soiled and torn that they issued him another—and forgot to have the rings painted on it. On holidays they had sports, races and football, and the commanding officer seemed a good type. One day, however, he lost his temper when the prisoners were brought in early on account of a rainstorm. He raved about it, and was jeered, whereupon he gave orders to fix bayonets and charge. The prisoners separated slightly and prepared to sell their lives dearly, and the soldiers hung back and did not charge at all.

The German non-com in charge of Higgs' party had worked in an English hotel, and he spoke good English. He carried a revolver but seldom threatened with it. The ditches the prisoners dug were five feet deep and four feet wide and always waterlogged. The guards had planks placed for crossing so that they could escape the mud and slime, and the prisoners were given clogs to wear, and leather gaiters. They resented working in such conditions, and loafed, making no pretense of action. The guards stormed at them and threatened to use force, but the prisoners merely crossed to the opposite ditch bank. The guards went around and charged, whereupon they crossed back again. This game helped pass the time.

At length the sergeants among the prisoners decided to attempt escape. Each working party was counted off separately, then marched away. The sergeants watched for their opportunity and joined in at the rear of a party that had been counted, and were not noticed. They were marched out to the heather-cutting, and hid there when the time came to return to camp. Of course the proper number was counted at the gate, and the trio was not missed until night roll-call. A frantic search was made, then the alarm was given. Three days later the three men were brought back. They had got lost and had wandered into the hands of the searchers.

Higgs was very friendly with Kittredge and they began to plan an escape. On damp days in March there was a heavy ground fog in the evening, and it blanketed all surroundings. If they could escape then they were sure of getting away from the district. And Kittredge had been lucky enough to get a pair of wire cutters.

There were five hundred mixed prisoners in the camp, and a road divided it into two sections. Both enclosures were strongly wired. There was another night of thick mist and Kittredge got to the rear of the barracks and cut through several of the lower strands of wire. A sentry patrolled very near the spot, however, and it seemed useless to try there.

On the other side of the enclosure, bordering a field in a rather exposed position, a drain ran under the wire. It was bridged where it crossed the sentry's path, then extended into an opening from which a man might get away. Higgs and Kittredge decided to make their attempt in that direction, and they agreed that in case of capture they would state that they had

got out at the rear of the barracks where they had first cut the wire. This would preserve the drain exit for future efforts.

Again the welcome fog descended and Kittredge used the cutters enthusiastically. It was decided that he would go out first, and he had the compass that had come to him in the loaf of bread. They would travel directly towards Holland.

Everything went well. Kittredge got under the wire, and under the bridge, and Higgs started to follow. He had got under the barrier and had just squirmed into the narrow confines below the bridge when—the alarm blared into the night!

Higgs could not retreat. It was impossible to go back from where he was. A sentry had come racing along the beat and was stopped within ten feet of the bridge, listening.

Kittredge was surely captured. They had caught him at once, and likely were watching the same vicinity until they could make a roll-call. For what seemed an eternity Higgs lay waiting, trying to draw his feet from sight, expecting every moment that he would be discovered. The bridge was only four feet long and three times the sentry paced across it. But nothing happened. The sentry walked away to the other end of his beat, and Higgs crawled along the drain.

He made his way for two hundred yards into the open, then rose and ran. It had been twenty minutes since Kittredge crept out, and even though they had not caught him there was no telling where he was. Yet Higgs paused at the place where they had planned to join each other. For a moment or so he lingered, then ran on. It was long after before he learned what had happened. Kittredge had made a safe exit. The alarm had been given from the enclosure across the road when it was discovered that a Belgian had escaped. Kittredge, thinking of course that Higgs had been caught, never waited, but raced away. And he had the compass with him.

Higgs had studied the stars, however, and now he used the north star as his guide. He travelled paths and lanes and crossed fields, being careful all the time, and at dawn hid in a wood. He had chocolate and Oxo cubes with him and he ate a ration of them, then slept. Every circumstance was more favorable than during his first getaway, and he determined to reach safety.

On the second night, after travelling three hours he reached a high railway embankment. Climbing up, he peered over, and saw a good highway on the other side. No traffic was in sight and after a moment's hesitation he resolved to go by way of the road as he would make much better time. He slid down the far side and stepped over a ditch and…

"Alt!" A German patrolman with a revolver, the muzzle a few inches from his face!

There was not a chance of fight or flight. The fellow was one of a bicycle patrol that guarded the railway and he had seen Higgs against the skyline. A moment more and they were heading into the nearest town.

There was another court martial, another twenty-three days in the punishment barracks, bread and water and darkness, and all kinds of threats. He endured it stoically, and his resolve to escape was stronger than ever.

Higgs was sent again on working parties and was given hard tasks so that he and three others refused to work, and were given a trip to a punishment camp. This only served to stiffen his determination to escape and he watched for an opportunity.

On the first of June he was sent to Saltau Camp where he remained only a short time. While there a large batch of Serbian prisoners was brought in, men so starved-looking that Higgs and other Britishers tossed their bread to them. The Serbs fought like wolves for each fragment, gulping and bolting the food. Before he left the Camp Kittredge arrived and gave a graphic account of his travelling for fifteen days before getting caught.

Unfortunately Kittredge forgot all about their plan regarding the exit back of the barracks, and so his story did not tally with Higgs'. There was a stern investigation. Higgs was questioned and threatened for two days, but stuck to his own tale, and was finally let alone.

On July 5th Higgs was sent to Vordenmoor, a smaller place containing about two hundred of the more desperate prisoners, those who were always trying to escape.

He was sent out on working parties, those used in cutting peat. It was heavy and spongy and the guards measured the amount to be accomplished. If this was not done three days in the cells resulted. A Russian was so sentenced and while undergoing the punishment escaped from the cell and ran into the barracks. Hard treatment had made him partly insane and he hid under the beds. The guards rushed in after him and six of them could not catch him until he had led a chase around the grounds. Then they beat him cruelly and the watching prisoners in the barracks booed loudly. The rest of the guard immediately fixed bayonets and rushed in, threatening everyone.

Higgs got into trouble again. He was working at building a bridge and a heavy rock had to be lifted. It was too large for one man and he refused to attempt to raise it. The guard argued loudly, then menaced him with the butt of his rifle, and was very angry. But Higgs would not scare and shortly the fellow desisted.

The camp they were in was surrounded by a high wire fence with fifteen-foot towers at each corner. For two months Higgs had studied the problem of escape and now autumn had set in. He must make his try or remain there for the winter.

On one side, beyond the wire, was a public road, and the main gates opened on it. Across from them was a long wooden building. Two-thirds of it served as a barracks for the guards; the rest was used as a kitchen with the exception of a small room in which the vegetables were stored and prepared for cooking. Kittredge had had a slight attack of fever, and after recovering was given light work in the kitchen, peeling potatoes. And, with his observations, plans were made for another attempt at escape.

At meal time the prisoners were formed in lines across the camp, and were marched out in single file, across the road and in one door of the kitchen where the soup was issued. This file continued out through another door, across the road again and into the camp, there being two guards stationed on the road to see that none made a break for liberty.

Higgs and Kittredge planned to escape a dark night in the latter part of October. Kittredge was working in the small room and Higgs was to slip out of the soup line and join him, trusting to luck that none of the cooks saw him. They still had the compass and had hidden chocolate and Oxo cubes in their clothing.

All went well. The man ladling the soup did not look up and Higgs dodged into the small room, his mates scuffling on the floor so that his steps would not be heard. Slowly the prisoners filed through, and at last all were gone. No one looked into the small room, and the guards went to their supper.

There was a window in the room and the sash raised easily. They propped it up and climbed through, then lowered it softly from the outside. It was a position of advantage, for now all the building was between them and the sentries about the enclosure. But it was still daylight.

They had figured all their chances and had resolved that as the guards set to their eating they would be too busy to look out of the windows. Such was the case. The two men were in plain view for a hundred yards from the guards' dining room, but no one saw them go.

The next greatest danger was from the sentries in the towers. As soon as they were away from the Camp they would have to cross a bare field and if a guard happened to glance that way they would be seen. Such a happening had been foreseen, and the prisoners in the camp assisted nobly. They started a quarrel that held the attention of all the sentries until the escaping pair had vanished.

Once across the opening Higgs and Kittredge began to run, heading for the edge of some low brushwood in the distance. On the far side of it stretched the moor, and soon they were jogging along in the shelter of the small trees, stopping occasionally to rest and listen.

As soon as it was dark they started to cross the moor, which was several miles across and bare of trees. They used the compass and headed south instead of going direct west toward the Holland frontier, feeling sure that in so doing they would avoid many pursuers.

The north star served as a guide when the sky was clear, and when it was cloudy they shaded the light of a match on the compass and got bearings by the reflection of electric lights in the sky, from some town in the distance.

After travelling a mile the moor became wet and spongy, and water squelched up at every step. This gave them a certain sense of relief as they knew dogs could not be used to trail them. After getting across the moor they kept on through the woods, over small canals, across farms and occasional roads. At daybreak they stopped in another small wood and hid under a heap of brush.

There they ate of their meagre rations and congratulated each other on the success that had favored their getaway, and made plans for the next day. They resolved that if seen by pursuers or sentries they would run for it. Both were fleet of foot and they would chance a bullet in the dark sooner than surrender.

They slept the greater part of the day and were only wakened by people talking as they travelled a road through the wood. Darkness set in early and they started on, going over fields and skirting villages. Everything seemed to favor them as they were able to keep on their course without making detours, and made a very considerable distance before dawn. Once more they found a grove and thick bushes in which they could hide, and there they ate and rested.

All day they heard distant traffic and several times it seemed that people were coming to the grove, yet nothing happened, and they set out the third night in high

Allied soldiers attack under a smoke screen in June 1916.

spirits. They now changed direction and travelled west, keeping the north star on their right as they headed for Holland. For four hours they swung along at a fine pace only having fences to cross, then were confronted by a double-tracked railway that ran north and south. A train came along as they made a reconnaissance and the headlight seemed to expose them so they lay flat in a ditch.

Each time they got near enough to make a dash across a train came along, and each time they had to run back and take cover until at last they grew desperate and hid at the bottom of the embankment. There they cowered as several trains rumbled by and at last there came a lull. Tense, ready for instant flight, they stole over the tracks and down the other side. No one challenged them and no shots were fired. In ten minutes they were far away. Luck stayed with them and once more they found a good hiding place at dawn, and there lay hidden through the day.

The fourth night seemed as lucky as the previous ones and they were swinging along at top speed when—they came to a river. It looked wide and deep, and there was not a boat or plank of any sort along the edge. For a time they travelled the bank, and then were desperate. They were being forced out of their course.

A hundred yards on, they saw a long steel bridge which spanned the river. It seemed deserted but they were suspicious and held a long consultation. Several times they had crossed small canals by bridges and not once had found them guarded. Should they risk this larger one?

They went nearer and nearer, and waited and listened. It was midnight and there did not seem to be a person within miles of them. There lay the bridge, and the river flowed silently under it. One minute, two minutes at the most, and they would be across it.

They stopped and took off their boots so as to make no noise on the planking, then advanced, keeping to the darkness of the steel work. No one challenged them as they reached the structure and, heartened, they stole over, silent as shadows.

"Alt!"

It was a loud startled shout. A sentry had been leaned against the steelwork, probably dozing, and he was only a few feet away. He had flung his rifle to his shoulder and had them covered. "Alt!" he shouted again.

Kittredge stood still, dazed, dumbfounded. Higgs sprang like a deer. He leaped and dodged and ran as fast as he could go, and the sentry yelled wildly.

But the man dared not fire. If he pulled the trigger Kittredge could leap on him, and most of the guard was some distance on the other side.

Higgs expected a bullet every second. He swerved as he neared the other end and sprang over the side, dropping ten feet below and falling with a crash. He was slightly stunned but soon was creeping away and then running along the bank. The guard had not even reached the bridge, and the sentry had stopped shouting.

There was, however, every chance that he would be caught, and Higgs circled into the country away from the river until he had gone several miles. Luck seemed to guide him for he did not encounter anyone and at last made his way back to the big stream that barred him from his route. No boat or bridge was in sight, no means of crossing. It was the first day of November and the water was icy cold, the air chilling. He must not have his clothing wet. A raft seemed the only answer.

A short distance away a board fence separated fields and Higgs went to it and removed a few of the widest of the boards. He then cut small switches in a grove and with them bound the boards together. Then, undressing, he fastened his clothing to the small raft so that it would be kept dry. He had made a tow rope out of the switches and, placing a loop of it over his head, he swam the river towing the raft.

The icy water chilled him by the time he was across so that he had to beat himself to restore circulation. He struggled into his clothes and then began to run, keeping it up until he was warm again.

He had crossed the river, so much for that, but now to his dismay he could not find cover, and soon it would be light. He crossed fields as fast as he could travel, ran down lanes, kept to fences, and it grew lighter. Only one move remained; he must hide in a building.

One farm was somewhat isolated from the rest and he headed towards it, keeping to the rear. Luckily a door was in the end and he found it unlocked. Shortly he was in the barn and had hidden deep in the straw.

He fell asleep almost at once, and had a great fright when later the farmer climbed into the mow and forked a quantity of straw over the beam. Twice the prongs came very near his hiding place.

Higgs was hungry, and after the farmer had gone he finished his chocolate and Oxo cubes. Then he slept again and when he woke it was getting dark. An hour later he was in the fields again.

Speed counted now. He had no more food and it was certain that a hot search was being made for him. All night he travelled, crossing several roads but keeping to the farmlands and skirting all villages. Before it was light he found a garden and pulled carrots and turnips as provisions for the next day. At dawn he halted in a wood and there had dry refuge. The day was cold, however, and he could not sleep much. Shivering, gnawing at the vegetables, he waited for night.

Once more he started out, and realized that he was fast nearing the limit of his endurance. Such travelling, with no food, was very exhausting, and the nerve strain was worse. He kept to a road in order to have smoother walking and all at once was halted by a blinding light. It had issued from a small building as a door was opened, and inside the place he saw several soldiers in field gray. He had reached a line of sentries and knew he must be getting near the border.

One thing was in his favor. The soil was poor and the farms were very scattered. Keeping low, he backed away, and was not seen by the man who had emerged. Then he climbed a fence and ran straight across country. Soon he was among sparse bushes, and his fright subsided.

Again he went on, and had to venture along a pathway as it led in his direction. All at once he heard footsteps and had barely flung himself into a clump of bushes than a sentry passed, pacing leisurely. The fellow carried a rifle and was evidently not aware of anyone in his vicinity. He stopped carelessly and rested a time, then resumed his beat, and Higgs lost no time in getting away. He was now in a highly nervous state and bordering on exhaustion. Instinct warned him that he must be more careful than ever, yet he continually found himself staggering on a direct road, only heeding an impulse to reach the frontier.

Daylight nearly caught him in an open spot. He had reached the banks of a small river and was looking for a place in which to hide when he became aware of two men with rifles about three hundred yards away. They had seen him and were coming towards him.

Higgs started on at a fast walk and the men began to run. His feet had seemed leaden a few moments before but now he ran like a deer and after a time had gained many yards on his pursuers. Ahead, he could see that the river curved and that the banks would temporarily hide him from view. Without hesitation he scrambled and slid down to the water and dove in. His clothing made a terrible load but he swam across and was over the far bank before his pursuers, German soldiers, arrived. One clear view of their field gray uniforms, and rifles, sent him on again at full speed.

The Germans shouted at him and then began shooting, but the light was not very strong and they did not hit him. Two hundred yards away was a wood and he dashed into it, then halted and watched to see what the soldiers would do. They had halted on the high bank and had begun to argue. One seemed in favor of taking a plunge into the water, and the other against it. Finally, after wasting time sufficient for Higgs to recover his breath, they turned and went back the way they had come.

Higgs kept on for two miles, travelling on sheer nerve, so spent that he was hardly conscious of what he was doing. The wood ended suddenly and he was in an open field before he realized it. A large straw stack was near and he went to it, climbed up and buried himself in the top. It would be a safer hiding place than anywhere in the wood. And in a moment he was sleeping the sleep of the exhausted.

When he awoke he was freezing cold, shaking, his teeth chattering. It was only noon but the chill of his wet clothing had roused him. People were at a farm close by and he could hear them talking. He lay and suffered from the cold, and hunger, and acute weariness. His mind was almost numbed and when a wind sprang up before evening he slid down, not knowing what he was doing.

The cold mastered him. No matter if he were caught it was impossible to remain still. He was in agony, blue with exposure. He realized what he was doing, but could not prevent his actions, and only took precaution enough to keep the stack between himself and the buildings as he headed into a wide field. There he rolled and beat himself in an effort to get warm, and at last the sun had gone down.

Once it was dark he started on. It was his last night. He knew absolutely that his strength had reached its limit; he could not last more than twelve hours longer. Then he would collapse where he stood.

There was a tower near the road where he was travelling but he had not enough energy to make a detour around it, and kept on. The man in the tower saw him, and shouted as he passed. Higgs kept on, only turning to shout "Yah—yah," as if he understood and all was right. The man made no effort to follow him.

On and on and on. Was it a mile, or two miles or ten miles, he had come? What time was it? Near morning? He had lost all reckoning of everything. Only one urge dominated, to keep on and on and on. Somewhere, away in the distance, at some time, he would reach Holland. He was on a road, and would not leave it. His dulled senses tried to warn him, to deter him, but he shambled on. All speed was gone. He could not run, could not walk fast. Just shuffle, shuffle, shuffle. He did not look around, because he did not want to see pursuers. Everything was dim, vague, and his hunger was like a vast sickness.

All at once he was conscious of farm buildings very near the road. Then he saw that a man was beside his path. But he kept on, lurching, stumbling, reeling.

"Das is Holland! Das is Holland!"

The sound beat on his brain, and at last Higgs knew that the farmer had stopped him, was trying to talk to him, was—telling him that HE WAS IN HOLLAND.

The next he knew he was in the farmer's kitchen and they were preparing him hot drink and food, and never in his life had he had such a feast as that homely meal.

At long last he sat back, for he had not eaten fast, but slowly, and he was very sleepy. The good farmer, however, tugged at him, protested, and led him out and down the road, and to another farmer who spoke English.

There he was told that the Germans often came into Holland territory and seized men who had escaped them, and they urged him to keep on until he was in a safe zone. Six miles away was a garrison city, and there no one could get him.

Somehow, during those dark night hours, he staggered on that additional six miles, and a crowd followed him in the lighted streets. The farmer had kept with him all the way, helping and encouraging, and now he explained things to the following crowd. Soon they had roused the officer in command of the garrison and Higgs was given a long-wanted bed. On the next day he was sent to Rotterdam accompanied by a Dutch sergeant.

The British consul supplied Higgs with boots and clothing and money, but he was too spent to travel and for four days he stayed at the Sailors' Home in the city, wandering about leisurely, getting his strength back. Then a passport was provided and he crossed to England on a merchant vessel, one of a small fleet that were met by British destroyers and convoyed to London. A few days previous one of these fleets had been captured by the Germans and taken to Ostend, and had Higgs been well enough to sail then he would have been re-captured. Such are the vagaries of fate.

Higgs wrote a long letter to his wife, telling how he had escaped, and mailed it in Rotterdam. The letter was sent back to his prison camp in Germany, and, two years after the war, was sent to the proper address in Canada.

However, he himself landed safely at Yarmouth on the second week of November, 1916 and was soon in London. He there met with Lady Drummond, mother of Captain Guy Drummond who fell so gallantly at the fighting at St. Julien, and was then introduced to the Princess Patricia and also entertained by the Duke and Duchess of Connaught.

After this great change from the German camp life, he was sent to a questioning bureau and there gave all possible information about conditions at prison camps and in Germany generally. And when, later, Kittredge escaped, Higgs' cup of joy was full to overflowing.

What price Liberty? ◡

PASSED WITH FLYING COLOURS
James Warner Bellah

The first time I met him was at an aerodrome in England during the last months of World War I. He was a slender young man with a nice smile and pleasant grace. He had infinite courtesy and a diffidence of manner that seemed quite natural.

Six or eight Canadian officers were stationed there, and like myself, they preferred coffee to the eternal tea that flowed so freely. But cream was hard to come by, on a subaltern's pay, so we would sometimes get a cupful from the mess by taking the cook up for a 20-minute flight in the back seat of a De Haviland 9.

On one occasion we obtained a whole bottle of cream at four a.m. from the diffident young man's doorstep by the simple process of stealing it outright. He was a captain, and we reasoned that his pay could stand the loss.

He had been in the British Navy and had seen plenty of action. After long and legitimate spells on the sick list, he had been transferred to ground duty in the Royal Flying Corps. He never talked of his navy experiences. We learned, however, that during the battle of Jutland he had climbed out of a turret and stood there calmly taking pictures until he was dragged back in.

The young captain didn't seem pleased with his lot, for prestige both socially and in a military sense was based on one's ability in the air. And that ability was hard to come by. Crashes were frequent, and we used to have collective funerals on Wednesdays and Saturdays for mistaken ability. Ahead of us lay France and the privilege of buying what was to be left of our lives across the sights of a Vickers gun synchronized with the propeller.

France actually came to us once or twice, when the Hun made night bombing raids. Country club though the place was in some ways, it had elements of realism.

There was a rumor that the young captain was begging for permission to learn to fly, and that his politically powerful father was refusing firmly because another of his sons, an army officer, was already

The young and humble King George during the First World War.

risking his hide in France. But the captain must have been persistent, for one morning he reported to Cy Caldwell, a pilot par excellence, and he presented orders which stated he was to take instruction in flying. Cy obeyed those orders and taught him the workings of a Handley-Page.

The captain proved he was a real Joe when Cy asked him how he liked flying. He answered, "Not too much," showing that he was far more honest than the rest of us.

From a real Joe he got to be a good Joe when his brother, returning from almost four years in France, came for a visit. His brother asked him if he knew anything about the De Haviland plane, and the captain said, "Practically nothing." That pleased us greatly, for neither did we.

But what promoted the captain from good Joe to regular guy was an incident that happened one night in the senior officers' mess, to which I had been invited.

Another guest was a famous air fighter who wore the ribbons of the Distinguished Service Order, the Distinguished Flying Cross, the Air Force Cross, the Military Cross and several French decorations. He had imbibed freely, in the Flying Corps manner, and his good taste had become dulled.

After staring for a long moment at the wingless ribbons on the diffident captain's left breast he said, "Captain, what are all those ribbons for?"

The Captain looked curiously down at his ribbons as if he had never seen them before. Then he looked up and smiled and said, "I'm not quite sure. The tailor puts them there whenever I have a uniform made."

No one present failed to feel the quiet lash of the remark.

I'd like to be able to record that our young captain became a great air fighter, but he didn't. He did get his wings however. Then his brother, after years of great prominence, stepped out of the picture and the diffident young captain, whose name was George, was promoted.

The last any of us heard, he was King of England. ౩

The King inspects the Women's Division at one of the stations of the Bomber Group in the Second World War.

ROYALTY NEVER FORGETS
D.E. Macintyre

I had a cousin named Harry Smith who was with the Canadian Railway Troops in France in World War I. Harry's job at Passchendaele was to get shells up to the guns located in the unspeakable morass of mud and water that made up the famous Ypres Salient.

He ran his trains up at night and they were always shelled. Sometimes the track before them was destroyed; sometimes they fell behind and sometimes they scored a direct hit on the train. But, no matter what happened, repairs were made in the dark and the ammunition was delivered.

When this horrible battle was over Harry was recommended for, and got, the Military Cross.

Now the protocol regarding decorations was that after the award had been gazetted the recipient was supposed to go and report himself to Canadian Military Headquarters next time he went on leave.

Harry was a rough and ready fellow who paid scant attention to ceremony and so he avoided CMHQ when he next found himself in London.

When the Germans broke through the British lines in a last great effort to win the war in March 1918 and penetrated for several miles through the Fifth Army front, Canadian machine gunners on motor bikes, cavalry and railway troops were sent south to help them.

Harry's job this time was to evacuate wounded from field hospitals and dressing stations as well as to save as many guns as possible.

He was working at top speed and for long hours when an orderly came running up and said, "Sir, you're wanted on the phone." Harry was furious at being interrupted and expressed himself in soldier's language, but he went to the telephone.

"Captain Smith speaking."

"Wales here, Fifth Army. How are you getting along, Smith?"

"I'd get along a damn sight faster if I didn't have to answer this phone so often." Then he hung up and ran back to the local railway station.

The Price of Wales and General Arthur Currie *(right)* consult during the First World War.

About an hour later he was again called to the phone. "Wales here again. When will your train be leaving?"

"Oh, go to hell, Wales! I haven't time to talk," said Harry and ran to his job, where he heard that German patrols had been sighted near the outskirts of the village. It was time he pulled his freight. A few nights later, when the situation was quieter a dispatch rider on a motor bike roared into the Canadian camp. "Letter here for Captain Smith," he announced. He was directed to Harry's tent and delivered an impressive-looking envelope with Fifth Army Headquarters printed in the corner.

A neatly typed note was enclosed which read,

"Capt. W.H. Smith,

"Canadian Railway Troops, France.

"Your presence is requested for dinner at Fifth Army Headquarters to-morrow night, the thirtieth March. A car will be sent for you. Please acknowledge by bearer."

Harry was astounded. Why should he, an obscure Canadian officer, be invited to such a gathering of important army officers?

Guns and weapons of the First World War.

A car came for him the following night and in a short time he was delivered at the front door of a large and impressive country house, or chateau, evidently the former home of a wealthy Frenchman.

Presenting his invitation at the front door he was soon approached by a young officer, who, with a friendly smile escorted him to an anteroom where a dozen or more senior officers were gathered, talking and enjoying their *aperitifs*.

His escort left him but returned almost at once leading a fair-haired young man whose face was known all over the British Commonwealth who said:

"I'm Captain Wales. I think that we have had some conversation on the phone." Harry was speechless; he was facing Edward, the Prince of Wales, whom he had never connected with the telephone incident. The Prince put him at ease by saying, "You did a fine job out there. Come

with me. The Army Commander wants to see you."

He was introduced to Lt. General Sir Hubert Gough, VC, and other senior officers and then they all went in to dinner. The atmosphere in the room was serious as the situation in France was critical and the Allies were facing possible disaster. It was no time for light banter.

The war came to an end in November and in the following year the Prince of Wales, who had always been popular with the Canadians, came over on his first trip to Canada. It was announced in the press that if veterans who had not received their decorations for gallantry would send in their names the Prince would present them on behalf of his father King George V. In Owen Sound Harry's father wanted him to go to Hamilton for the investiture but Harry was against making a fuss about the medal and dismissed the subject by saying, "Let them mail it to me."

MARKED MEN
Will R. Bird

The Prince of Wales attends the funeral of Major-General L.J. Lipsett in the First World War.

"No, Harry, that's not the proper attitude to take. This young man will be our future king and to please me I must insist that you go. I will drive you to Hamilton." And so Harry agreed.

The day of the Prince's visit came and he appeared before a huge crowd in Hamilton. Veterans were paraded and as their names were called they mounted the dais where the Prince pinned on their decorations. At last Harry's name was called and he marched up and saluted the Prince, who showed no sign of recognition. Edward pinned the purple and white ribbon with its silver Military Cross on Harry's tunic and then he smiled and shook hands with him, at the same time leaning forward and whispering in his ear, "Go to hell, Smith." ॐ

Sambro and Kennedy and I kept together. We went down a side street of Mons where we saw Belgians peering from their doorways, and asked them where the Germans were. They pointed in different directions and shrugged their shoulders. A woman brought us hot coffee, and another brought wine. We heard shouting and saw a soldier who called that he had seen two Huns but they had escaped him. A dignified Belgian in a frock coat and top hat guided us to a building and into its cellar. It had been a German billet and many tumbled beds were there; the enemy, however, had flown out one of the windows.

We went on up the street. Women and children cried welcomes as we passed and a group of them corralled Sambro and Kennedy. I went on alone, then at last entered a home to accept more coffee, for I was utterly weary. I had seen "Old Bill" with the Mills brother, trying to console him, for the fellow was half-crazed by grief and swearing vengeance on the first "brass hats" he saw, blaming them for the order to fight again.

The old lady who gave me coffee suddenly jabbered something and pointed excitedly. I looked out the window. A German soldier was escaping out of a house further up the street. He was unarmed and was watching some officers who were coming toward him, probably meaning to surrender to them. He had to pass a big gate to get outside the yard and as he did a burly Belgian rose from where he had been waiting and struck with a sledge, crushing the German's head like an eggshell. No one rebuked him or went near the body.

When I left the house I went to the Square where many of our boys were resting. The new men were talking loudly and a photographer was there taking pictures. I left and went away back to the little building where Jones and Mills were lying. A sergeant was there, with others, helping to get the bodies from the shed. "Know them?" he asked me.

"I was with them when they were killed," I answered curtly.

"Phew!" he said. "Close enough. Well, considering everything, we got off light. And now she's ended. They're going to give these boys a bang-up funeral and…"

"What good'll that do?" I snarled. Something seethed within me.

The sergeant looked at me. "The best thing you can do," he said, "is to get some liquor and find a bed somewhere. The brass hats are coming into town as soon as it's safe and there'll be all kinds of ceremony and all that."

"I'd like to shoot every blasted one of them," I grated, and left him.

I walked on and on, thinking of Jones, his kissing the little girl, drinking that mocking toast…had he known? Away on the outskirts an old man hailed me from a little cottage and I went in. He and his wife could not speak English and they were very deaf, but they wanted to do something for me. I told them I was very tired and they offered me a bed. I had a good wash and then promised I would go back to them if possible, after I had seen the orders of the day.

Down on the Square I met Tommy. It was the first time I had seen him since the previous morning. "Where have you been?" I blurted.

He looked at me oddly, and flushed. "I'll tell you the straight truth, Bill," he said. "I steered clear of you. Did you ever stop to think about all the fellows who've been killed alongside you? Every time it's the other chap who gets it. I've thought about it and this time I wasn't taking any chances."

We looked at each other a moment, then grinned in a confused way, and I went on. "They want to watch that Mills don't plug some of them gilded guys," he called after me. "He's in the humor to do it."

Everywhere there was wild celebration. The new men were drinking and laughing and shouting with the Belgians. Officers were posing in the public places. The older hands were conspicuous by their absence. Mostly they had found places to sleep and were sleeping, indifferent to everything. Other soldiers were crowding into the city, riotous, loquacious, wine-mettled fellows, and were shouting things about the Kaiser and the German navy. "Nothing ahead but home now, Jock," one shouted at me, and I wanted to hit him.

An inexplicable bitterness had seized me, gripped me. I hurried away from them, walked the streets until I found my way back to the little cottage. There I went into the room the old Belgians had given me, kicked off my boots and sat on the bed, thinking, thinking. I was needing sleep more than anything else, and yet I did not lie down. My mind was a turmoil of visions, vivid pictures. I was back again on the Ridge that first winter, with Mickey and Melville and MacMillan, shooting rifle grenades, seeing Burke sitting in the mud, trying to form fours in a rain of gas shells to please a small-brained major. I crawled again on my first patrols and felt the muddy ooze under my knees, wet grass and weeds against my face, saw red-eyed rats creeping away from nameless things among the slimy craters. The pictures would not fade nor remain definite. They swung to a long line of snaky trenches with chalk parapets, to old ruins, shell-battered villages, gaunt ribs of shattered roofs, the sunlight catching bits of glass that remained whole. What sensations! Thrills! Horrors! Chills! Dreads!

I saw undergrounds, dugouts, tunnels, stinking, rat-ridden places; an existence among mud; mud and rusting wire, mud and rain, mud and sodden sandbags, mud and mire, always mud…war! Brick dust and ashes and broken timbers, and twisted iron and gateways into houses that were not there; gaping cellars, bedding and toys and clocks and cradles in a chaos of destruction; a lone crucifix at a cross-roads where all else was ruin. War! A plot of white crosses sandwiched among heaps of rubble, and a sign board saying "Dangerous Corner." War! Hollow, reverberating sounds, the steady, measured tramp of marching feet, the dazzling floating whiteness of a flare, twisted long-barbed black wire, gray sand-bagged trench walls, a desolation that seemed increased, that seemed peopled with grisly spectres when the Very lights became fewer just before dawn. War—I hated it, despised it, loathed it—and yet felt I was a part of it.

I saw Mickey's white face close up to mine, felt him in my arms. "And we—go—on." What a hopeless, gasping surrender his had been! And Melville going steadily forward, set, composed, ready, Ira beside him; Sparky's sudden tremors, the questioning in his staring eyes; Eddie coming and saying "goodbye"; Sidall in that old foul Somme trench, murmuring, "Stay close beside me, Bill—till I go—to sleep." I could see…

"Kamerad!"

I sprang to my feet. A closet door I had not noticed was suddenly ajar. I jumped to it, flung it open. There, blinking in the lamp light, cringing, white-faced, stood a German!

He was a young fellow, and his eyes held the fright of a hurt animal. "Kamerad!" he said again, in a whisper.

Still I did not speak. All that day I had burned with rage and bitterness. Why did they stay and shoot till they had killed Jones? Why did they keep on fighting if they had decided to stop? The German, watching my face, huddled, gasped "Kamerad," and offered me his red and gray cloth cap. "Souvenir—Kamerad." I motioned him to put it on again.

All at once there were ribald shouts in the street, the sound of many feet on the cobbles, a rollicking song.

"I'm out to catch a Hun, a Hun,
I'm out to get the son of a gun;
And when I do I'll bet he'll rue
The day he left the Rhineland."

The German, listening, whimpered with fear and stood watching me, dry-lipped, wide-eyed, terror-stricken.

"Kamerad?" he whimpered. I shook my head, motioned him to be still. No use to put him out on the street for that crazed bunch of celebrators. Even the Belgians would kill him. I made him sit down beside me on the bed and we waited. He lost some of his fright. I did not like the stale smell of his dirty gray uniform or admire the cut of his bulging trousers, but his face was clean and boyish and he might have looked well in a kilt.

Finally the town grew quiet, the long day of rejoicing had taken its toll. I got up and looked into the closet where the German had hidden; probably he had ducked in there during a mad flight and had not been heard by the old couple. The place was partly filled with old clothing. I searched among it and found a long blue coat and a limp cloth cap, and handed them to him.

The German's eyes lightened. He understood, and slipped the coat over his tunic. It fitted well and he put on the cloth cap. The change was effective. He appeared a young Belgian and would never draw a second glance. It was only a short distance to the open and beyond that the outposts would be relaxed, scattered, easy to avoid.

I opened the door of my room and saw that the old man and his wife had retired. Outside, the way seemed clear. The German stepped out hastily, then hesitated, turned and held out his hand. I gripped it with a warm pressure.

"Kamerad," he said with a soft accent.

"Good luck to you," I answered, and he was gone.

↔

A PADRE AT THE FRONT
George Frederick Scott, C.M.G., D.S.O.

August 22nd, 1918

Well, we have had another splendid victory and the old 1st Division has once again made a record and covered itself with glory. It made the biggest advance in one day that has been made by any Division, British or German, since the war began. We are more than ever proud of the old Red Patch…

August 24th

To return to the great attack. We were moved hurriedly and silently and with great secrecy to this front. I travelled for about 60 or 80 kilometers in my sidecar. Then we prepared for the attack. On August 7th in the afternoon I heard that the attack was going to take place the next morning at 5 o'clock so I had dinner with the officers of the Trench Mortar Battery and shaved and then started for the trenches to be with the 16th Battalion as the 3rd Bde. were going over first. I left our H.Q. in a certain wood and then rode to the barrier in the Roye Road. There I got out and in the twilight made my way to the 15th Battalion.

From the 15th Battalion I made my way to the 16th and finally, after losing my way many times around the back of this Battalion, I came to Col. Peck's H.Q. They were all in a trench on a hill facing the wood which the Germans held. Here Col. Peck and two of the officers were crowded into a little hole in the trench and they took me in for a while, but I wanted to go and see the men in some trenches further forward so I got out and followed a party down to the trench. It was a time of great excitement and delight. All our men were as keen as mustard and all enjoyed the sport of the thing. We had fooled the Germans completely.

Fitful search-lights went up every now and then from the German line and there was intermittent shelling and machine gun fire, but otherwise all was quiet. I saw the boys and shook hands with them and gave them my blessing, and just about half an hour before the attack was to begin I left them and went back to Col. Peck. He

was just going off with his piper. I saw the 5th Battalion and Ian Crawford, afterwards wounded. At 4.20 a.m. our batteries opened up. It was a lovely night. The stars were clear and I saw the Pleiades.

Before us sloped the great plain and at the end a wood and a hill above it. We could see this in the dim light. Then the thunder of the guns began and shells hissed over our heads by the thousand and shrapnel burst on the German lines. The sound of a barrage always has an intoxicating and delirious effect on me. They all laughed at me, for as I sat on the edge of the trench I kept saying, "Glory be to God for that barrage." Then we heard the sound of tanks, and on turning I saw all along the lines things like beetles coming from the slope. It was a weird sight. I believe one thousand tanks were employed in the whole operation. One tank was heading for our trench but it would have cut our telephone lines so a man was sent out to turn it off to the right.

Then the 5th Battalion went off and I went over with the stretcher-bearers. We found a good many wounded, and some killed near the wood, for the Germans were now replying with their guns. An amusing thing happened here. The German shells were falling pretty thickly and the smoke they made hung around so thick that you could not find your way. I came across an old shell hole and in it I found three apparently dead Huns, all huddled together. While I was looking at them wondering how they had been killed, one moved a little and I called out, "Kamerad!" Then the three prostrate men, thinking I was going to bomb them, held up their hands most piteously to me and said, "Kamerad, Kamerad! Mercy! Mercy!" Wasn't that funny? Fancy the Rector of St. Matthew's Church being appealed to by three Huns to spare their lives! I looked very severe and said, "Venez avec moi," and I called to a sergeant who was following and we took them through the smoke till we stumbled on the 2nd Battalion and handed them over.

One of them cut off his shoulder straps and I sent one to Mary the other day.

It was rather hard to find your way, for the sun had not risen and there was such a thick smoke and guns seemed to be going from all sides. I had to go back to the battle, so I got on a tank and had the novel experience of riding into the battle on a tank. We went over the trenches and shell holes without any trouble.

The sun now rose and the smoke began to clear away. We got off the tank and followed with our men. It was hot and dusty work. The rout had been so complete that our men simply walked over the ground unimpeded. I found some of our wounded and a good many Germans. Poor fellows, they were generally terribly wounded. A good number were R.C.'s and I gave them the Crucifix which I wear to kiss. It was quite pathetic to see them take it into their hands and kiss it and say their prayers. I did what I could for them and then went after the men. The Germans were "beating it" as fast as they could. We had a magnificent view from a hill of the cavalry advancing. Thousands and thousands of horsemen made their way over the plain. All the great cavalry regiments were there—Dragoon Guards, Lancers, etc.

By the afternoon the 2nd Bde. had advanced so far that I got a ride on an ambulance and got out to Caix, the final objective of the day, about ten miles from our starting point. There I found in the new front trench the 10th and 7th Battalions. Opposite I saw the Germans bring up reserves on the Rosiers Road. We could see the buses loaded with men; still no counterattack was attempted that night. I slept in a sort of cellar with the runners of the 10th Battalion. As the floor was only earth and rather damp I got two sandbags for a mattress and had two bricks for a pillow and then slept till "morning light." I got full of cramps when I tried to turn in the night.

Next morning our 2nd Bde. was going to make another push to the right so, after breakfast with the 7th Battalion, I shaved and went off through the wood. Here I was eating my lunch and wondering where I could find our men when I saw the 22nd Bn. going over the hill. No sooner did the Germans see them on the other side than they put up a heavy barrage, but our French-Canadian regiment behaved splendidly. They never budged but came on in high spirits. I got up and went over to them and found some fellows from St. Sauveur who knew St. Matthew's Church.

Then I went off to the right and saw Clark-Kennedy with the 24th Battalion and he told me that the 8th Battalion were not far off. I went over in the direction he told me they were and finally came up to a group of them behind some buildings by a track. Here a cavalry patrol rode up and reported to me (I suppose they thought I was a combatant officer) that the wood in front of us was heavily held by machine guns. It sounded like it, for every now and then machine guns would open up and little puffs of dust would start up before me.

I saw young Boswell of the 8th (he was afterwards wounded) and he and his men were just going to attack the wood. I told him what the patrol said. He replied that he was going to go round the wood. I gave the men my blessing and told them they were all right. They were in fine form but their Battalion had lost its colonel—Col. Raddell—and also had lost many men. I went up the hill facing the wood. Here were a good many wounded. One man, who was dying, I baptized. Then I saw to some wounded Germans. I looked over towards the wood and to my delight saw the Germans running out of the other side and our men going through, so I ran back and shouted to a company of the 14th, "The Germans are running away!" The officer ran out to see, for he was waiting to follow up the 8th, and he gave orders to his men to charge and the wood was ours. All sorts of stores were found in it. I went on then to Warvillers where I had a lunch of onions and lettuce and bully beef in the garden of a chateau which in the morning had been the H.Q. of a German Corps Commander.

The chateau was used as a dressing station and at night the wounded were being brought in. A nice fellow—a doctor called MacDougall—was in charge. He was so good to me. I had some sleep there that night.

The next day I was not feeling very well but I went off to Rouvroy, our new front. I saw Armitage and the 3rd Battalion H.Q. I got some writing paper from an old German bookshop. I began to feel very seedy and got back to our advanced H.Q. which had not seen me for three days. I had dinner with General Thacker, but he thought I was looking so ill that he went and fetched the A.D.M.S. and Col. Wright of Quebec. He took my temperature and, finding it 103.5, he ordered me, much to my dismay, to an ambulance. I was carted off in the middle of the night and taken from place to place until at last I found myself in a British C.C.S. in Amiens. When I was carried into the reception room the Major told me I was to go to the base. I was in despair for I knew that my temperature was only caused by drinking water that shells had burst in. However, there was a railway accident that day so they could not send me. The next morning I got up and shaved in the garden where I had lain with a lot of wounded heroes. I put on my best tunic (I had my kitbag with me) and put one of my brother Frank's cigars in my mouth and strolled off to the Major in the reception room and asked him when he was going to send me to the base. He looked up and laughed and said, "I don't think I will send you now. You may go back to your Division."

I was much amused. I really did feel rotten and nearly keeled over. Well, I got a lift back with Sharples and then I found to my dismay that MacGreer had put another man in my place and the latter had established himself in my room. I felt like Enoch Arden but did not have his self-denial. I turned poor Emmett out. Thacker said I came back "upsetting all the pet schemes of well-ordered minds." Poor Wright was surprised to see me.

He said he thought I had gone down with pneumonia.

Well, when we came out of the lines I came into this C.C.S. and they took me in and inoculated me and gave me a nice bed.

Dr. Martin of Montreal is here now and Sir Edward Kemp has just had lunch here. I am now going back to our H.Q. feeling quite well. ✑

Part II

The Second World War

THAT OTHER SEPTEMBER
Ben Malkin

In Canada, World War II began in an atmosphere of quiet acceptance. In Parliament, only J.S. Woodsworth, the CCF leader and a pacifist to the end, broke with his party to vote against the war. In the country, young men joined up in numbers large enough to fill, within a few weeks, the ranks of the two divisions that had immediately been mobilized.

Although I had been a pacifist during my late teens and early twenties, I also joined. Pacifism among the young had been a strong movement in the 1920s and early 1930s. In the aftermath of World War I, popular books, plays and movies like *All Quiet on the Western Front*, *Journey's End* and *What Price Glory* had expressed the reaction of the post-war generation to war as an unmitigated evil. Britain and France had each lost a whole generation of young men. Canada was not far behind. But by 1939, that mood had almost completely dissipated.

War was still evil, but it had become a necessary evil, with survival of the free world clearly at stake. Arriving in England Dec. 17, 1939, with the first contingent, Gen. A.G.L. McNaughton put it succinctly: "We've come here to do a job, then go home." No glory seeking. No flag waving. Just a necessary job to do.

The pacifist mood began to change visibly by 1938. Only two years before, in a widely publicized debate, members of the Oxford Union voted not to fight for King and country. In France the feeling among the young was the same. It was perhaps not so clearly articulated in Canada, yet anyone brought up in the post-World War I period with its disillusionment, its skepticism about false slogans (remember "the war to end wars," "a country fit for heroes," "making the world safe for democracy" followed by more wars, dictatorship, widespread unemployment) had to sympathize with the sentiments expressed at Oxford University.

There was some erosion in the pacifist sentiment when Japan attacked Manchuria, and later China. But while Canadians condemned such action they didn't see it as a danger to Canada. In Winnipeg, to be sure, John Dafoe, editor of the *Free Press*, thundered that only a policy of collective security, especially through the League of Nations, could stop aggression and ensure peace. Yet Asia was far away, we didn't seem threatened, it was none of our business.

Even the rise of Adolf Hitler and the Nazis in Germany, and the aggression of Benito Mussolini in Ethiopia, didn't immediately alter the mood. Hitler's march in to the Rhineland, and even in to Austria, and Mussolini's incursion in to Ethiopia, were also to be deplored. But at the time few saw these actions as a threat to Canada. The pacifist mood remained strong.

The turning point came with the Spanish Civil War. Had it remained between Spaniards alone, the conflict probably wouldn't have mattered to most of us. But it heralded the greater struggle to come. Air and land forces of Italy and Germany fought on the Fascist side, while the Soviet Union supplied arms to the Republican government. To avoid a wider war, Britain and France, still licking their wounds from World War I, remained neutral, as did the United States and Canada.

But that was only at the official level. Individual Britons, Frenchmen, Americans, Canadians went to Spain to join the International Bde., with the Canadians forming the Mackenzie-Papineau Bn., the Americans the Abraham Lincoln Bn. Many were no doubt active Communists, but many were not. They were men who saw, somewhat sooner than most of us, that a new, aggressive force was loose in the world, and that it had to be stopped if we were to enjoy any security at all. The massive bombing of Guernica foretold what was in store for those who resisted the Fascist march.

I began to change at that time. By late 1938, when Hitler swallowed the Sudetenland, and early 1939, when he took over the rest of Czechoslovakia, the change was complete. War was inevitable because it had become plain that, though Hitler was still moving toward the east, our turn would come. Even in the United States, with its Neutrality Act, that mood had begun to take hold. As a reporter on the *Winnipeg Free Press*, one of my chores during the royal tour in May, 1939, was to cover the arrival in Winnipeg of a special train from Minneapolis-St. Paul carrying hundreds of Americans who wanted to share the King and Queen with us. Chalked on the sides of the train, in foot-high letters, was the message: "Britain and Canada we're with you." They, too, knew that the war was coming.

Perhaps because so many young men had, long before the outbreak of war, already made private commitments to join, no special government exhortations were needed. The climate was sober. Though pacifism was an honorable position to take, even then, the pacifists had become a small minority.

On Sept. 7, I joined the 19th Field Battery, a militia unit that was to become part of the 3rd Field Regt., RCA. It was located at McGregor Armory in Winnipeg's north end, within walking distance of my home. The recruiting officer was Charles de Pencier, a young subaltern. He set the tone.

"I'd like to join," I said. He looked moody as he doodled with a pencil. "You know," he warned, "we've been assigned to the 1st Div. We'll be going over soon."

I didn't know, but the news suited me fine. I had no wish to soldier in Canada. "That's O.K," I replied, and signed the form.

The Nazis had accused us of being warmongers. But looking back today, our lack of preparation was laughable. We were issued cavalry uniforms of WW I vintage—breeches, long puttees, brass-buttoned tunics, bandoliers—and boots that we dyed ourselves with thick, black army issue coloring. We had no barracks and lived out. That made the conversion from civilian to army life a little less bumpy. It was something like having a new job, with first parade at 8 a.m., an hour for lunch and dismissal at 4 p.m. The hours were better than I was used to as a reporter.

Rifle drill, foot drill, gun drill, with the signallers learning Morse and flag drill. Once a week, a lecture from the battery commander to explain military etiquette.

He had started as a WW I gunner and was now a major. He knew how to talk to the fledgling soldiers in their own language. It was effective.

"Some soldiers," he said, "have been getting on street cars without paying. Just because you're a soldier and there's a war on doesn't give you special privileges. Pay your way."

"There's been a certain amount of stealing going on around here: badges, shoe polish, stuff like that. When it comes to stealing around an armory or barracks, soldiers are sitting ducks. They can't keep their stuff locked up. If you must steal, steal from civilians.

"I've had complaints from some of the officers that there's too much saluting going on. You don't have to salute every time you see the same officer, all day long. Pay your respects in the morning, and again when you go off duty. That should be enough."

All of this was very good advice to a bunch of greenhorns. I suppose it was being given at the same time to other Winnipeg units, because reports of soldiers trying to get a free ride on street cars dwindled, petty thieving—euphemistically but inaccurately defended as "borrowing" or "finding"—disappeared and officers stopped complaining about their arms getting tired by the end of the day.

It was a green and balmy autumn, one of the most benign any of us in the west could remember. By the first days of December, it hadn't even snowed. When we entrained for Halifax, where we were to set sail on Dec. 10, it seemed like a day in September.

We were able to use the outdoors constantly, to practise our drill so well that, eventually, we were able to march to the railway station in a reasonable facsimile of military order.

World War II training under fire at Camp Shilo, Manitoba.

By the time we entrained, we had been issued with the new uniforms and caps, but no gaiters. Canada's clothing industry, caught as unprepared as our government, for reasons that were never made clear, could cope on short notice with blouses and pants, but not with gaiters. And although we had learned the elements of foot, rifle, and gun drill, army administration officials still had to learn—and this was a long-drawn

process, never quite completed—that it's folly to try to fill every round hole with a round peg.

I was among the first to be trapped. I naively gave my true occupation: journalist. I was put to work as a battery clerk. What else to do with a man who could type? It was a job I came to loathe. Once you've typed one nominal roll, you've typed them all. The only good word I had for a battery clerk's job was that it was a cure for insomnia. Counting nominal rolls is even more effective than counting sheep.

It took two years of importuning and pleading and losing files to convince the authorities that I wasn't cut out for the work, and I got transferred to a gun crew. Army administrators are something like Hollywood movie directors: once they put you in a certain slot, they think it's forever.

At that, I wasn't as badly off as one fellow who was driving a brewery truck when war broke out. On the September day he decided to join, he left his loaded truck parked at the curb of a downtown street, phoned his brewery to tell them where they could find the vehicle and what they could do with it, and came to the armory to join up. As innocent as I, he gave his occupation as truck driver. They put him to work driving a truck for the duration, causing him to mutter from time to time that this wasn't what he had joined up for and that it was a hell of a way to fight a war.

The smart men said they had no occupation and were put on general duty, which meant a gun crew. That was the best posting because you weren't at everyone's beck and call, and because that seemed to be the purpose of joining up in the first place.

In the early days of the war, a friend who had enlisted in the PPCLI told me that one day the company sergeant major, who had been laboriously writing out company orders by hand, had paraded the company and asked all men who could type to fall out. No one moved, though my friend said he knew of three, besides himself, who could type. The hapless sergeant major had to go on writing out his own orders, until eventually he found a round peg willing to fit in to the orderly-room hole.

So many men had privately committed themselves to war many months before the actual outbreak that the emotional conversion from civilian to soldier came easily. When we left Canada, we were not ready to meet the enemy in the military sense. But in spirit we were, and that stayed with us throughout the war. ✍

THE INQUISITION
Dave McIntosh

Would they hand out white feathers to army-age young men who hadn't or wouldn't join up? I'd heard that young women used to do that in WW I and it worried me.

It was 1940. I was 19 and still a civilian. I had to shave only every two or three days but I was over six feet tall and healthy. In the winter I could double up my wrist inside my overcoat sleeve and pretend I had lost a hand in some dreadful accident. But here it was a warm fall day and I was standing beside a dirt road on the Alberta prairie trying to hitchhike from Calgary to Hanna and there wasn't a cloud of dust, marking the advance of a car, between me and the horizon, which was a long way off.

I didn't have much faith in cars by now. They worried me even more than white feathers. I had stood outside Banff with two soldiers when a car stopped. The driver told them to hop in and drove off, leaving me standing in the rain. Half an hour later, a farmer picked me up in his truck. "Goin' in to Calgary to join up?" he asked, shooting me a piercing glance like a bayonet thrust.

"I'm trying to make Hanna right now," I said non-committally.

"To join up there?" he queried.

"No, I have to see a relative there before I push on east."

"You from the East?"

"Yes."

"Maybe you're going to join up when you get back East," he persisted, shooting me another of those unsmiling, recruit-drive looks.

He took me as far as Calgary. I walked to the eastern outskirts with my cardboard suitcase in which I carried the $80 I had made working at Jasper all summer. But I couldn't get a ride. The Fords, Chevs and Hudsons, the DeSotos and Studebakers just kept going by, not in a steady stream by any means because there weren't that many cars then. I walked back into town and used a precious $1 bill to get a room at the Hotel Noble. The rooms on the outside, with window, were $1.25 a night but rooms on the inside, with transom only, were $1. I sat in the lobby beside a spittoon until the clerk finally sang out: "Room on the inside." I had been third in line for an inside room.

I got on the road early Sunday but still couldn't get a ride all day. Not wanting to waste another $1 on a hotel room, I walked to the railway station and sat on a bench till morning, keeping both arms wrapped around the suitcase in case I dozed off.

The first train out was a milk train headed toward Stettler. I asked the conductor if he could let me off where the railway crossed the road to Hanna. He agreed and sold me a ticket for 25¢. After an hour or so, he said "Here you are" and I stepped down on the gravel beside the train. Just behind the train, the road crossed the track. Well, it wasn't raining and I was out of Calgary.

Cooks enlist at the RCAF recruiting centre in Toronto, November 1941.

I soon got a ride. He was a middle-aged man, probably a salesman because he had a lot of boxes in the back seat.

"How old are you, son?" The same sharp glance accompanied the question.

"Nineteen."

"Just military age." He didn't beat around the bush. I twitched my face to make it appear I was under some terrible stress.

It didn't fool him. "You look healthy enough," he said.

He stopped at the next village. "If you're still on the road when I finish my business here I'll pick up you again."

I went into the Chinese restaurant. I was the only customer. I was looking at the list of sandwiches on the menu when the counterman said: "It's cheaper if you get a full-course dinner." It was. I got rice soup, sausages, mashed potatoes, carrots, a piece of pumpkin pie and a glass of milk for 30¢. The counterman didn't ask if I was going to join up. When I left, the salesman's car was gone and I stood at the end of the village. The next ride got me to Craigmyle. I sat in the back seat because the farmer had his wife with him.

"Our oldest son is already in England with the army," the woman said. The farmer chimed in right behind: "Which service are you going to try for?"

"The air force, I think," I said. It was the farthest thing from my mind.

I made Hanna by evening and found my cousin John, who had been working around the Prairies since well before the war. I stayed at his boardinghouse for three days. It was a good break. Around the table for the heaping meals were 10 people, including a bank clerk, a store clerk and two or three guys working with John putting in a sewer. Joining up was never mentioned.

I pushed on to Saskatoon where I stayed with an uncle for two days. The people in Saskatchewan who gave me lifts found it possible to introduce subjects other than my enlistment. But in Manitoba the inquisition resumed. Some were subtle: "There are some mighty fine regiments in Winnipeg." Some were more direct: "I'm driving right by the barracks, if you'd like me to let you off there." And some were fairly blunt: "Strapping boy like you should be helping out more" or "When I was your age, I'd been in for two years, right up in the trenches, too."

It was a relief when I got on the train at Winnipeg, even though I had to sit up all the way to Toronto. I knew I would soon be back among all the other young slackers at university.

The university, however, had a nasty surprise for most of us: we were expected to join the reserve Canadian Officer Training Corps and train a couple of evenings a week and Saturday afternoons. The COTC uniform, I figured, would eliminate questions about the timing of my embrace of the colors. It did, but it brought something worse.

I had two part-time jobs that kept me in university. One took me downtown after the COTC evening sessions at the University Armories. Regular soldiers would be thick on the street near the taverns and restaurants and movie houses.

"Hey, get a load of the officer," one would call out.

"He is real pretty," another would say.

"Even after a hard evening of drill," came another.

"Yoo-hoo."

But it was worse when they decided to be formal. They would crash their feet to the pavement and throw up an exaggerated salute in which you could almost hear the arm twanging.

"Good evening, sir," one would bellow.

"All accounted for, sir," another would shout.

"Your driver will be here in a tick, sir."

"Grand evening, isn't it, sir."

"Will there be anything else, sir?"

I wanted to go back to my civvy clothes and dare the white feather. ⌇

THE ONLY WAY TO GO
Ben Malkin

"Is everything to your satisfaction, sir?" bellowed the chief steward as he hammered on the door of the state room. The soldiers within, ignoring the heavy sarcasm, said no, it wasn't; the ship's crew was too noisy.

This was the first convoy to sail overseas in 1939, on a voyage almost unique in military annals. Five passenger ships—the *Aquitania*, the *Empress of Britain*, the *Empress of Australia*, the *Monarch of Bermuda* and the *Duchess of Bedford* (the *Drunken Duchess*)—had been assembled at Halifax, N.S., in such haste that they had not yet been converted to troopships.

Vessels that would later carry thousands of soldiers apiece now carried only hundreds. It was a classy way to travel, whether first, second, or third class. State rooms were allotted on a first-come, first-served basis. My unit, headquarters of the 3rd Field Regt., RCA, along with several of its batteries, had been among the last to arrive, resulting in the allotment of four persons to each small state room on the lower level of the *Empress of Britain*.

Before the war, teachers and clergymen would travel in this kind of state room on their once-in-a-lifetime journey to Britain and Europe. More affluent pilgrims inhabited the upper levels. However, the ships still had their peacetime crews, and on the *Empress of Britain*, a splendid Canadian Pacific vessel which, unhappily, was sunk off the Irish coast in October, 1940, they wouldn't let us do anything. Perhaps the management feared we landlubbers would damage their property while performing ship's duties.

Except, that is, for the passageway in front of the state rooms. We were supposed to sweep that up, but in the seven days until we sailed up the Clyde on Dec. 17, some of us became so lazy we wouldn't do that much. The chief steward's angry frustration resulted.

We had sailed on Dec. 10 under what was presumed to be tight security. We were told to draw the blinds on the train windows 30 miles from Halifax. The fact that most of the people living along the country's main railway lines already knew that troop trains were heading east evidently didn't matter. At Kenora, Ont., for example, where we stopped for a few minutes on our way from the West, the local ladies loaded boxes of apples on our train. All that an enemy spy needed to do in those days was visit any small town along either of the main railways, pick up a telephone on a party line, listen in, and he'd know when the next troop train was coming through.

Despite the "tight" security, when we slipped our lines and began to move away from the pier, a grand cacophony of car horns burst from the shore. Most of Halifax seemed to be on the dock to wish us Godspeed. In security as in other military matters, our amateur standing was still unimpaired.

The voyage was pleasant. Like peacetime passengers, each of us was seated at the same chair, at the same table in the dining room for all our meals. The steward who served us was polite, though not noticeably deferential. The food was regular CPR fodder, plentiful and nourishing, if unexciting. The sea was calm, and the only relief from boredom were the nightly bingo games, as well as sing-alongs conducted by an auxiliary services officer.

He was zealous, but had a limited repertoire. Not an evening went by that he didn't lead us in half a dozen renditions of "Home on the Range," a song for which, by the time we reached Scotland, I had developed a lasting hatred. After being home on the range so long and so repetitiously, after never having heard a discouraging word night after night, even Aldershot seemed a relief. At least it was a change. ॐ

The passenger ship *Empress of Britain* (the larger ship) at Quebec City in 1935.

THE LONG AND THE SHORT AND THE TALL
Ruth C. Auwarter

I grew up in an unsophisticated atmosphere and in an uncomplicated way. Until I was nineteen or so, I grew like the wild rose that sprawled on the stone fences of my grandfather's Yarmouth, Nova Scotia, farm. I was aware that my parents loved me deeply and I loved them in return.

Somewhat immature and gawky, I began to realize that all the tender loving care that had been lavished on me was stifling. Rather late, my adolescent revolt overtook me during World War II and went under the convenient guise of patriotism. Abandoning home and mother for my country, I enlisted in the Canadian Women's Army Corps in Halifax and cheerfully lied about my age, claiming to be a vastly more worldly twenty-one. I was quite unconcerned about the fact that the new date for my birth ante-dated that of my mother's wedding by some fifteen months.

So there I was, a bumpkin by nature and a bastard of my own contrivance, the unreadiest creature imaginable to be thrown to the CWAC.

The plunge was shocking. My existence was so altered that it was like learning to live under water. I moved slowly, heavily, uncomprehending, through an opaque world, gaping and mouthing like a carp until I broke surface and became myself again. I vaguely remember stumbling in and out of hospital ante-rooms during my physical. At one point I opened a door on a room where some men were standing about…Oops! wrong door!…these seemed to be urine donors.

I staggered blindly back to our group in time to undress in a blue-cold hall and to be fitted out in a sheet-like gown for a series of needle punctures, and probes which left no orifice unexplored. (What feminine mystique?) Numb with embarrassment, we all moved from orderly to grinning orderly like sheep through dip. We were afraid to ask whether the x-ray technician needed to be so helpful with the fronts of our sheets.

Our first quarters, emptied to accommodate us, had been part of the RCASC's Cogswell Street barracks.

Barracks life took some adjustment. It was somewhat like summer camp, except that our cross-section cut into a broader segment of humanity. I soon realized how colourless and inadequate a vocabulary I had had, and how dull my adolescent dating had been.

Eventually a few of us formed a group to protect each other against the consequences of our own naïveté, especially in new situations like gang showers. A sign in the shower-room read, PLEASE USE FOOT-BATH BEFORE AND AFTER USING SHOWER. However, the trough for the antiseptic foot-bath had been drained, so the sign didn't mean much to us. I found someone even greener than I who carefully washed her feet in the urinal before and after her shower.

My earliest snarl in army red tape came in a most innocent way. Before we had our own mess halls, we ate in one of the Service Corps' messes. Nasty rumour had it that the diet for the men was spiced with salt-petre. (There was more gaping and mouthing when we discovered all about that!) The cuisine was otherwise unimaginative, ranging from nebulous to catastrophic.

At any rate, whether by diet or trauma, I incubated two giant boils, one under my left armpit, the other on the left side of my neck. My sergeant promptly consigned me to examination along with the early V.D. aspirants. There were not yet any army hospital facilities provided for women, but being military personnel, we were sent to the Cogswell Street Military Hospital, even though we could not be kept there.

After the most cursory examination, I was sent to Victoria General Hospital. There I was tucked neatly away in bed—no patients could be ambulatory without a doctor's consent.

At first it was luxurious. I spent about thirty-six hours sleeping off my accumulated weariness, waking only for meals. The bland diet was so well prepared that what it lacked in spice, it made up for in careful and attractive preparation. I was so touched I almost cried in my custard. I was so content I scarcely noticed that I hadn't seen a doctor in days.

In fact, no doctor had come to see me. Shrewd cunning had elicited from me my name, rank and serial number and other pertinent information. My daily progress was charted and my sheets were regularly changed and smoothed, but nobody from the army seemed to care enough to find out how I was coping with my infirmity or even to bring me my pajamas.

On the third day I began to chafe; on the fourth to fret; on the fifth day I was so desperate for companionship that I remembered that it had been almost two weeks since I had written to my mother. By coincidence, the lady across the hall had ordered a telephone for her personal use. I had been unaware that such refinements were available. Not to be outdone, I ordered a telephone and made a (collect) call home.

I knew that I had conferred a great favour on my parents in calling, but I was totally unprepared for their response. Mother cried and said incoherent things. I was touched, but still out of touch. Then my father, with his cool, incisive manner, took the phone.

"Where the hell are you?"

Dad was seldom profane…it took a lot to make him say "hell"…but what? I knew the tone, but I couldn't think what I'd done to provoke it. Craftily, I decided to make him suffer.

"I'm in the hospital," I reproved, in what I hoped was a weak and pathetic tone.

It's a wily child who knows her own father, and my comment had the desired effect. A hurried conference on the other end of the line, then the sound of Mother's new burst of weeping buoyed my confidence. I had my finger on the pulse of the family. I explained the situation to my father.

I was still flattered at the stir I had caused until my father began to speak. Because I had not written them, my parents had telephoned me two days before. By that time I had been absent from my barracks for another two days.

My sergeant, the one who had sent me to the Military Hospital, informed Mother and Dad that I had been sent to the hospital for diagnosis and

An illustration of members of the Canadian Women's Army Corps preparing for an injection.

treatment of venereal disease, and that, further, I had not arrived with my little group. According to my sergeant, I was Absent Without Official Leave, a deserter, and very likely an infected deserter, a menace to the citizenry and a drain on the war effort. Hitler, she had implied darkly, would have been proud of me.

"Now," said my father in his quietest, most terrible tone, "where are you and what are you up to?"

That shattered my composure and I began to blubber incoherent protestations of my innocence into the horrible little black device in my hand. I sobbed my compliance with his ill-disguised "suggestions."

Yes, I would immediately call my sergeant. No, I did not have V.D. Yes, I would see that nothing on my medical record would imply that I did. Yes, I would take care of it right away. Yes, I would call back as soon as I had phoned my sergeant. Yes, I really was in the hospital. NO, it was just boils! Yes, boils. How should I know how I got them? No, I hadn't been to church lately. Yes, I would call back right away. Yes, yes, yes, no, but yes.

A call to my sergeant got immediate action. It took several days to effect my release from the hospital, but eventually I was once again a regular in His Majesty's forces. My boils had been lanced and were healing and all the implications that I was medically undermining the war effort were deleted from my record. The notice of my absence without leave was rescinded. I was ready to continue my basic training.

A few days later, I was re-united with my friends at the Cogswell Street barracks and it wasn't long before I was "pickin' 'em up and layin' 'em down" on our fine parade square.

Hup! Two! Three! Four! Ha-a-a-a-alt! ॐ

THE BATTLE OF B FLIGHT
Gerald Wright

In the heart of the beautiful habitant country, jokingly referred to by the airmen as "Unoccupied France," on the southern shore of the Gulf of the St. Lawrence, No. 9 Bombing and Gunnery School trained the air gunners who later manned the turrets of the Lancasters and Halifaxes of Bomber Command. From the Anzac countries, from the British Isles, from every part of Canada and many of the occupied countries of Europe the trainees assembled at Mont Joli, Quebec, for a few weeks to learn the culture of the Browning gun. Here, in the late summer of 1944, in a small barrack room, I met and lived with as colourful an assortment of characters as I ever met anywhere.

Outside the barracks, the lovely green hills sloped down to the blue water of the St. Lawrence River. The multi-coloured sunsets matched for splendour anything seen in Canada, including the prairies. Life inside the barracks drew its colour from the inimitable antics of the characters who comprised B flight. These consisted of a New Zealander, a Cockney, a Welshman, and a Yorkshireman whom no one could understand without an interpreter. A Jew from Cambridge University, two Scotchmen, a full-blooded Chippewa Indian, and an odd assortment of Canadians, including a schoolteacher and two ministers' sons, completed the list.

Two days after our arrival one of the ministers' sons, who had a great taste for booze, landed in the digger for "borrowing" some boxing gloves. His punishment was later commuted to four weeks at shelling eggs in the kitchen for four or five hours each night. From then on life in B flight was like going to the circus. Kiwi, the New Zealander, had a habit of advertising the glories of New Zealand and the beauties of Karanaki at night when the rest of us wanted to sleep. One evening he had just come to the oft-repeated sentence, "Boy, you should see Karanaki," when he was suddenly seized and launched down the fire escape in his birthday suit. Kiwi, being a good sport, took it in good part, having received only one or two scratches.

Directly under me slept the schoolteacher from Saskatchewan, an ardent member of the C.C.F., whose strong political opinions stirred up some red-hot controversy in the barracks. Ranged at the opposite end of the room, the conservative faction from Britain hurled a barrage of imprecations across the room at the socialists. Taffy, the fiery-tempered Welshman and a rabid communist, sided with the socialists. Taffy had one redeeming feature, however; he was an excellent singer. When he wasn't too angry over some supposed social injustice, he entertained B flight with his music. Even the *Internationale*, anthem of Marxism, sounded all right when Taffy sang it.

Sometimes big Jock, a six-foot ex-policeman from Glasgow, regaled us with stories of adventures in the slums of the Scottish metropolis. Wee Jock, his inseparable companion, came from a farm in the Highlands and scarcely measured five feet, even when he stretched.

An Avro Lancaster from the RAF Central Navigation School in Shawbury, England, visits Boundary Bay, B.C., in February 1944.

Then there was Cambridge, so called because he had attended the university of that name. Born in Egypt, where his father was a British diplomat, Cambridge professed the Hebrew religion. He held to a strong dislike of socialists of any kind, which fact accounted for some of the most ear-blistering debates. As his special pride and joy, he sported a woollen muffler composed of the Cambridge colours. Cambridge lost no opportunity to wear this snobby neckpiece.

Cambridge's neckpiece became the target for the ridicule of Blondy, eighteen-year-old son of a trade union organizer, who had clearly defined ideas of class. Blondy made repeated attempts to have the Air Force organized along the lines of a trade union, with more privileges for the A.C.2's, no saluting, etc. Of course, these attempts weren't too popular with the C.O. and Blondy frequently found himself on the peg. The whole political issue ended up one night in a fierce pillow fight, resulting in considerable destruction to His Majesty's linen. Of course, when the facts leaked out, B flight had to foot the bill.

The character of them all, however, was a Cockney from London, answering to the name of Lamb. Possessed of a good voice, he knew just about every song that was worth knowing, and several of doubtful worth. Mr. Lamb claimed to be the grandson of Charles Lamb, the English poet, and I don't think anyone doubted his claim. In any case, he had a remarkable gift of the gab and formed numerous friendships with the single W.D.'s on the station. In addition, he broke the hearts of several of the local mademoiselles. The last time I saw him, some months later, he was walking arm in arm with a member of the C.W.A.C. down Granville Street in Vancouver.

One night an electric failure threw the camp into total darkness. Taffy, Charles Lamb's grandson and another bloke went out on the fire escape to sing some songs of the black-out. About halfway through "The Lights of London," the music degenerated into a frustrated

A Lancaster bomber during the Second World War.

gurgle, as a well-directed stream of water from another section of the barracks soaked the musicians to the skin. B flight retaliated swiftly with our own fire-fighting equipment and trained a shower of cool water into the bunks of the boys below. Ironically enough, the only casualty in B flight turned out to be the schoolteacher, who had taken no active part in the fight. While he lay peaceably in his bunk a direct hit from the enemy's fire hose caught him and flooded him out of bed.

As in most barracks, there had to be the inevitable ladies' man who wore silk pyjamas and nursed a cute little officer-type moustache. He announced publicly that he intended to snag himself a commission when he graduated, and he cultivated the friendship of as many officers as would put up with him. This attitude didn't go over too well with the rest of B flight. Our

officer candidate pal spent most of his spare time in town treating the "belles femmes Canadiennes." After one such sally into town, Casanova returned to walk into a little surprise, devised by some of his comrades. Inserted cleverly into his bunk, an ingenious contraption full of water lay concealed beneath the blankets. A slight amount of pressure would have flooded the place. Unfortunately, the wee Scot, who occupied the bunk below, had taken the precaution of covering his own bunk with two raincoats. Casanova inadvertently discovered the raincoats which aroused his suspicions and destroyed our joke.

A few days after this incident, graduation arrived and the Battle of B Flight ended. If nothing else, it had served to strengthen Commonwealth relations and enlarge our insight into human nature. ❧

ROAD TO THE ISLE
Rosemary Hutchinson

My friend Charlie and I are drinking milk shakes at a soda bar in Toronto, 1942. "I think I'll have a hamburger," she says. "When you're in shock you gotta eat."

Charlie and I are very new, very shiny drivers in the RCAF, greener than grass. We have just learned our first posting is to Newfoundland, when we had expected Trenton or Dunnville, Ont. We could not be more surprised had Ottawa sent us to Zanzibar or Katmandu.

"Where exactly is this place then?" Charlie asks. She is from the West, so cannot be expected to know any geography east of Winnipeg.

"Oh," I say vaguely, "it's an island somewhere off Nova Scotia, the nearest point to Europe in North America. If you walk too far east you're liable to fall off the end of it and have to swim all the way to Scotland."

She looks at me suspiciously. "Why can't I swim back?"

"Impossible, you'd be dashed to pieces on the rocks along the coast. Newfoundland is nothing but rocks and bush."

"You paint a beautiful picture," Charlie says drily. "I don't think you know what you're talking about."

I slap mustard on my hamburger. "I'm only quoting my Uncle Wally. He was there in 1913, but he's a bit flaky and he drinks a lot."

Charlie gurgles up the last of her milk shake. "Well, I hope they make good shakes there."

We leave the restaurant and trek down Jarvis Street towards Manning Pool. It is a warm autumn day; tomorrow at dawn we leave for Halifax.

I had met Charlie on my first day in the air force while we were at the counter in the mess hall trying for a second piece of butterscotch pie. She is a tall, good-looking girl with great hair that springs from her head in a wild mass of curls, waves and fetching tendrils.

Somewhere in this hirsute jungle is her cap, whose peak can be seen perched on the end of her nose. She is in constant trouble with Authority for "wispy bits," the euphemism for hair touching the tunic collar, a real air force no-no.

You could be loping along minding your own business, and whip up a smart salute—longest way up, shortest way down—passing Authority, when suddenly you are commanded to stop.

"Airwoman, you have wispy bits."

So you say: "Yes, ma'am," and go to chop off a few more strands.

Not Charlie though. She is a bit like Samson—she believes in her hair.

Next afternoon there are about 30 girls in the Newfoundland draft sitting in Montreal's Windsor Station surrounded by kitbags and assorted luggage. Cooks, drivers, wireless ops, hospital assistants, riggers, clerks, telephone ops and parachute packers are all raising the dust in the old station with their yackety-yack.

For a change of scene Charlie and I head up Peel Street to St. Catherine and peer in a shoe-store window. She digs me in the ribs.

"Will you look at those black penny-loafers. Wouldn't they go great with the uniform?"

"But they're not issue. Where would we wear those?"

"To dances of course, and on heavy dates with wing commanders."

"But I don't know any wing commanders," I complain.

Charlie casts a withering glance at my shapeless, black issue lace-ups.

"You never will with those beetle-crushers. Wincos like girls with neat feet. C'mon," and she dives into the store. Moments later we emerge, each clutching a big box.

"I hope you're happy," I tell her.

"Yup!" she replies. "Happy, but broke."

We rush back to the station to find our train boarding. I lug two kitbags, a badminton racket, a holdall, the shoe box and my shoulder purse endless miles down the platform and collapse exhausted on the train, which is absolutely packed with aircrew. They surge up

CNS *Lady Rodney* at Montreal in 1929.

and down between the cars in a ceaseless parade. As the train rattles on we all get jolly and friendly together and it's well after midnight before irate conductors shove this young, male mass back to its own carriages. We airwomen have been allotted berths—it sometimes pays to be female—and sleep the night away in innocent tranquillity.

The war really hits us in Halifax. On this warm, foggy morning we are dragging our kit up the gangplank of a great, grey ship with canvas-colored guns fore and aft.

"Lordy," pants Charlie, "this thing's big enough to sail us to England."

"We can't go on the ferry any more," I remind her. "The *Caribou* that went between North Sydney and Port-aux-Basques was torpedoed a few weeks ago. Remember?"

Charlie stares at me in consternation. "Gosh, I'd forgotten that."

So we board, chilled by the grim facts of war. The harbor is full of grey ships and in the distance I can see a super-size one looming over the rest. I think it must be one of the Queens.

Later, as we forge into the open sea, Charlie and I lean on the rail watching the land disappear. Surging along beside us is another grey shape.

"That's the *Lady Rodney*," she tells me importantly. "We're on the *Fort Amherst*. Before the war they both cruised around the Caribbean."

Charlie should have been a reporter, she goes after the facts. If I don't stop her she'll tell me their tonnage, registry and the passenger list for June, 1936.

"I bet they were painted white with red funnels," I cry enthusiastically. "The passengers sat around the swimming pool all day drinking rum punch."

"With no life jackets," Charlie says gloomily, jerking at the one clamped on her chest.

We have been told to wear these and to sleep in our clothes. It has begun to dawn on us there are submarines out there: German ones.

It seems a pleasant ship, not too crowded. The passengers are a mixed bag—military and civilian— the bulk being airwomen. There is a big room with tables and chairs we learn to call the saloon. It has a bar, unfortunately closed. Our sleeping quarters are deluxe—four girls to a cabin—although I wouldn't realize how deluxe until much later when I sailed to England on the *Queen Elizabeth*.

Time passes. At the end of the third day we are still sailing with no land in sight. That evening some of us slip through the blackout door on to the deck for a breath of fresh air; the saloon tends to be very hot and stuffy. We are met with an astounding sight and stare in stunned silence across the water at the *Lady Rodney*. She is covered with dancing lights. It is as though millions of fireflies have settled on her every railing, spar and mast and clicked on their tiny bulbs. From bow to stern she glows in the blackness and even the waves are flecked with light.

Finally someone whispers, "What on earth is it?" then adds, "Oh! What a lovely sight."

But it takes a girl from Alberta to bring home the awful truth. "God!" she says, "I bet you can see us for miles."

This casts such a pall on us we scuttle back to the muggy light of the saloon. As expected, Charlie dashes off to get the facts. On returning, she says: "It's St. Elmo's fire—something to do with climatic conditions and phosphorus, very rare." She does not have to add it is not a happy wartime condition. We have realized that ourselves.

Some of us start a game of crazy eights. Charlie deals. "Deucys wild, a nickel a game."

There are five of us around the table and I would be surprised if our combined ages add up to much more than 100. Most of us have never seen the sea before, let alone the North Atlantic in the middle of a war. We may be frightened but we don't let it show. We fight over every hand as though nothing in the world mattered more.

After the game Charlie and I stay at the table. "Scared?" she asks. "Are you thinking great thoughts of eternity? Is your life unrolling before your eyes?"

I unwrap an O'Henry bar, hoping my hands are steady. "You know there are two shiny ships out here; we must be lit up just like the *Lady Rodney*."

Charlie peers at me through her bramble-bush hair. "I got a bottle in my holdall. How about a smash? Then we'd be lit up too."

I think this pretty funny and we both start to laugh. "Na," I say, "save it for the lifeboat."

The next day we sail safely into St. John's harbor. As we wait to disembark Charlie heaves her holdall on to her shoulder and cracks it on the deck railing. Goodbye bottle.

"My pennyloafers are in there," she wails. "They'll get soaked."

I can't resist it. "Too bad," I tell her. "No dates with wincos now. They don't approve of alcoholic loafers."

GARBAGE RUN
Rosemary Hutchinson

Charlie and I are sitting in the cab of the old dump truck. We idly watch the sleet hitting the windshield and the sea fog gathering round us. It is November of 1942. The place is RCAF Station Torbay, Newfoundland. Charlie and I are motor transport drivers.

Charlie is in charge of this ancient dumper. Shortly, she will drive it a mile or so along the cliff road, near the fishing hamlet of Torbay, and dump a load of garbage in to the sea.

We can hear the clatter as the civilian helper empties the trash cans on to the back of the truck. Charlie is pooped out: she has been helping heave junk all day, her parka is soaking wet, and water drips from the peak of her cap on to her nose.

This is the last call of the day, the station hospital, where she has acquired me as a passenger. I have spent a much warmer day than Charlie, as duty driver on the ambulance. A "stand down" has been called—there will be no more flying today—so I am free early. If I go back to the transport section, I may have to take some duty run in to St. John's. Anything is better than that, even accompanying Charlie and the garbage to the cliffs at Torbay.

Corncob bangs on the door. I open it and shove over to give him room to get in. "Yer finished, B'y," he says, taking out his ancient pipe, whence his nickname, and lighting it. Acrid smoke mixes with damp clothing but the pipe is the only hot spot in the cab, the powers-that-be in Ottawa not providing heaters in their military vehicles. Corncob is the civilian helper, a tough little man, his years many, his energy unflagging.

Charlie starts the motor in a miasma of fruity tobacco. She clashes the gears back and forth.

"This is a frightful old bucket," she remarks. "I never know whether I am in low or reverse." With this she rams home the gear, we suddenly lurch backwards and crash with a fearsome rending of wood in to the side of the hospital, narrowly missing the steps to the back door but squashing flat two large tin pails. As we sit there somewhat surprised at this reversal, the door to the hospital kitchen is flung open and the rotund figure of the cook appears, waving a carving knife.

Charlie quickly jiggles the gears again and this time we proceed forward in good order in the direction of the station's main gate, en route to the cliffs.

During the drive Corncob reaches in to the depths of his vast and filthy parka and produces a large vinegar bottle. On ascertaining that it contains rum, Charlie and I join him in a couple of belts. He always travels with some liquid; when it is only tea, we don't partake. There is a lot of trench mouth on the station, and there is probably no better source than the unsanitary top of Corncob's bottle, but rum is a different story. I figure it can kill the most determined staph germ.

I ask after Corncob's "wumman" and his numerous offspring and subtly seek out any station gossip he may know, but he is not forthcoming today. He is too cold. On the return trip we will drop him off at his house. He lives at Torbay in a tiny dwelling hanging on to a rock and boasts that he can fish from his back door. Some day the sea will pour up over his whole establishment, taking away Corncob, his wumman and assorted children. "Don't worry me none," he says.

We grind up a long hill to the cliff top and Charlie backs the truck smartly to within 6 feet of its edge, pulls the dumping lever and the garbage slides, with a roar, 30 feet in to the sea.

Corncob and I stand and watch the swirling mess below. The word pollution is not in my vocabulary. I only look across the surging water, thinking how great it would be if I were to sight a submarine. I hear the thud as Charlie retracts the dumping platform. She leans from the cab and bawls through the fog: "Let's get outta here." Letting out the clutch, she prepares to move ahead, but the truck jerks backwards a good three feet before she jams on the brake. Appalled, I rush over and hang in the window.

"Jeez, Charlie, what are you doing? For the love of Mike, go forward." Charlie stares back at me, her pretty pink and white face somewhat green. Even with her sodden cap, her hair hanging in wet strings about her face, she is a very good looking girl—what my old granddad used to call a "stunner."

"I can't get the blasted gear out of reverse," she wails. "Here, you try it." She vaults to the ground, holding the cab door open for me. I nonchalantly climb in, shove the gear in to what I know is low and confidently acceler-ate. I shoot back another two feet and hastily withdraw from the cab. My cap is now dripping water too and the toes of my flying boots are beginning to turn up in the wet. I am very proud of these boots. They are the old RAF fighter-pilot type, and I've ferried many bottles of hard-to-get scotch from St. John's to a boozer I know to effect a trade.

"My boots are getting wet," I announce. Charlie glares at me: "I don't give a damn about your bloody boots. Just what would you suggest I do now?"

The three of us stand in contemplation. Corncob passes his bottle. "Eeh B'y, thassa problem," he says. Charlie turns to me. "Do me a favor? Walk back to the station and get the wrecker." This good idea has one drawback. By the time I return it will be pitch dark on the cliffs and the Newfie blackout is so profound it would be easier to try hitching up the dumper in a clothes-closet.

We might be standing there still, covered with salt and a national historic site, had a figure not loomed out of the mist—an American soldier carrying a rifle under his arm, a great dog on a chain by his side. He is one of a patrol that regularly checks the byways on the coast.

I can't see what he looks like, he is so muffled in clothing, but he has a voice like Humphrey Bogart: "You got trouble, gals?" Charlie falls upon him as though heaven-sent. If that dump truck goes over the edge, there will be one furious sergeant major in the transport section. Charlie is more expendable than the truck.

This is one cool guy. He hands me his rifle and the dog's chain. "Stay, Buttercup," he says to the beast and takes Charlie's arm affectionately. "Nothing to this, Sweetie, we'll just take it slow."

He starts the motor, eases in the gear shift and lurches back another foot. The rear tires are now poised on the brink.

"Holy smoke!" he yelps. "This old bastard should be in the junk yard." Charlie is braced against the front fender, as though she alone can stave off the dumper's plunge to a watery grave.

The Yank sits in the cab, obviously in deep thought. Suddenly jiggling the gears, he waves and shouts, "OK, Kid, I got it," grips the steering wheel, accelerates and the truck lurches forward to the safety of the road.

"This gimmick on the gear is busted, you oughta get it fixed," he tells Charlie, who is so overcome with gratitude she isn't listening.

"Oh," she trills, "that was magnificent. How can I ever thank you?" Our soldier takes back his gun and dog, for which I am very thankful. "You can," he says. "I'll buy you dinner Saturday at the USO." He jerks his thumb at me. "Bring her, I got a buddy." With that he and his dog disappear in to the gloom.

Of course we go. Dinner at the USO, the American servicemen's club in St. John's, is not to be sneered at. Steaks, french fries, chocolate malts and sundaes don't come our way at Torbay. Charlie brings her hero a pair of socks she knitted for some pilot who will no doubt have cold feet for some time as she is a very sporadic knitter.

There are no shocks to our virtue; in fact, we spend the entire evening admiring photographs of our boy-friends' wives and children. We escape early, blunder over to the Newfoundland Hotel in the blackout and hasten to the bar. Admiring other people's kids is thirsty work.

Pettigrew, one of the night shift drivers, picks us up. The barrack block is dark and quiet. Charlie lies in her bunk above mine, laughing at some guy talking on her little radio.

"He must be very funny," I tell her.

"Naw," she mumbles, half asleep, "just some announcer. His name is Joey something. Smallwood I think he said."

"Turn him off," I say. "He should be in politics, he's got so much to say." ॐ

THE COAL-OIL KIDS
Rosemary Hutchinson

Bussy Bodine and I are up on the runway laying the flare-path. My friend Charlie has come along to assist. Night is falling on a cold January day at RCAF Station Torbay, Newfoundland. It is the Year of Our War 1943.

If I write to my mother tomorrow about this flare-path job, she will be so impressed. She will tell all her friends: "Rosemary is doing such marvellous war work. The other day she laid the flare-path!" Later she will ask my father: "What's a flare-path?" If she were handy, I could explain that the whole dirty business is nothing but mud, wet and swears.

So here I am driving the tired old pickup, the rear loaded with oily flare-pots, alongside the runway at a snail's pace. I can hear the thuds and scrapes as Bussy and Charlie, working feverishly, pull them off the truck.

When Charlie gets cold enough, or angry enough, she will bang on the window and, with a fierce jerk of her thumb, indicate that it is her turn to drive and mine to unload. Bussy gets no such respite. Being assigned to general duties, which means he does anything, anywhere, any time, he is a permanent fixture on this job. Charlie and I get involved only when we are not smart enough to escape the beady-eyed transport section dispatcher when he is looking for a driver.

Inching slowly along, I wonder if I have perhaps made a mistake in my choice of a wartime occupation. Maybe I should have been a Wren or CWAC, a genius in some naval plotting room or the veritable right hand of a red-tabbed army officer. "Give that girl an instant commission," some senior type would say. "Her intelligence and devotion to duty are an example to all!" Then I tell myself to stop dreaming. I would probably mix up all the ships on the plotting table or drive my red-tabbed officer crazy.

I am really quite happy, though in truth Bussy, Charlie and I occupy very lowly positions on the air force social scale. There is hope for Bussy: he is waiting to remuster to aircrew and may end up a squadron leader covered with gongs. But Charlie and I are doomed for the duration, like worker bees in a hive with all sorts of irritating people buzzing over our heads.

These sombre thoughts are interrupted by Charlie banging on the window. As we change places I idly wonder if I look as awful as she does, and sadly decide that I do. She is wearing a dirty brown parka, a long tartan scarf around her neck, the oily ends flapping in the breeze, and a WAAF cap. The new hat, somewhat resembling an inverted cooking pot, has, thankfully, not yet made its appearance at Torbay.

"Your cap looks like a pea on a pumpkin," I shout, because the wind is getting up, making it hard to talk. Charlie is taken aback by this uncalled-for remark. I can see her trying to think up some withering retort, but all she finds to say is quite unprintable. She clambers into the truck and, laughing, shakes her fist at me.

When all the pots are out in more or less straight lines, Bussy lights them. This is in the hopeful expectation that they will continue to fizz and flare, providing enough illumination for some poor sod to land his aircraft in the right place rather than removing the top of the control tower or pancaking on the roof of the officers' mess.

We get the OK sign from the control tower and leave hastily in the pickup. I park outside. For some reason this decrepit old bucket is not allowed house room in the transport section, but must sit by itself in oily isolation like some leprous pariah. We hurl our gloves (No. 273, gloves, yellow, airmen for the use of) on to the cab floor and depart for the canteen. The gloves don't fit and are as waterproof as paper. Our hands stink of coal-oil.

We sit for an hour in the canteen eating hotdogs and drinking pop. We note that those at adjoining tables leave abruptly, making nasty remarks, presumably because of our smell, a penetrating Nuit de Coal-Oil. Charlie, fond of the going air force jargon, remarks: "We pong."

A woman in uniform polishes up a window on an aircraft during the Second World War.

Bussy is on his fifth hotdog. Charlie and I are very fond of him; he is bright, witty and has the kindest heart in the world. He also talks a lot and is very politically minded. While the cigarette smoke swirls about the table he expounds on taxes, conscription, the war in general and Social Credit in his native province. This erudition falls on deaf ears. Charlie and I are too lulled by heat and hotdogs to even hear him. As far as I am concerned Mackenzie King is indestructible, he will just go on forever, marching eternally with Churchill and Roosevelt—as permanent as Mount Everest, like the war. I suppose it will end one day, but my narrow little mind can only encompass my own affairs, such as flare-paths, flat tires, dirty cars and will someone ask me to the sergeants' dance next Friday.

Bussy now regales us with stories of Bella. Bella lives in St. John's and they are to be married shortly. Charlie and I are quite stunned by this girl's accomplishments. She is not only beautiful but cooks like Escoffier and sews like Coco Chanel. "Can she lay a flare-path?" Charlie asks nastily. Bussy thinks this very funny, and departs for a heavy date with his beloved. We tell him to wash. If Bella could see him now it would put the romance back 10 years.

Charlie and I repair to the recreation hall to see *Casablanca*. We peer through the gloom at Ingrid and Humphrey. What a problem this girl has! Will she go with Paul? Or will she throw honor and virtue to the winds and stay with Bogey? Charlie is so entranced she drops her popcorn all over the floor.

After the show we return to the barracks. From the depths of her locker Charlie unearths a jug of home-made wine, a gift from Bussy. We suspect that Bella has brewed it, not in her bathtub, we hope.

I peer at the label. "Why is it this funny yellow color when it says blueberry 1942?"

"Gad but you're fussy," says Charlie filling two large chipped glasses. "The color doesn't matter, it's taste that counts."

We lie on our bunks, refilling the glasses several times. Charlie smiles across at me. "This glop doesn't taste half bad," she says.

"Yeah," I reply. "Didn't you know? 1942 was a very good year!" ❧

A woman, perhaps a member of the Women's Auxiliary Air Force, fuels up a truck.

HOME PORT
Hugh Garner

St. John's has always held a special spot in my wartime memories. It served as an oiling and supply station for Royal Navy and RCN escort forces almost from the outbreak of war and I sailed in and out of it many times.

Newfyjohn, as we called it, though not a Canadian city at that time, is the only Canadian city today that can boast of really taking part in a World War II combat zone. It is our only city that was blacked out during the war years, and to my knowledge the only North American one. Even Gibraltar flaunted its lights throughout the war, defying German and Italian planes to bomb it.

Although U-boats laid an extensive minefield outside Halifax harbor, and other German submarines landed enemy spies on the Gaspe Coast and penetrated the St. Lawrence River far inland, St. John's—situated hundreds of miles east of any other mainland Canadian or U.S. city—played a stellar role in the longest battle of all, the Battle of the Atlantic.

On one occasion at least, whether in 1942 or 1943 I no longer remember, a German U-boat stood off the city's harbor entrance and fired a spray of torpedoes that exploded against the anti-submarine net and beneath the coastal guns below Signal Hill and its twin headland to the south. I remember this occurred one afternoon because the destroyer and corvettes of the escort force I was serving in were sent out to search for the sub, but we failed to pick it up on our radar or asdic gear.

The escort ships making the Triangle Run—St. John's, Halifax, and a U.S. eastern seaboard port were the triangle's corners—waited in St. John's to pick up ocean convoys from their escorts, which then took their places in the small harbor. It was also the home port when Canadian escorts ran only to Iceland.

When Canada later took over a large share of the mid-Atlantic merchant convoys between St. John's and Londonderry and the Clyde, the harbor entrance of Newfyjohn was a welcome sight, the first sign of land we'd seen, with the possible exception of the flashing beam of the lighthouse on Cape Farewell, Greenland. I read somewhere once that the RN supplied 50 per cent of the WW II Atlantic convoy escorts, Canada 49 per cent and the United States 1 per cent.

A convoy could only steam across the ocean at the speed of its slowest ship and the horrifying losses of tankers and merchant ships to U-boats forced the Allies to resurrect some old, broken-down turkeys that held many convoys to a speed of only five knots. When it took us 26 days to escort one convoy across the Atlantic, we jokingly renamed our ship the *Santa Maria* after one of Christopher Columbus' ships.

There were times when Canadian escort forces were engaged in battle with German submarine wolf packs. Probably one of the worst attacks took place between Christmas, 1942, and New Year's Day against a convoy we were escorting north of the Azores. At the time I was a new petty officer, who'd received my promotion by signal from Canada while we were tied up in Londonderry, Northern Ireland.

I was serving on the flower-class corvette HMCS *Battleford*, part of No. 1 Canadian Escort Force that consisted of the river-class destroyer *St. Laurent* and four more corvettes, *Kenogami, Shediac, Chilliwack* and *Napanee*, when we took a shellacking from a couple of U-boat wolf packs, and lost 14 of the 44 ships we started out with from the United Kingdom.

One of the first ships sunk was our fleet oiler, the *Scottish Heather*, and as we'd been fighting heavy gales for about 10 days rounding Ireland the corvettes were running short of fuel. The *Chilliwack* had just completed fueling from the *Scottish Heather* when she was torpedoed. Among the others we lost that holiday week were the *Fidelity* and a rescue ship code-named *Stretcher*.

The convoy broke up and the ships chose their own routes to the ports of Canada and the U.S., aided by the arrival of fleet-class destroyers from Gibraltar. Because she was out of fuel, we towed the *Shediac* into the oiling port of Ponta Delgada on the Azores island of Sao

HMCS *Battleford* (a corvette) on patrol in the North Atlantic.

Miguel. Portugal was a neutral country, but seemed more neutral to the Germans than to us; we were given about 48 hours to refuel and take on food.

Coming back to St. John's towards the end of the war was a nostalgic experience. The city hadn't changed much since I'd last been there—the Newfoundland Hotel and the spire of the Roman Catholic cathedral still dominated the skyline.

At anchor in the middle of the harbor was a captured German tanker where some ships still oiled up. The jetties built by the RCN on the south side of the harbor were now the berths of destroyers, frigates and castle-class corvettes that were formed into hunter-killer groups to go looking for German submarines.

To the south of the harbor across from the city, a large oil-tank farm dotted the hills where the shantytown we called Dog-patch once stood.

Canadian sailors and airmen now shared the streets with American servicemen on pass from the camps, airfields, coastal guns and signal stations along the coasts of the island.

One thing that hadn't changed was the friendliness and decency of the Newfoundlanders who had accepted our comparatively overpaid arrogance when we first arrived there shortly after the war began.

There were many Newfoundlanders serving in the Canadian forces, but a great many more had been shipped to Great Britain when the war broke out as members of the Royal Newfoundland Regiment and the RAF. And a number of Newfoundland girls had married Canadian, British and American servicemen stationed there.

St. John's pubs—and remember that pubs or beer parlors were still not allowed in Canadian provinces outside of Quebec—still served Canadian beer. Many of the city's bootleggers still flogged 'screech,' the rum-based local drink more potent than Quebec 'caribou' and powerful enough to derail the Newfie Bullet.

The surviving RN and RCN destroyers, flower-class corvettes and Bangor minesweepers, as well as Norwegian, Dutch and Free French warships that had fought the U-boats when they outnumbered us five to one in the North Atlantic, were now tied up beside U.S. Coast Guard cutters and U.S. Navy destroyer escorts.

The seagoing naval officers' club, The Crowsnest, was still going strong, and Canadian Wrens were seen all over town. It reminded me of the time when our corvette pulled into Jetty Five in the Halifax Naval Dockyard after a fairly long spell at sea and one of our seamen, spotting some Wrens on the parade square, shouted: "Lookit all the double-barrelled ABs!"

Officers and gentlemen had their own drinking club, and chief torpedo gunner's mate Popeye Chambers from North Vancouver decided that the chiefs and POs would have theirs too. He formed one in the chief and petty officers' wet canteen, sold membership cards for a buck apiece and named it, rather indelicately, the Gag and Vomit Club. A bunch of us stalwarts whose iron-bound stomachs matched our brains gathered every evening.

Unlike the top brass in Halifax who crazily shut up all the wet canteens on VE-Day, triggering the biggest Bacchanalia since Canada became a Dominion, the officers in command of things in St. John's kept them open. I have a hazy, somewhat delirious recollection of May 8, 1945, but I'll bet it was a great day for those who remember it well.

Around the tables in the chief and PO's wets we members of the Gag and Vomit Club, ably abetted by every

nationality of Allied non-commissioned officers from most of the ships in the harbor, sang every dirty service ditty we could think of, including "The North Atlantic Squadron." We interspersed the service songs with "We'll Rant And We'll Roar Like True Newfoundlanders" and "The Squid-Jiggin' Ground."

Shortly after VE-Day I was given the job of shutting down all the naval wet canteens around St. John's. Though to me it was a lead-pipe cinch that the canteen wallahs who'd inveigled themselves into jobs in these joints throughout the war had all filched enough dough to buy themselves a house on civvy street when the war was over, I gave them a cursory inventory and made out reports that their books balanced. Actually, sending me to inventory beer stocks was like sending Jack the Ripper to run a girls' school, but the free beer alleviated my terminal hangover for a while.

When some clown tried to pressure me into signing up for the Pacific war I told him that he should sign up himself, after all he'd joined the navy in 1944 just to miss the army's 'zombie' draft, but I'd paid my dues, having joined up Sept. 11, 1939, was now 32 years old, and had a wife and two small kids who hardly knew me.

In August, 1945, some of us naval odds and sods in St. John's were given passage on the destroyer *Saskatchewan* to Quebec City and then sent home for discharge. We happened to tie up in Quebec on VJ-Day, and were confined to ship while civilians held their 'victory' parades through the city.

In Montreal's old Bonaventure railroad station the next day we split into two groups, one for the train to northwestern Ontario and Western Canada, and the other for southern Ontario. That morning I'd discovered that my gas mask bag was the perfect container to hold eight pints of ale, so I shoved the gas mask into my duffel and filled its container.

And that, kiddies, is how grandpa spent the war. And you keep your lip buttoned, Johnny, or I'll send you down to the cellar to polish them medals! ॐ

A STAR IS BORN
Vic Cousins

England in 1943 was reeling from long years of war. Its supply line was fed by an endless stream of ships from North America. Our corvette, HMCS *Pictou*, was one of the feisty little watchdogs escorting the full ships across the Atlantic and the empties back for refills.

On Dec. 8, 1943, we left Londonderry for St. John's, Newfoundland, leading a convoy of empty ships bobbing like corks into the howling hell of a North Atlantic gale. There were broken backs, crews to be rescued and tow lines to be rigged for the rescue tugs. As three different storms raged at us, it was almost impossible to attach lines to the refuelling ships and we only managed to refuel once.

For 23 days we battled our way across the Atlantic. Food stocks were so low in Ireland, we had taken on barely enough for the nine days of a normal trip. Christmas was celebrated with dehydrated cabbage and dehydrated potatoes. We even used up the emergency supplies in the lifeboats. The only warm things in those raging storms were our memories of Christmas past. We were so cold, hungry and miserable that often only three or four diehards could find the courage to muster for 'up spirits.'

A cook on board a Canadian navy ship poses with a cake in November 1941.

We limped into St. John's on New Year's Eve, just as dusk was beginning to gather. Our heads were filled with visions of leave, booze and girls, but mostly food—any food but dehydrated cabbage and potatoes. We'd been eating that for years, it seemed.

As we tied up, the quartermaster's voice came over the intercom: "Now hear this. We are so late arriving, we have to go back right away. We will be loading supplies right now. There will be no leaves. The supplies are waiting on the dock. We start loading in half an hour."

A heavy coating of ice covers the superstructure of a Canadian corvette on the North Atlantic in the Second World War.

A view from HMCS *St. Croix* of a merchant ship convoy heading to Britain in March 1941.

HMCS *Snowberry* guards the flank of a convoy headed overseas.

Wearily we began to load. Morale, already at rock bottom, sank even lower as we toiled through the bleak December night. Tempers were short. "Some Christmas. Some New Year's," we grumbled.

Suddenly there was the boom of a four-inch gun. The ship shuddered in recoil and the rank smell of cordite drifted down the harbor on the December wind. For a few seconds there was silence, then the whole of St. John's was visible as a star shell began to drift slowly down. The twin towers above the city and the snow-covered houses below, etched in the stark white flare, made an unforgettable sight. We stood in awestruck wonder.

In a minute or so, the footsteps of the shore patrol were thundering down the dock. "Who the hell fired that star shell?" someone shouted. Of course, we were as innocent as the newborn New Year. Besides, the harbor was filled with ships. It could have been any of them.

Dawn saw us back on convoy duty. As we cleared The Gates, we were a softly smiling crew who'd just ushered in the New Year with the whole of St. John's. Morale had never been higher. We were a happy band of brothers. ⌁

An aerial view of merchant ship convoy HX-188.

CRUISING ON THE *QUEEN E*
Rosemary Hutchinson

When the alarm goes off, we are playing our 55th game of crazy eights hunched on the cabin floor.

We grip our cards, and flip them on to the dusty carpet as though we were in the world's greatest gambling casino. The nickels and dimes are in little piles in front of us, though my pile is noticeably small. It must have been a beautiful cabin before the war, but now its sides sprout tiers of bunks that house 16 of us on this all-expenses-paid trip on the *Queen Elizabeth*.

Two days out of Halifax, steaming at full boil for the U.K., we are hoping that speed alone will outwit the lurking submarines. The time is 4 p.m. on a November day in 1943.

As the alarm shrills on, the girls who have been reading and sleeping start jumping down to the floor clutching life-jackets and greatcoats. They disturb our cards, and we four pick up our money in a big hurry.

"Now listen," says Curtis, peering through all the feet and legs stamping about the floor, "I have one great hand here, and I am not about to lose it, so put your cards in your pockets, and we'll finish this later."

Curtis is the cool cat in our foursome. A good-looking, dark-haired girl from Alberta, she works in the accounts section. The other three of us are drivers in the motor transport section. I tuck my cards away, hoping all this is some sort of nightmare, and that I'll wake up soon in my own little bed at home in good old Montreal.

As some sort of action seems indicated, and we've certainly been drilled for it, I seize my life-jacket and greatcoat and struggle towards the corridor. The top bunk next to the door is still occupied by the glamorous member of our cabin society who is languidly pulling dozens of metal curlers from her head, which seems to be covered with little hairy sausages.

"Hey Plunkett," I shout, "get a move on. The ship's probably sinking!"

"Well, I just can't go 'til I get my hair fixed." She gazes at me with wide blue eyes, a comb in one hand, a little mirror in the other. I shrug and press on. If there's one thing the air force has taught me, it's self-preservation. Obviously the girl is either as dumb as a doorknob or as brave as a lion.

In the corridor people are surging towards the stairs. As there are about 15,000 soldiers, airmen and airwomen on board, it makes for one mighty surge, and I am borne effortlessly forward and up, then deposited on the deck not too far from my lifeboat station.

There I meet my card-playing buddies, shrug in to my coat, adjust my life-jacket to the official position and test its little red light, which is supposed to be switched on the moment I hit the water, making sure I will be seen as I soar up and down on the waves of the limitless Atlantic.

But, with approximately 15,000 other red lights blinking away, give or take a few people who will presumably go down with the ship, get hit on the head by a falling spar or get their big feet tangled in a rope, my chances of survival on the briny don't look so good. All the bright hopes of Canada's future are milling about on the deck and important-looking sailing types are dashing about shouting at each other, but apart from this everything seems serene. I note that the lifeboats are still in their davits, which makes me feel more cheerful.

Smitty starts to light a cigarette, but Curtis clutches her wrist: "You can't do that, you dummy. You'll pinpoint us and the sub out there will blow up the whole ship."

"Oh let her have it," says Charlie. "It may be the last fag she ever has."

"Well thanks a whole lot!" Smitty glares at Charlie, hands me a cigarette and lights it with the fake-gold lighter her bowling club presented when she left Fairy Dell, Sask., to give her all in the service of her country.

A very fat army major comes charging down the deck. "Here comes your boy-friend, Curtis," says Smitty. "Tell him we want to be saved."

We've been kidding Curtis a lot about this fat boy.

When we're not playing crazy eights she's been walking the deck with him, and we find this very romantic.

Right now, though, he is all business. He shouts something in Curtis' ear, she nods, and he barges on. I notice that he is smoking too. Curtis beckons to us and we follow her to the corner of the deck, where a pile of life rafts are stacked. She is feeling pretty important, being singled out for command, so to speak.

"If there are three short blasts from the funnel, we are to start chucking these rafts over the side," she tells us.

"You don't call them rafts, Curtis," says Charlie. "They are carley floats." Charlie is from Halifax, and we bow to her superior knowledge in all things maritime.

I heft the rope handle attached to one: "Well, if you expect us to heave these things in to the water, you'd better get some more bodies."

Curtis has no time to reply. The *Queen Elizabeth* suddenly heels sharply to the left and we are all flung helter-skelter on to the carley floats. The guns start up, the Bofors at bow and stern, and all the yackety little pom-poms amidship.

The noise is absolutely horrendous. As I taste the blood in my mouth—I've given my lip a good bite—the ship suddenly heels over the other way and the whole bunch of us nearly shoot in to the water. I wedge myself behind the pile of rafts and stare gloomily out to sea. Night is coming on fast, but I can still see vast quantities of heaving grey water.

I look across at Smitty: what a nice gal she is, I think. We had met at initial training, where she'd been a class ahead of me. We'd gone our separate ways and now a year later had met again in Halifax, posted overseas on the same draft.

Now, it seems our friendship may come to an abrupt end. I can see the newspaper headlines: Queen Elizabeth Lost Through Enemy Action, No Survivors.

Women's Division personnel are inspected by Princess Alice in August 1942.

The pity of it all, and I, only 20 years old, doomed to end my days deafened by guns and either frozen on this chilly deck or drowned hanging on to a carley float.

I start to wonder if this is a U-boat giving us so much trouble. Hopefully her captain is one of the old school, with duelling scars on his cheeks, an Iron Cross strung round his neck and steely-grey eyes with wrinkles at their corners from all his sea time. He really doesn't like Hitler very much, but when his beloved fatherland called, what could he do?

Besides he has a mother, who, at 92, lives in the ancient family *schloss* in Bavaria, and if he doesn't do what he is told she may get chopped. To make things even more difficult, his *mütterkin* is the only one who knows where the family jewels are hidden. Surely such an upright officer and gentleman wouldn't knock off a whole ship.

I am really getting interested in this character, when Charlie thumps me on the back. "Come to," she shouts, flapping a hand in front of my eyes. "Heaven doesn't seem to want us today." Now I realize the guns have stopped, and the all-clear is sounding down the deck.

Smitty stands up, tips her hat over her eyes and lights a cigarette, though her hand shakes somewhat. "We live again," she remarks nonchalantly.

Curtis looks at her watch: "Do you know we've only been up on deck for 20 minutes?"

"It felt like 20 hours," replies Charlie.

It takes a further 20 minutes to push and shove our way back to the cabin. Plunkett is still sitting on her bunk, her hair a glossy halo. She regards us with large and vacant eyes: "Jeez, you all back already? I was just coming up to join you."

Curtis sits down on the floor, takes the cards from her pocket and fans them impatiently. "Come on, let's get playing." ✺

CHASING THE MARGAREE
C.L. Carroll

"Jolly nice for some people I'd say. Lying there with nothing to do but stare at the ceiling. Hear you won yesterday's raffle too. Some people have all the luck."

The crisp London voice of the young nursing sister startled me into the present. I'd formed the annoying habit of lying on my hospital bunk, staring into space and reviewing in my mind all the details of the few frantic weeks that had led to my collapse on the streets of Plymouth, England, and my two months' enforced rest in hospital at this port. What a rest! It was late summer 1940 and the German bombers came day and night. At first we scrambled to basement shelters. Later we just crawled under our bunks, and now we didn't bother to move. We contented ourselves trying to guess the number of enemy planes downed and running a daily raffle on the results.

The nurse was standing by my bed waiting for some sort of response. With a conscious effort I came back to the present.

"I won? My luck must be turning. Let's see now, where's my ticket. Here—total 40. How many did we get?"

"Fifty-one! Isn't it amazing? They've raised the number every day for the raffle and we've never yet made it high enough. You'd think the Germans would run out of planes. Here, put this in your mouth."

"Here's hoping they do," I muttered as she slid the thermometer under my tongue.

"H'mm." She peered at me. "Time you were getting some colour back into that face—and some flesh too. You look like death warmed over."

And with that cheering remark she walked briskly away.

I took my shaving mirror out of my drawer and had a look for myself. My God, she was right. My last birthday had been my thirtieth, but I'm sure no one would believe that now. Normally the whitish blond hair combined with my tanned skin and blue eyes to give me a boyish appearance. Now it had the opposite

HMCS *Restigouche* takes part in D-Day operations.

effect. My skin was pale, my eyes were pale, with circles under them, and my hair was white. I put the mirror away in disgust and went back to my thoughts.

I'd joined the Canadian Navy as a boy cadet when I was just over sixteen. I was now a radio officer and my most recent posting had been aboard the destroyer HMCS *Restigouche*. We had joined with the British fleet after the evacuation of Dunkirk, scouring the French coast to rescue broken fragments of British and French divisions at isolated bays and harbours.

At many points I had gone ashore with small groups of engineers and technicians to conduct vitally important demolitions. The enemy were close, often arriving at a port just as we were scrambling aboard ship and our launching would be completed under enemy fire. When, in accordance with their armistice with Germany, the French turned their guns against us, we had started back across the Channel for England.

My ship and the senior Canadian destroyer *Fraser* had been assigned, along with Royal Navy destroyers, the task of protecting the British cruiser *Calcutta*, laden with refugees and high officials of both the French and Allied governments. We were travelling at high speed and in close proximity in sub-infested waters. It was about ten o'clock in the evening. We were in the process of manoeuvring into a straight line behind the *Calcutta* when there came a sharp warning blast from her signal, then a horrible crash and grinding of steel. The giant cruiser had ploughed into the *Fraser* and sheared her in two. Men shouted from the water. We could see the bow of the ill-fated ship floating away, carrying the cries of its marooned occupants into the darkness. The jagged mass of steel that was the afterpart writhed in the choppy sea.

It was recorded later that we completed an amazing rescue under the circumstances. But many were lost and some had to be left. I had to board the wreck to retrieve the radio log and confidential books, and the scene in the radio cabin will never leave my mind. The radio officer, a friend of mine, lay decapitated on the floor. Another buddy lay close by, his body skewered by a spike of steel. He was breathing his last and all I could do was fulfill his request for a cigarette and leave him to go down with the ship. He couldn't be moved and there wasn't time to get rescue equipment. We had to open the seacocks to sink the ship, and then get on with the convoy.

Now as I lay on my bunk in the hospital, the scene on the wrecked *Fraser* came back to me again. There was nothing more I could have done, but in an irrational way I felt responsible for I should have been the officer lying dead on the radio cabin floor. Orders had been received transferring me to the senior ship, the *Fraser*, as I was the senior wireless officer. I had never gone. We had been too busy.

When we got back to England we had to help with the relatively mechanical job of capturing the French fleet in Plymouth harbour. The *Restigouche* then put into port for repairs and outfitting. I had a few days' leave in the port city and it was then, on the first day, I collapsed with an attack of violent pain and ended up in the naval hospital. I think the diagnosis was peptic ulcer but it didn't quite conform to the accepted pattern and so it was left to heal with time and a bland diet. The doctors were fully occupied with concrete cases of broken bones and warwounded bodies. I wasn't having pain often now but I couldn't get a clear bill of health. I knew I wouldn't be well until I could get back to work, to doing something useful. If nerves had contributed to my illness, the condition was certainly not being improved by my having so much time to do nothing but think.

The day I won the raffle I had a visit from an old friend, a visit which led to my release from hospital. Scotty Macpherson had joined the Navy as a boy when I had; he'd left to take training as a medical doctor and had then returned to the Service in that capacity. I thought he had been lost on the *Fraser*, and I greeted him as one returned from the dead. He told me an incredible part of the collision story. He had been on the bridge of the ill-fated ship when the *Calcutta* sliced through her forepart.

Her entire bridge was lifted onto the *Calcutta*'s bow, and the captain and others on the bridge were able just to step aboard the cruiser. I also learned that we had acquired another destroyer, the *Margaree*. She was just being commissioned and, to as great an extent as possible, was to be manned by survivors of the *Fraser*. Scotty was to be the medical officer aboard.

"We've got to get you out of here," he said. "Headquarters have been asking for your whereabouts. They need you in Canada to outfit the new corvettes with radio officers, and that's really why I'm here today, to see if you can be released."

"But this place won't clear me."

"I know, but I think they will release you to me as a patient and you can go back on the *Margaree* under my care. I'm almost sure her first trip is to Canada. I'm willing to bet the RCN will let you go back to work. You'll never get better here, lying around thinking about that damn collision."

Scotty was successful in making the necessary arrangements, and in a few days my orders came through to report to the *Margaree* as soon as possible. But I had to go through a Medical Board at the hospital first and this procedure seemed endless.

Three weeks later I emerged from the hospital with the discouraging Category E—unfit for service. I felt that way too, not that I had pain or felt particularly weak, but my confidence in my appearance as a naval officer was sadly lacking. This was mostly because my uniform was hanging on me like a tent and I felt like a little man inside it. I remember it was raining when I got to the dockyard. I was challenged, presented my credentials, proceeded to the proper authority, again presented my orders to report to the *Margaree*. I was told she had sailed the night before.

I couldn't believe it. I stood there for a moment looking blank, trying to focus my mind on what to do next. Then I heard the Movements Officer muttering, "Sorry, old chap, but I guess it's back to hospital with you"—and that did it. My thoughts clicked into place, my old confidence returned, and I heard myself telling him I wasn't going back to hospital and I had to catch the *Margaree*. It took a bit of arguing and protesting,

HMCS *Fraser* at Vancouver in April 1941.

but eventually I found out she would be docking at Liverpool, and I walked away with a railway pass to that city. I had to catch that ship. It might be months before I'd have another opportunity to get across the Atlantic. I wanted so badly to get back to work.

By the time I got to the railway station I was soaked to the skin. The station was crowded and so was the train, but I managed to get on. The evacuation of women and children from the south was in full swing. I stood in the narrow corridor of the train beside compartments of crying children and distraught mothers and looked out the window. The soggy countryside began to move swiftly by, and then dusk and rain blurred it altogether. I sat on the floor and dozed a while, and then woke with a start. The train had stopped and we were in complete darkness. There was excited chattering, then some lights, and then explanations from the railway men. We were in the tunnel under the Bristol Channel. A heavy air attack was in progress over Bristol and we were staying put until it was over. Hours later we emerged and continued our journey. I had managed to get a seat by holding a child on each knee.

A grey morning was replacing the darkness as we approached Liverpool, and what a sight of chaos it revealed! This port had also been bombed. The ruins were still smoking and the station was a shambles. The train stopped just outside the station. Hastily I retrieved my baggage, found transport, and made for the dockyard. The rain had pursued me relentlessly. I had a feeling I would never be dry again. And I had missed the *Margaree*! The delay in the tunnel had done it. The ship had sailed just at dawn. My mind seemed to function automatically now and it had only one purpose—to catch the *Margaree*. I ignored the suggestion I go back to Plymouth. I insisted on a railway pass to Greenock, the next port of call, and again I got it.

The train wasn't due to leave until late afternoon. I walked around in the rain and when I got on the train I was incredibly wet.

At Greenock it was raining harder than ever. Mechanically I gathered my baggage and made my way to the dockyards. Once more I went through the familiar routine of presenting credentials and waiting for direction to the proper authority. The only difference in the verdict this time was that it was delivered in a rich Scottish burr.

"The *Margaree* has sailed. I'm feared you'll have to go back to Plymouth."

I wasn't going back. I knew now I'd never catch the *Margaree* but I was determined this miserable chase wouldn't be in vain. I asked to see the shipping master and pleaded with him to get me aboard anything going to North America.

After two false starts, I was able to get aboard a little armed merchant ship, the *Rawalpindi*, which was leaving for Halifax, all on her own.

The ship had been instructed to pursue a zig-zag path and to switch to a southerly course because German pocket battleships were thought to be in the North Atlantic. I got into the habit of going up to the ship's radio office each day to chat and exchange shop talk with the boys, and I often saw the news releases as they were received. One day when I went in, the radio officer looked up from a message he was reading and then handed it to me.

"My God, Sparks, wasn't that the ship you were chasing?"

I started to read. It was an Associated Press release.
CANADIAN DESTROYER MARGAREE SUNK IN MID ATLANTIC.
RAMMED BY SHIP IN CONVOY. VERY FEW SURVIVORS.

It couldn't have happened again! The words blurred before my eyes and I leaned against the wall for support. I guess I turned pale for the radio officer got me a chair and called to someone to get some brandy.

"Fate."

I said over and over to myself, "Those men were meant to die. We rescued them and now the accident has been repeated. And what about me? What kept me from getting on that ship? God knows I tried hard enough."

Ten days later, and some eight weeks after I left hospital to join the *Margaree*, we reached Halifax.

I didn't see Scotty in Halifax and I was sure he had gone down with the *Margaree*. I didn't ask about him or my other friends. I didn't want to know the details and avoided any discussion or inquiry about the collision or about the previous *Fraser* episode. Then on a quick duty trip to the West Coast I walked into the wardroom of HMCS *Naden*, and there was Scotty!

"I thought you went down on the *Margaree*," I faltered. "I looked for you in Halifax but I was afraid to ask."

"I was on the bridge again," he said quietly. "Just as on the night the *Fraser* was rammed." He put his hand on my shoulder. "How the hell did you miss that ship? You would have been in the Sick Bay and that's where she was hit. Everyone there was lost."

"I didn't know that," I answered weakly. "Let's sit down and have a noggin."

Over a drink I explained why I wasn't on the *Margaree*. At least I recounted the sequence of events that kept me from being aboard. I don't suppose I'll ever be able to explain why so many things happened at just the right time to cause me to miss the *Margaree* and death in the Atlantic. ✑

A wartime scene at Greenock, Scotland, in 1941.

WAR GAMES

Ben Malkin

For the 3rd Field Regiment RCA, the disjointed summer of 1940 began at the artillery ranges near Larkhill, on Salisbury Plain where, to adapt some lines from George Bernard Shaw's Pygmalion, the rain at Salisbury falls mainly on the Plain.

We had left Lille Barracks at North Camp, an Aldershot suburb, three days after the Germans invaded Holland. We were to complete our training at Larkhill by firing a few rounds, then proceed to France, where 1st Canadian Div. would join the entrenched British Army. For us, that was to be the start of the shooting war.

Despite the invasion of Holland, despite the earlier, successful invasion of Norway by the Germans, we still based our judgments on the 1914–18 experience. We assumed the Germans wouldn't get very far, and that after Larkhill we'd still have France ahead of us. In the event, it would be three years before we'd see action. But we couldn't conceive of it at the time.

Hardened by a winter of sniffles, coughs, frozen water pipes, plugged toilets, largely unheated barrack rooms and the British Army's daily menu—sowbelly, porridge, beef or mutton stew and the eternal rice pudding, none of which even the most ardent anglophile could consider a coup de cuisine—we felt at least physically qualified to face any enemy. An English spring had spread its beneficence early. Where Browning wrote, "Oh to be in England, now that April's here," the sun warmed the green March grasses.

Through April and early May, we felt good. So good that we had a most convivial celebration the night before our departure, replete with many toasts to assured victory, and with amateur dramatics in the form of such heroic, if theatrical, utterances as "Death, we are about to salute you!" Unhappily, after we entrained for Larkhill our paymaster-captain, who had remained behind in charge of the rear party, reported to Lt.-Col. Bob Wyman, our commanding officer, that we had left our barracks in unconscionable chaos:

The Battle of Britain rages in the skies over London.

broken bottles, damaged furniture and filthy rooms. Like most paymasters, ours was a precise man who regarded a column of figures with rapture and exactly balanced accounts with worshipful awe. He was not given to exaggeration, and his report was to be taken very seriously indeed.

Wyman had little choice but to act. He ordered the entire regiment confined to barracks, or camp, the dictate enveloping the just and the unjust alike. Since we were isolated on the ranges, and were to be there only 10 days before leaving for France, confinement would have been normal, and there was really nowhere to go. But to be confined by order was a different matter.

Being temperance minded, some—and there were more than one might suppose—had not sampled strong drink the night before we left North Camp. Others had drunk peaceably, sung a few songs, then slept it off. Yet the order applied to everyone, and since some orders are in any case regarded as a kind of challenge, certain tensions could be sensed.

Our padre, a man of great ingenuity as well as charity, found a solution. Besides his commitment to look after the souls of those who wished it, he was charged with helping to maintain our morale and educating us. He pointed out to Wyman that we were close to two famous English structures: Salisbury Cathedral and Stonehenge. Why not put the regiment in his care on Sunday, and transport the men to both places in pursuit of higher education?

The colonel was only too pleased to comply. Almost all the regiment volunteered for the educational excursion, and made for Salisbury. Almost all those who had left camp entered the cathedral, where we received an erudite lecture on the historic building. Many of those who had entered the cathedral departed with the trucks for Stonehenge, where we enjoyed—if that is the right word in the circumstances—a learned discourse on the meaning of these ancient rocks. We discovered that nobody knew their meaning, a piece of useless but interesting intelligence I carefully stored away.

When we mounted the trucks for the return trip to camp, the padre's army had shrunk noticeably. However, no one said anything and by morning, having walked most of the night to reach camp before first parade, the stragglers showed up, their education no doubt much advanced. It was a most satisfactory resolution of the confinement issue.

The disorderly summer began in camp. The Germans, having overrun Holland, had driven in to Belgium and France at a speed as frightening as it was unexpected and unprepared for. We were ordered to draw two blankets each, on the assumption that we would now head for France. By the time we drew the blankets, German armor had advanced a few more miles, creating great uncertainty as to whether we could get to France in time to accomplish anything. OK, came the order, turn in the blankets.

A pause in the German advance, and perhaps we could get to France in time, after all. OK, draw two blankets. A further German push. Turn in two blankets. For the better part of two days we drew and returned our blankets with such regularity that we began to wonder whether anybody up there knew what he was doing. Since the war, it has been revealed that our leaders did, indeed, know what they were doing. It's just that they didn't know what the Germans were doing.

We left Larkhill and after several days encamped on the grounds at Blenheim Castle, near Oxford, while the generals tried to decide what to do with us. We travelled to a reception centre near Aldershot, where we were to prepare to sail for an area west of Dunkirk. Again, chaos. The 1st Bde. did sail, landed at Brest, and later returned without firing a shot. The 2nd Bde. was at the coast, preparing to load. Our brigade, the 3rd, was packing to go to the coast. The King and Queen and Gen. A.G.L. McNaughton visited us, presumably to dispel the feeling, by now fairly general, that no one was in charge. McNaughton taped a prepared statement while with us, and I overheard him saying we were now "battleworthy." Considering the way the Wehrmacht was knifing through professional British and French troops, McNaughton's judgment was charitable.

Then it was finished: Dunkirk, the west of France, Paris, everything. Night descended on the continent, and now it might be our turn. Although somewhat buoyed by Winston Churchill's rhetoric, which was about all we had to sustain us at the time, I didn't really feel anything. I don't know of anyone else who did either. Perhaps, finally, we were beginning to develop the numbed fatalism of the professional soldier, a safeguard against a hostile world. But we were only beginning.

Possibly as a public relations exercise, we were sent to Northampton for a short time. Battleworthy though we were supposed to be, we still relied on civilian trucks for much of our transport. I don't know whether we very much impressed the people or any enemy agents lurking in the vicinity, but we did our best. In convoy, we drove through the town several times, evidently to spread the notion that we were a far larger force than we actually were. Then the regiment settled down for a few days in Northampton, where we were billeted on the cordial, kindly civilians of this workaday industrial town.

We left Northampton and headed south, still not knowing where we were to go, or what was expected of us. Once, when the convoy paused, our battery commander said he thought we would make for the south of France, invade, then fight our way north. That seemed a welcome decision, because at least it was something definite to do. But what we actually did was stop on a wooded common near Guildford, dismount and learn that this was to be our home.

Here was an anti-climax to six weeks of hectic and seemingly purposeless activity, of movement and countermovement and the false expectation of imminent warfare and heroic deeds. We looked at the surrounding woods, at the sun-dappled ground, heard the murmur of the forest, and some of us, perhaps suffering from nervous exhaustion, fell to the ground and laughed uncontrollably.

We played games. The regimental sergeant major, inevitably, became the Sheriff of Nottingham. The padre, of course, was Friar Tuck. A couple of fellows, preferring not to sleep on the ground, built a tree house, which they found comfortable enough. However, the games of July-August didn't last long.

First, the realization was driven home that we were still very much in a deadly war, more so than ever. We were a mobile reserve, to be trained to dash to any part of the coast struck by invading troops. It meant much intensive training, especially in new techniques learned by the British Army from the disaster of May-June.

Second, the Battle of Britain began. Located as we were near the London-Croydon area, the war was immediate in the trailing exhausts from the embattled aircraft overhead, and the occasional encounter between RAF and Luftwaffe.

Third, we didn't remain in the isolated woods more than a few weeks. We were moved to Roedean, on the edge of Brighton, where we took over anti-invasion chores from the 38th (Welsh) Div. Our passes were

St. Paul's Cathedral during a German bombing raid, circa 1940–41.

limited to three hours' absence and I, for one, hoped the Germans wouldn't come. For if they landed despite the opposition of the RAF and the Royal Navy, we had little to stop them with. By now, we knew that much. We knew our equipment was insufficient and outdated, our tactical training still inadequate.

The Battle of Britain won by the RAF, the daylight assault by the Luftwaffe ended, we moved in to quarters at Coney Hall, near Hayes, Kent, about midway between Bromley and Croydon in the London suburbs. Here we were again a mobile reserve. We were billeted in requisitioned houses, where we were to remain for more than a year. Here a considerable number of men married and, once the immediate invasion threat had passed, we settled in to a stable routine for the first time since spring.

Hayes was the last stop on the suburban line to Charing Cross station, reached in 15 or 20 minutes by fast train. We could get an evening pass, see a London show, and return in plenty of time. Being in the army became almost like having a civilian job, especially if you married a neighborhood girl and became entitled to a sleeping-out pass. A henhouse on Hayes Common, where our guns and vehicles were kept, served as our guardroom, but it had a gas fireplace and, once cleaned out, was as comfortable as any soldiers or hens could wish.

The night bombing, which had begun by early fall, preserved our perspective. Maybe there wouldn't be an invasion—at least, not yet—but the war was still very much with us, and we knew that somewhere, sometime, somehow, we would make a U-turn, and go to the continent. Meanwhile, we prepared, and gradually our equipment and professionalism improved for the day when, in Gen. McNaughton's words, we would indeed be battleworthy.

Back in Ottawa, we were not forgotten. In early February, while still at Aldershot, I had received a form letter from the federal tax collection people, addressed to my Winnipeg home and forwarded to me. It counselled me to remember to file an income tax return for 1939, and then to pay Caesar his due.

At that time still easily unhinged by official correspondence, I asked our battery commander what to do. With military crispness he said: "File it." "File it? I haven't got files." "Here, I'll file it for you." And threw it in to the fireplace.

In October I received another letter from the national revenue department. It was filled with veiled menace.

I had ignored their earlier warning, said the letter, more in anger than in sorrow. If I did not file an income tax return for 1939, action would be taken. I could face grave consequences.

By this time, many bombs had fallen in our area. As I read that letter, I could hear the bark and thunder of nearby anti-aircraft guns. Later, my own billet was to be hit, with four killed and several badly hurt. In this environment, I felt I could cope with threats from the tax collector.

I flattered myself—and still do—that my reply was suave. I was interested in helping to win the war, I wrote smoothly, and wanted to co-operate. For 1938, I explained, my income tax payment had come to about $23, though I couldn't remember exactly. For 1939, it would naturally be somewhat less, for although I had received a $2-a-week raise that year, I had worked only nine months, being on the government payroll for the final three months at a somewhat lower emolument.

I reiterated: I was most anxious to co-operate. But there was a difficulty. I didn't really know how much I had earned in 1939. If the tax people could arrange for me to return to Canada where I could unravel my complicated financial affairs and make out a return, a mutually satisfactory conclusion would result.

I didn't hear from the department again. After the war, I met a fellow from the department and told him my story. He said some functionary in the department had noticed that the men overseas had failed to file 1939 tax returns and had sworn that just because they were overseas, they weren't going to get away with it. Thousands of threatening letters were therefore mailed.

The answer I sent, he continued, was very mild compared with some of the replies. The minister heard of it, and went through the ceiling. He ordered the 1939 files closed, and persons in the armed forces were to pay no income tax during the remainder of the war.

On that encouraging note from the home front, 1940 ended. ✌

Vincent Massey, High Commissioner for Canada, inspects Canadian soldiers in England in 1940.

THE OLD PUB GAME
Ben Malkin

Men accustomed to the bleak Canadian beer parlor of the 1930s experienced culture shock when introduced to the English pub. In late '39 and early '40 we emerged from the Stygian gloom, the heavy breathing, the guilt-ridden atmosphere of the all-male beer parlor. We entered the quiet companionship of the pub where, in light and airy surroundings, we could enjoy an exchange of views and trade lies with the men and women of the neighborhood.

We found that some pubs permitted singing around a piano, considered sinful back home. In all of them, without breaking the law you could play darts and other games of chance—though some said it was a game of skill. Above all, we found that to the shrewd youth seeking quick acquaintance with a shy and reticent young woman, the pubs became targets of opportunity.

One had to be subtly devious. In the opening move, the trick was to show an interest in culture, rather than in the young woman herself. Let's say you were on manoeuvres near Sevenoaks, Kent, and the tacticians had decided that the enemy had stopped your advance, and you could now bivouac for the night. You were in a field a couple of hundred yards from a country pub, and it was early evening.

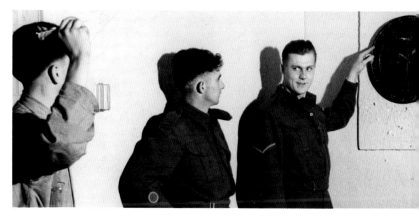
Service personnel enjoy a game of darts in a Canadian Legion War Services hut in Calgary.

Entering the pub with a companion, you got your drink, sat down at a table, and noticed a pair of young women, who seemed well worth meeting, seated nearby. Being well brought up, they appeared a little standoffish. Were it not for the cultural approach, that might have posed a problem. As it was, there was nothing to it.

You walked over to their table and hesitantly, not wanting to look too pushy, you said: "I do beg your pardon. I don't want to intrude, but my colleague and I are having a rather difficult dispute. How old (pointing to the rafters) would those beams be, do you suppose?"

There's nothing an Englishman or Englishwoman is more interested in than heritage. Old buildings are treasured, old pubs doubly so; they seem to have a mystique of their own. With an opening like that, you and your friend are invited to join the ladies. Especially if you can make comparisons with other pubs you've visited, an animated conversation follows, and you finally return to your bivouac ready for more manoeuvres.

The oldest pub I visited was Ye Hostel of God Begot in Winchester. Ye Hostel claimed birth in 1067. A friend, Frank Brazier of Regina, and I travelled there from Aldershot on rented bicycles one Saturday in March, 1940. The weather was sunny and warm, making cycling hot work. We found that at almost every mile there was an intersection marked by a church, a graveyard and a pub. The closing hours were evidently staggered, so

Service personnel outside a British pub.

75

that there was a pub open all the way along, and it took us eight joyous hours to pedal the 32 miles.

After booking in at a hotel, we made for Ye Hostel, which, disappointingly, turned out to be a very modern pub, almost a cocktail lounge. As we sipped our beer, the publican said we were the first Canadians he had encountered, and would we like to see the original tavern.

It was below ground. The weighty, locked door required a key four inches long. Inside, long, highly polished wooden tables and benches lined the walls, with metal tankards on the shelves above. We didn't mind the musty smell as we pondered the people who had drunk there almost a thousand years ago.

Upon our return to the cocktail lounge, a Royal Marines sergeant wearing blues plaintively complained that he had tried for a long time to see Ye Hostel's underground tavern, but had consistently been refused. Now a couple of Canadians showed up and were given instant attention.

The publican tried to pacify him, and we thought we were helpful when we pointed out that we weren't looking for special privileges. We were just interested in history, like. "Ah," said the marine, "come off it. I know that game. Now you've got an edge. I could have used the information myself."

Service personnel relax with a game of darts in a Canadian Legion Recreation Centre in the United Kingdom.

AGONY AT ALDERSHOT
Douglas How

In those long years when Canadian soldiers waited in England for WW II action, something happened that was celebrated and, in a way, still is: The troops booed their prime minister at Aldershot.

It was immediate front-page news back home. Though there was both booing and cheering, it is referred to in the published version of the 1939–44 Mackenzie King diaries as "the notorious 'booing' incident."

To this day it is difficult to gauge its significance. I have talked to men who were there, and gotten a variety of interpretations. But it is doubtful that many of them ever realized, then or later, what the experience meant to King. His diary makes clear that it shook him to the depths. For that rain-soaked Aug. 23, 1941, crystallized all his doubts and even terrors about his relations with the men he'd called to arms.

If America's Roosevelt was magnetic, Britain's Churchill revered, King was neither, and he knew it. In a military atmosphere in particular he felt uncomfortable, alien. He'd spent much of WW I as a labor-relations consultant to American millionaires. He was nearly 40 when that war started, and our top military historian says he can hardly be faulted for what he did to keep production rolling. But memories of taunts clung to him, and to them were added an heirloom of the blood: His grandfather, William Lyon Mackenzie, had led the abortive 1837 rebellion against autocratic rule in Upper Canada (Ontario). The faint taint of family disloyalty hurt. His sensitivities about both these things would blurt out at times but in 1941 his sense of the gulf between him and all things military was larger than either.

Bruce Hutchison says King had "come to feel a burning pride" in the forces. But J.W. Pickersgill, King's wartime assistant, says that even before the prime minister left for England "he was worried about the reception he would get from the Canadian troops." He flew over in a Liberator bomber, flew for the first time, at a moment when the war still seemed like some endless process of defeat. The Russians reeled before German attacks. Less than four months before Pearl Harbor, people speculated about Japan, and Churchill said Britain couldn't win unless the Americans entered the war. Iran was on the front pages then too: British and Russian troops had invaded to clear out German sympathizers and seize vital oil wells.

King had good, encouraging meetings with Churchill. They even did a little dance together at Churchill's home, and reduced the audience to hysterics. Then King was off to Aldershot for a Saturday with the troops, and luck was against him from the start. It began to rain. Insufficient time had been allowed to drive there, and a passing train slowed them even more. So he was late. He lunched with Lt.-Gen. A.G.L. McNaughton, the beloved overseas commander, and others, then went to a field where thousands of soldiers were gathered for a sports meet already under way.

No sooner had he arrived, says the Canadian Press story, "when the mood became apparent." Mixed cheers and boos greeted him, "then the boos subsided and there was much applause" as King set out to inspect the guard of honor. Hand-clapping, cheering and boos broke out again after the inspection. As McNaughton finished introducing him, "booing from the rear of the grandstand drowned out the handclapping and cheers from the front row. His first words did not reach the crowd and there were shouts of 'Speak up, speak up.'"

King said he brought the soldiers "a message from their homes…day in and day out they are in the thoughts and prayers of those nearest them." Never had Canada been prouder "of the men who crossed the seas to play their part alongside the Mother Country. We shall never forget you and when I return I shall be able to give a message about the strength and appearance and spirit of the men who are exhibiting it in such noble fashion."

Canadian prime minister William Lyon Mackenzie King. This is a photo taken during the Second World War.

At this, says the CP story, "he was interrupted by loud booing. Mr. King hesitated momentarily and as the booing subsided he resumed, 'I gather from the applause that many of you are impatient and would rather be engaged in more active operations than you are today.' This was greeted by loud cheers, whistling and applause. Mr. King shouted into the microphone: 'That is the spirit to which I am referring.'" But when he finished speaking "another chorus of handclapping and booing broke out."

Though King was apt to see the Toronto *Globe and Mail* as a Tory arch enemy, its correspondent John Collingwood Reade put the episode into a perspective he could hardly have found harsh: "It should not be supposed the booing was evidence of a particularly hostile spirit. From such conversations as I had with members of the various units I gathered the impression that the troops had no love for politicians as such. Men mobilized for action grow impatient of long speeches, and need a heroic figure to move them to enthusiasm."

Reade said King, "after a lengthy preamble," struck the wrong note by referring to the spirit of the troops, then "showed some of his mettle." His rebuttal "drew cheers, and from then on the tension was eased. Certain units of the 1st Div. continued to boo at intervals but it was generally felt that he had been pretty game, and he was quite warmly cheered at the end. The mixed boos and cheers were evidence of nothing more than the indifference to politicians among men who were in carnival spirit anyhow.

"The prime minister is not universally unpopular with the men. There are some who have little liking for him without quite knowing why. There are others who are inclined to hold him responsible for the continued inactivity of the Canadian Corps, but have no grounds for their belief. To the remainder King is

prime minister of Canada, which is enough in itself to give him some claim to their respect. Hence the mixed boos and cheers."

Whatever the correct interpretation, the effect on King was devastating. Even before he went out to the field "I was really so tired by the long motor trip (he was 66) and being late, and as a consequence the disconcerting effect, and with continual rain that I found it extremely difficult to keep clear from an appalling depression. I would have given anything to not have to speak but, as McNaughton said, it would never do for the PM to be present on such an occasion and not address some words to the troops."

When the booing started, he later recorded, "quite clearly it had been organized, but I think what occasioned it was that the teams were in competition and

The Lord Mayor of London, England, receives Canadian prime minister William Lyon Mackenzie King and British prime minister Winston Churchill. The photo was taken in the early years of the Second World War.

there was both booing and applause with respect to the different events. It was a little disconcerting and in my heart I knew it to be unfair and Tory tactics, but I ignored it altogether." He got, he felt, "a splendid hearing" despite some "very limited" booing.

"I felt that what I said was very inadequate. In fact it had begun to pour rain when I started to speak and everything was as unpropitious as it possibly could be." He noted that when he turned the men's reaction "quickly the other way," it disclosed "their eagerness to fight." There was one interruption: "One man asked me when they were going home. This I ignored."

But the real impact of it all became obvious three days later when King visited the 1st Div. and McNaughton unexpectedly said he should speak again: "I felt what was like a dart pass through my bowels. It made me quite sick and faint and to break out into a cold perspiration." There was "nothing to do but face the ordeal" but that "was the least part of the terror"; he was "astonished" to find he would have to speak not once but four times, to large but scattered formations.

By the time he faced the first "I was really in a state of agony and fright." He felt he made "a poor if not painful impression. It was pretty much the agony of Aldershot all over again." Twice more he did it, then confronted Toronto regiments. "I again felt I would be confronted with a Toronto atmosphere and was sensitive thereto," but he managed to make "fairly appropriate remarks" and enjoyed inspecting the men.

Now his diary strikes to the heart of things: "I really felt too moved at the thought of all this young life being possibly destroyed to be able to give proper expression to my thoughts. I cannot talk their jargon of war. There is no use attempting. My words inevitably get into those of thought, and prayer, and providence, which is not the conventional thing, but the only thing that I feel at heart. I have held to these words, rather than to others. I cannot tell them what we are

expecting of them in the way of service. Offering their lives is infinitely greater than anything I myself am called upon to do, except to suffer perpetually from a Tory mob."

That was the day King made clear that the government placed no restraints on use of Canada's army, that it was Churchill who wanted it kept in Britain. It was a day too when "there was nothing to suggest any ill will at all. On the contrary it was quite the opposite. The cheers at the end of the visit to each place were obviously wholehearted." He even speculated that his flight on a bomber, the "obvious sharing of their risks," had "increased the respect of the forces for myself." He felt he had shown "a friendliness and a readiness to hear what was to be said, which, in the long run, will do good."

In the long run, it didn't. What happened at Aldershot was a harbinger. For in the June, 1945 election it was the services vote that defeated King in Prince Albert, Sask., and a sign soon rubbed it in: "This town liberated by the Canadian Army."

Nevertheless, his government survived while the electrifying Churchill's did not, and personal defeat didn't stop King. He simply outflanked the forces, found a safe seat and went on ruling for another three years—reaching a record 22. It is not the least of his many mysteries that, in the words of the late Tory senator-journalist Gratton O'Leary, he taught his enemies "the meaning of eternity."

Yet to this day his name stirs anything but affection among many of the men who went to war. A few years ago I was invited to address a Remembrance Day dinner. Since I'd been reading a great deal about this enigmatic man, I decided to risk speaking on the war as he saw it. Five minutes in to my speech I knew it was a disaster, and when I finished the feeling was confirmed by a man who'd been at Aldershot that rainy, distant day.

"You made just one mistake," he said. "You should have sat down 20 minutes earlier." ॐ

THE DARKEST YEAR
F.C.L. Wyght

When you are 19 the next few years tend to loom large. For me, those few were 1939–45.

We landed in England on my birthday, December 17. I wangled a Christmas leave and visited my wife-to-be's cousins near Bournemouth. Assuming that as a Canadian I had spent my life in the saddle they arranged an afternoon's ride in the New Forest. My experience being limited to nodding a polite 'Good morning' to the dobbin pulling the milk wagon, that became my broken-bottomed Christmas.

1940 was my Protestant Christmas. We were in Eastbourne, relieving a battalion of the Manchesters, when well after one midnight I was sent off with two 30-cwt. trucks to refuel the company. All map references were encoded and because someone had added in his girl-friend's chest measurement or something, we spent half the night wandering around in a light rain. On the way back around 0730 I stopped off at a fine old stone church for Christmas Mass. Dog-dirty and tired, I sat well to the rear. About halfway through, at communion, I realized I was at a High Anglican service. And lovely it was—the ecumenical bit started earlier than some think.

Christmas '41, in the South Downs around the little village of Fulking, I was again on a night trip to deliver a message to our three platoons in the area. It was black as the inside of a bear, with a howling wind, and the hammering bark of a 500-cc Norton drowned a sentry's challenge. I took a burst of Bren gun fire through my front wheel and lost the only new bike I ever had.

In '43, back home in Smith Falls, Ont., for Christmas—and the great national registration card hoo-haw—I went to the in-and-out store for a bottle of Christmas cheer. The pea-headed twit behind the counter wanted my permit before I could make a purchase. To get a permit I had to produce my national registration card—something that came out long after I had gone overseas. Well, talk about it hitting the fan! It took the local constable to agree that my RAF 1250, complete with photograph, was pretty good identification.

1944 was special. On December 19 my wife produced the ultimate in Christmas presents—a beautiful pink and blonde baby who grew to a delightful girl and then to a strikingly attractive woman with her own children.

By Christmas '45, I was discharged and in Calgary starting training as an air traffic controller, while my family was back home.

But I've left out the Christmas of '42. I visited my old buddies in the regiment now stationed in the village of Petworth. They had invited all the youngsters—about 60 or 70 aged between 6 and 11—to a party. The QM, who could whip the hind teeth out of a skunk without promoting a whiff, from somewhere produced a turkey that was converted to a mountain of sandwiches. The village bakery produced more than enough cookies and cakes. A tree was found and decorated.

The entertainment was a most catholic offering. Eddie Watkins, probably the finest pianist in 1 Can. Div., led the kids in a great sing-along and two girls played very creditable Spanish guitars.

Another of the older girls, a flawless, classical beauty with long golden-blonde braids, put on a one-girl show of gymnastics to rival June Pressier, who reigned in those days. Somehow Eddie picked up her cadence and gave

Canadian soldiers entertain evacuated children.

Above, below left and below right: Christmas parties are held for children in Paris in December 1945.

her a background rhythm. Almost 40 years later I still remember that performance. It was a great party and all went home happy.

The following quotation belongs to the early days of '43:

"The village of Petworth in West Sussex became almost as childless as Hamelin after the Pied Piper had taken his revenge. A scared German pilot, to gain speed, dumped his bombs during lesson-time on the local school."

Our company was on the scene within minutes and out of the ruins took 47 forever-still small bodies.

I never asked about the blonde gymnast. I never will. In my mind she had to go on—to survive and become the beautiful woman she was promising to be, to marry and have dozens of beautiful children and so close the gap that particular horror created in the lives of so many. ❧

THROUGH ENGLISH EYES
Ben Malkin

During our years of waiting in Britain, Canadians were, on the whole, well thought of by the people. It's true that, one evening during the winter of 1942–43, when my wife and I spotted one of my compatriots trying to go up on a down escalator in the Underground, she sniffed: "I have never seen a sober Canadian." But the remark left no sting. I was feeling pretty good myself, and in the circumstances it seemed fair comment.

While moving in to Coney Hall, between Bromley and Croydon, in late summer of 1940, we in our billet were busy unpacking when the civilian living next door came in to get acquainted with the new neighbors. He was soft spoken, earnest, resembled Clement Attlee, down to the moustache and bald head. It was about 6 p.m., and he asked whether we'd be eating shortly. We said we'd had supper an hour earlier, at our usual time.

He was appalled. "And you get nothing else," he exclaimed, "from 5 o'clock until next morning?" "Right." "We'll soon fix that," he assured us.

He disappeared, to return shortly with a pitcher of hot cocoa for the Canadian starvelings who had come so far to fight for freedom. We accepted his largesse gratefully, almost fulsomely, for it was well meant and kindly. Our relations with the people of that community remained friendly throughout our stay of more than a year. They always liked us, and once they became used to our casual manners, and the egalitarian way in which officers and other ranks mingled in the local pub, they came to consider our behavior quite normal.

An amiable lady kept the tea shop in Stewarton, Ayrshire, the village where we waterproofed our guns and vehicles before leaving for Sicily. Her attitude was typical. One morning I'd had a wisdom tooth pulled, and being too distraught to face the battery cook's lunch, asked her whether she could fix me something. "Aw, my poor laddie," she teased, "and you so far from home." She warmed a glass of milk, stirred a raw egg in and handed it over. I was impressed. It may well have been the only fresh egg in Ayrshire that day, and perhaps represented her week's ration.

Nor can I forget the long-distance telephone operator on the Glasgow exchange. We had shipped our heavy equipment to Liverpool, and were ourselves in Airdrie, a Glasgow suburb, waiting to embark in troop ships. Each evening for a couple of weeks I would telephone my wife in London from the same pay booth at 6:01 p.m., when the night rates took effect. One evening I phoned at 6:15 p.m.

The long-distance operator in Glasgow, through whom my calls went, came on the line as my number was being dialed in London. "Aw, laddie," she reproached me, "ye're late tonight."

Of course, it wasn't all strawberries and cream. There were exceptions. Not long after our arrival in England, the *News of the World*, a paper favored by sex-and-violence junkies, began to pay close attention to us. It seemed as though every time a Canadian got in to trouble with the civil authorities, the *News of the World* had to print the story, and above all had to identify his nationality. Indeed, the fact that he wasn't British was evidently what made the story newsworthy. The paper

Sandwiches and other goodies are served up at the Cartwright Gardens Leave Club in London.

A woman helps prepare and serve sandwiches at the Hastings Club in the United Kingdom.

became known among us as the unofficial Canadian war diary.

Representations about racism, about the misuse of national identity to blow up otherwise trivial events, about the false stereotyped image, unbalanced in its perspective, being created in the minds of the *News of the World*'s readers (it had the largest circulation of any British weekly) must have been made to the editors. After a time, the Canadian label was dropped and, instead, miscreants before the courts were referred to as Dominion soldiers. Since we were the only Commonwealth servicemen in the United Kingdom, apart from a number of airmen in the RAF, the camouflage was pretty thin. But I suppose it was better than nothing.

Fortunately, when the Americans arrived the *News of the World* lost interest in us, and it became as difficult for a Canadian to receive mention in the *News of the World* as it had been previously to keep our identities out. The Americans had far more glamor, being responsible for Hollywood and scandals which, in the opinion of the *News of the World*, were much more titillating than anything we provincials could produce.

All of which indicated to me, at any rate, that when the *News of the World* was watching the Canadians' every move, there was nothing personal in it. Among those to whom national identity is important, we were merely a target of opportunity. Such people are eclectic, and generally choose widely among their villains, lavishing their dislike among many groups.

Once I was alone in a train carriage, travelling south from London, when a civilian entered at a suburban station. He was a tall, plump, comfortable-looking man. Later, I recalled whom he reminded me of. It was a character in Ignazio Silone's book *Bread and Wine*, a novel popular in the 1930s, in which Silone describes an Italian Fascist functionary as having "a mouth shaped like a chicken's ass."

He opened the conversation. "We've Canadians in our area," he smirked, "and they're dreadful. Got their lorries parked on lawns and everywhere."

I turned my shoulder toward him, and he noticed the Canada patch. He was equal to the occasion. "Of course," his tone was soothing, "these are French Canadians."

"I'm French Canadian," I said.

There was a moment's silence. But he soon recovered his composure.

"I work in petrol rationing," he said, changing the form though not the substance of the subject. "You'd be surprised at how difficult it is, everybody wanting extra petrol. The Jews are the worst."

"I'm a Jew," I said. It appeared as though he might be starting to lose his aplomb. "I thought you said you were a French Canadian." "That's right. I'm a French Canadian Jew."

Fatso left at the next station. I suppose that if, out of 100,000 applications for extra petrol, one came from a Jew, that's the one that would stick in his mind. It's the kind of principle on which the *News of the World* had seemed to operate with regard to the Canadians, or the Americans, or whatever. Happily, there was very little of this mentality around.

At the same time, there were no doubt occasions when it didn't harm us to have our self-esteem reduced somewhat. Deflation can sometimes be useful, especially if accompanied by a subtle sense of irony.

I was an escort at the court martial of one of the men in the battery, accused of taking a 15-cwt. truck without authority, driving it without authority and, finally, wrapping it around a lamp-post and walking off, also without authority. The star witness was a civilian who had seen the mishap, and the offending soldier walking away from the truck. The other potential witnesses weren't of much use to the prosecution, being the soldier's pals who lived in the same billet and who, like the traditional three monkeys, had seen no evil, heard no evil and could speak no evil.

Finally, the star witness was brought in. In his early questioning the prosecuting officer established that the man had, indeed, been at the scene of the accident, and had seen the soldier-driver get out and walk away.

"Now," asked the officer, "can you identify this man? Do you see him in this room?"

The civilian, who had served in the British army during WW I and clearly knew something about courts martial, swept the room with his eyes. Then he peered intently into the face of each man in the room, including that of the presiding officer, a colonel. He again did a sweeping look around. Again he peered into the face of the presiding officer, more closely than ever. The colonel began to fidget uneasily.

Satisfied that he had done his best to identify the offender, the witness snapped to attention and testified: "I'm sorry, sir, but all Canadians look alike to me!" ↷

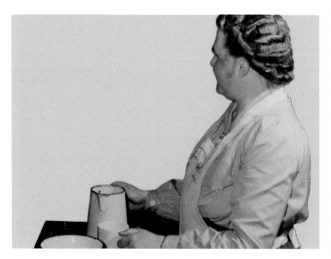

A tea lady at a club in the United Kingdom during the Second World War.

THE WEDDING CAKE
Joy Smith

Many young people today probably have never heard the word "rationing," but back in the "old days" of 1943 it had a very real meaning, particularly to those of us who were living in the U.K. Living in the south of England, and being exposed to many "elements" of the Canadian Army, Nature eventually took its course and I fell in love. My husband-to-be was a member of a famed Canadian regiment, and, though quite shy at first, very soon made it apparent that he meant business!

Ask any British war-bride, and she will tell you it just had to be love when a girl had to go through all those preliminary questions, blood tests, and supplying of references and still came up smiling and wanting to marry the man who had popped the all-important question.

Ask any man in the Forces who went through the same routine, and he will tell you the same thing. Eventually, however, our permission came through. But then came the snag—a three-month waiting period from the date of the written permission, a period in which the records were double-checked in Canada to make quite certain there were no "forgotten" wives conveniently tucked away in some remote spot!

Unfortunately we had not known about the three-month waiting period, and, by much begging and scraping around of ration "points," my family had managed to get together the ingredients for a real wedding cake. "No wedding cakes with icing," said the law, but somehow we were going to have it. Somebody knew somebody who had a brother who was a chef, and the carefully hoarded currants, candy peel and icing sugar left our house and came back in the form of a wondrous cake complete with a huge sugar Maple Leaf and little silver horseshoes. The eggs? Strictly rationed again, of course, but a farmer friend of my father's had known me since I was a little girl and his chickens suddenly put in some overtime! So there it was, my wedding cake, shining and beautiful, and now we could not use it for three months!

Being on the South Coast, not far from the famed "Bomb Alley," air raids were practically a daily occurrence, and, like everybody else, we had a Morrison table shelter in the house—a sort of oversized billiard table with a heavy iron top which could, and often did, take the weight of a two-storey brick house crashing down on it. Ours was in the living room, the wire mesh sides heavily draped with blankets against flying glass and other odd little bits of nonsense that came calling once in a while. On the top, in solitary glory, reposed the wedding cake in its cardboard box. Whenever a raid got really noisy we took cover inside the table-shelter, and the first in was the wedding cake.

Time dragged on somehow. We lost part of our roof, a few windows were broken, but still the cake remained intact in spite of many hurried trips under the shelter, usually in the middle of the night.

Then tragedy really struck. The regiment was moved out of town and all leave cancelled. It could only mean one thing—they were going overseas and we still had another month to wait. Everything was ready, the licence, my dress, and the cake. I was too sick at heart to even cry. One day my husband-to-be managed to get into town by volunteering to drive a truck which was to pick up some forgotten kit. He told me he had spoken to the padre, who was interceding for him and several others whose "waiting time" was nearly up. Hope flared again. Would we really get to cut that precious cake?

Two, three more days. How could they do this to us? Then one miserable, wet night when a proper gale was blowing, I was just about to crawl into bed when the bell rang. It just couldn't be, but it was! As I fumbled with the blackout curtain over the door—no lights, of course—my fiancé called through the letterbox opening: "I've got 18 hours' leave. We get married in the morning!" Then, as an afterthought: "Don't be frightened, but I've banged up my face a bit in the blackout."

By this time my dear Mom was out of bed and into the kitchen for the coffeepot (practical soul), and we were able to survey our battered hero. Running like mad with four other soldiers, also wedding-bent, through the pitch-black village to catch the one and only train, he had slammed into a garage door blown open by the gale and now had a lump the size of a hen's egg on his forehead and a cut above the mouth, partly hidden by his moustache. I got busy with antiseptic and bandaids while Mom whipped up some scrambled (powdered, of course) eggs—our wedding breakfast in reverse.

Just then, as though anything else could happen, a really dandy air raid got going in spite of the storm. There was only one thing to do and we did it. Under the table-shelter we went, wedding cake, scrambled eggs, coffee, Mom, bride, groom and dog—in that order.

The next morning a very surprised Dad came home (he had been out on fire-watch duty all night) to be told that his ever-lovin' only daughter was finally getting married that very morning. Now according to the etiquette books the bride and groom never see each other before the ceremony, but this pair did. In borrowed slacks the groom pressed his uniform, as all his kit was packed for the move back at camp and he had had to come just as he was. The bride frantically washed breakfast dishes as Mom had dashed down to the florist's. "No, we couldn't possibly deliver any corsages today," they had told her over the phone. "There's a war on, you know. You'll have to pick them up."

Suddenly, in the frantic rush, I cut my finger on the bread-knife—a deep gash that bled and bled. Now I would never get married, I wailed. I couldn't get my dress on, the finger wouldn't stop bleeding. And the groom? The lump on his forehead was turning blue-green. Oh, we made a handsome pair all right!

To further complicate matters, everyone else had been confined to camp because of the impending move, so our best man was not available. Poor Charlie, he would be disappointed, and it meant my husband would not have a fellow-Canadian to stand up with him. But my cousin Bill was home on leave from the R.A.F. and a quick phone call to him soon settled that. "Get up, you dope. You've got to be best man!" And to his sister Betty who was just leaving for the office: "But you can't, you've got to be bridesmaid—NOW!"

A 1940s-style wedding dress. Modelling the dress is Corporal Sherry Atwell of the Canadian Women's Army Corps.

Somehow the chaos was sorted out. My finger stopped bleeding, the lump on the groom's forehead did not show too much with the familiar black beret pulled down, the taxi appeared, and we were on our way.

The brief ceremony at the Registry Office was soon over and we drove back to the house. Mom had performed another minor miracle. Somehow she had got there first and the table was spread, with a long-hoarded bottle of champagne and the famous cake holding the place of honour. My aunt and uncle, and a couple of neighbours were there, and Dad collected my grandmother in one of his delivery trucks. A great little lady of 83, she stepped out and shook her fur stole with dignity, as though arriving for a wedding in a delivery truck was an everyday occurrence.

The champagne was popped, and just as the knife was poised over the wedding cake there was a squealing of brakes and an army ambulance pulled up outside the house. Out stepped Charlie, in dirty old "fatigues," with a big grin on his face. He had been detailed to drive to the village to pick up the last of the regimental laundry and somehow got "lost" on the four-mile trip. So he just kept going and drove another 20-odd miles to ask my husband about the way back! The party was complete, and never had a cake tasted so good! After the celebration the remainder was divided, part to go back to the camp, and part to be mailed thousands of miles across the sea to far-off Canada.

Our very brief honeymoon was soon over and it was 22 long months before I saw my husband again. During that time he did the "grand tour" of Europe— Sicily, Italy, France, Belgium, Holland and Germany. Then he came back to England on leave, and it was with great pride that I watched while he was decorated with the Military Medal by His Majesty George VI—a truly memorable moment in our life.

To this day I still carry the invitation card from Buckingham Palace, and a little silver horseshoe from that famous wedding cake. ॐ

No Secrets

Dave McIntosh

I suppose it was only prudent that the Allies try to keep Jerry from knowing about D-Day in advance and also how the invasion of Normandy was going for our side after it started.

But censorship changed our squadron's small society. Let me explain.

No. 418 City of Edmonton Sqdn., night intruders equipped with Mosquitos, was stationed at Holmsley South near Bournemouth in southern England. In the days before June 6, 1944, England, especially southern England, was bottled up by the censors. Nothing moved except, of course, the troops motoring surreptitiously to their landing barges. Leaves were cancelled. Mail was stopped or held up. The censor bore down with an even heavier hand than usual, even in the weeks after D-Day.

The only person on our squadron who might be classed as a likely censor was the intelligence officer, and he rarely did little else than answer the phone when intruder control in London called or listen to our combat reports, usually heroically embellished, when we returned from operations. As we were mostly a night-time unit, the IO had to stay up, like an ill-tempered chaperone, until after the last flier was in and could not be expected to be clear-headed enough to handle the demanding role of special censor during the emergency.

The CO asked for six volunteers, got no response and automatically appointed six who happened to be in his presence at the time, including my pilot, Sid Seid, and me as we were preparing for our routine night-flying test.

I understood why nobody would volunteer for our censorship board. My letters were deadly dull and I imagined everybody else's were, too. Long after the war, I read my father's letters home from overseas in WW I. They were almost as dull as mine. Our purpose was obviously the same: don't tell them anything, it will only alarm them. I didn't even let on to my mother for a long time that I had joined a squadron.

The censors met in our flight operations room. The squadron's outgoing personal mail was dumped in the middle of the plotting table where we navigators worked out devious routes to targets. The unsealed letters, mostly blue airmail forms, were divided equally among the six of us and the adjutant, who was our umpire, so to speak. We each had a razor blade (used) to expunge any mention of people, places, material, casualties, strategy, tactics, morale (unless good) and the general progress or otherwise of the war.

I was right. The first letter I picked up, from a member of the ground crew to his parents in Saskatchewan, comprised an interminable series of questions about the crops and the weather back home. I mentally noted a couple of flaccid phrases I could use myself.

Across the table there was a sound between a choke and a cough. I glanced up. Rodney's face was red and getting redder—an air force officer blushing!

"Hey, what's up?"

Rodney gulped. "It's a rather full description of the writer's last week-end in the Strand Palace with—" Rodney broke off abruptly before giving a name.

All the other censors were leaning forward, staring at Rodney, willing him to talk.

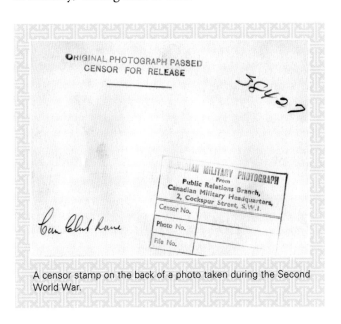

A censor stamp on the back of a photo taken during the Second World War.

A De Haviland Mosquito aircraft in July 1944.

"Who? Is she on the squadron? Do we know her? Where does she work? What's her name? Who? Who?"

The adjutant cut in: "I must remind you officers and gentlemen that these letters are private."

We ignored him, and anyway his sarcasm was lost on us. "Are there any photographs?"

Rodney read on, moving his lips and occasionally wetting them. "Oh, my God," he breathed.

His neighbor tried to grab the letter but Rodney hung on tight.

"No war secrets," he said, sealed the letter quickly and passed it to the adjutant who stamped it "Passed by Censor."

"Why, you selfish s.o.b.," Mike said.

There was a small pause. The rest of us looked down at our pile of letters and then frantically began riffling through them looking for something at least titillating if not pornographic. Perhaps Rodney's author had played show-and-tell with another girl.

"Wow!" said Hammy after a minute or two. "Listen to this."

"No tattling," said the adjutant. Hammy didn't even hear him. He read: "'I couldn't believe my luck when Mort took his clothes off the first time.'"

"It's a girl writing," some of us screamed.

Hammy read it all, panting slightly.

"What's her name?"

"Private information," Hammy smirked lasciviously and sealed the envelope.

I zipped through my dwindling pile again. They were all letters to mothers and fathers and sisters.

A few moments later, one of the other censors yelled: "Hey, here's one from ——————" and he named the most gorgeous girl on the squadron. His hand shaking, he read greedily about a voluptuous Saturday night in a Christchurch hotel.

"Better pass that to me," said an older and married member of our eagle-eyed group. "That stuff's too advanced for you."

"You find your own dirty letter."

Sid spoke up: "Here's one from a girl you'll like."

He began to read: "'I thought I'd go out of my mind.'"

Oh boy, oh boy, I thought.

Sid continued: "'It's a month since he went missing and I still cry all the time.'"

We looked shamefacedly at each other. We finished the letters quickly, nobody saying anything. Our few remaining censorship meetings before the end of the D-Day emergency were conducted in silence.

But the squadron had been changed. There were those who did and those who didn't. And there were those who knew who did and those who didn't. And all the fun had gone. ☞

PUBLIC RELATIONS, ARMY VERSION, OR HOW THE COLONEL GOT HIS CHRISTMAS PRESENTS

Doug Smith

Every now and then someone pops up with the question, "I hear that you are in public relations. Just *what* is public relations?"

Well, fellas, I reckon I could give you a long-winded spiel but, s'truth, it's often I don't know myself what it's all about. However, whatever measure of success I may enjoy in the grey-flanneled field, I owe a certain tribute to the Old Man of my unit. They say that necessity is the mother of invention. Well, to put it mildly, my Old Man was one proper bawstard who made you invent and produce necessities.

A real big-shot was my Old Man. At least he played the part of the big-shot and it was surprising how many people fell for it. Well, let's say they fell for it hard enough to give him his red tabs, which ain't exactly peanuts in our khaki-covered league.

It was only after the war was over that I learned what the Old Man had done in civvy street before '39. It

Foodstuffs are stored overseas in the warehouse of the Canadian Legion War Services Inc.

turned out that he had been a sales manager for crews of salesmen who peddled waterless cooking utensils from door to door. I can well imagine how this gave him the necessary brass and gall to handle men without too much compunction for their feelings.

Anyhow, as I said before, my Old Man was a proper bawstard. I think he must have written his own dictionary in which words like compassion, kindness and consideration were stricken out. On the other hand, like a real production man, he was strong on words like success, results, achievement, etcetera.

Fall down on one of his assignments, and you wrote your own ticket to a holding unit. Do a good job for him, and out of the blue would come a 72-hour pass with a travel warrant.

A queer cuss, who would just as soon put his own father on latrine duty if he didn't measure up to standard.

So it was around about this time of the year in '42 that I stood before him in his Nissen hut at Box Hill, a few miles this side of Dorking.

"Smith," says he, "I'll put it to you straight. Christmas is only a few days away. I have been invited to have dinner with Sir Thomas Hawkins and his charming daughter Barbara. They have been very kind to me. I would like to repay that kindness. I have prepared a Christmas shopping list that I would like you to fill. Here it is."

I pick up the list, read it and go pale. It says:

1 bottle Scotch.

3 sirloin steaks, two inches thick.

1 tin Turkish cigarettes.

1 pair nylon stockings, size 10.

In wartime England you might as well have asked for the plans for D-Day.

Not giving me a chance to recover my breath, the Old Man cuts in, "Here's five quid; see the adjutant, get a 48-hour pass, some transport…and get cracking!"

Rallying a little, I stammer, "Bbbbbbut, sir, this is impossible."

The Old Man raises one eyebrow. "Impossible???" says he. "I understand you know a cute cookie who does a buck and wing at the Windmill Theatre. I also know that you have been soft-soaping her old lady with tea, sugar and eggs from our kitchen. Now get t'hell out of here before I throw a court martial at you for purloining army property!"

Now, you guys see what I mean by a proper bawstard? The bloke ran his unit like a door to door sales outfit. He knew everything and everybody. Probably would never qualify for the old school tie at Sandhurst …but then again he did get his red tabs.

By now a desperate strategy was beginning to shape in my mind. And here, my friends, was how you operated in wartime U.K. when you had to take emergency measures.

In my pocket was the colonel's five quid. But to buy such goods as he demanded, money wasn't worth its weight in feathers. So you developed the cunning, the avariciousness and the deviousness of an Arab trader.

In nearby Leatherhead lived Marj of Windmill Theatre fame and her mother Mrs. Parkinson.

"Marj," says I. "I gotta have a pair of nylon stockings, just for 48 hours. I'll pay them back, honest I will."

"You gone crackers, mate?" says she. "Really, Smithy, sometimes I think you have gone balmy, simply balmy. I'll give you anything we have, but not my precious nylons."

It was Mrs. Parkinson, bless her, who—after a pound of tea—saved the day and kicked through with a pair of nylons on a lease-lend basis.

Jeeping to London, I made straight for the Horse & Dolphin in Chelsea.

Two gin and tonics later I drew Joe, the pub-owner aside. "Joe," says I, "I need two bottles of Scotch; desperately I do."

Joe looks at me with closed eyes. "I daresay you do, mate, and so do thousands like you. Ever hear there's been a war on?"

He starts to walk away. This is no time for niceties. I saunter over to Mrs. Joe who is beaming at the cash till. Flipping open my tunic in my best black market manner, I reveal the pair of glorious nylons.

Canned goods and other foodstuffs are stored overseas in the warehouse of the Canadian Legion War Services Inc.

Workers load cigarettes onto the shelves in the Canadian Legion War Services Inc. warehouse overseas.

I won't bore you with the details. Three minutes later the brow-beaten and muttering Joe is handing me two bottles of Scotch in a paper bag at the going rate of twenty-seven shillings and six pence each.

Now then—move number two. Two mild and bitters later, with a friend from C.M.H.Q. I locate the nearest R.C.A.S.C. unit where the meat rations are handled.

It's a funny thing about rations for the troops. Never in all of my five years in uniform did I ever see or hear of a sirloin steak appearing on any table—other ranks' or officers'. And yet a cow does have steaks. So who to see? The colonel? The adjutant? Don't be silly. The key-man in any such unit is the sergeant.

Now, to approach a sergeant and offer him filthy lucre for the purchase of a steak is crass madness. He would either call the Military Police and have you arrested for trying to bribe a servant of the King, or he would boot your posterior so far up your back you would look like the Hunchback of Notre Dame.

You do neither. I flip open my tunic and there, staring at the poor, thirsty, prohibition-confined man is a Heaven-sent bottle of Scotch.

Thirty minutes and six steaks later I am wending my way down past Lyons' Corner House in Leicester Square. Nearby is a tobacconist's shop.

"I'd like a tin of Turkish cigarettes," I say to the tobacconist. With a resigned stare he looks at me, pitying-like. Then he peers at my shoulder flashes. "Oi, a Canaidyun! Well, well now that accounts for it."

I haven't time to argue, so I flip behind the counter, whip open my haversack and flash him the sight of a juicy, two-inch steak. The poor bloke's jaw drops, he slavers at the lips, and shakily he reaches beneath the counter for a tin of Turkish cigarettes.

One more call to make. This time at the Red Cross centre for U.S. servicemen. The corporal at the door gives me the "Beat it, buddy. No Canadians allowed."

"I don't want to come in," says I, "I only want to get two pairs of nylon stockings, size 10."

Food rationing is introduced in 1942. The photo was taken in Montreal in 1943. Rationing was an inconvenience rather than a hardship.

The corporal's jaws tighten on his well-chewed cigar. "You shacked up with some broad?"

"No," says I, "I want them for my Old Man."

"Oh," says he with a leer. "You two goin' steady?"

This, fellas, is where public relations begins. You don't sock the guy. You carry on in the noble tradition.

Again I flip open my haversack to reveal the juicy two-inch steaks.

The Yank goes limp. His eyes bug out. "Brrrother! You just sit right down here. Don't you go away. I'll be back in two minutes flat."

Minutes later he and another corporal return and between them they have two pairs of good U.S. nylon stockings.

And so a few days before Christmas Day, 1942, I return to Box Hill and to my Old Man…mission accomplished.

"Good boy!" says the Old Man. "Good boy. You may have Christmas Day off." And he chuckles with his own peculiar sense of humour.

I turn to leave and am passing through the door when a voice barks:

"Hey, you! How about it?"

"How about what, sir?" says I.

"My change," says he.

Bewildered, I fork over four shillings and thruppence—all that was left of the five quid.

As I said before, my Old Man was a proper bawstard…and that's how I broke into public relations. ✑

Donated coffee is distributed to troops overseas by the Canadian Legion War Services organization during the Second World War.

RITCHIE'S SNACK BAR
Doug Macbeth

Lieutenant-Colonel the Honourable Basil Munn was truly a *pukka sahib*. I ran into him at the Senior Officers' School at Earlstoke in Somerset. My Boss had gone there to take the course, and I went with him—to look after him, as it were. To put you in the picture, as the books say, I should tell you that on account of overcrowding at the main school, five or six officers were living in a small estate a few miles away. It was really a posh place, with beautiful lawns, a rose bower, a vegetable garden and, mark you well, a *goldfish pond.*

Munn's batman and I lived there too. There wasn't much to do all day, bar sun bathing, and I had plenty of time to introduce myself to the neighbours—especially the one that had laying hens. What with the Boss's chocolate bars and my personality, I was a pretty popular visitor.

The officers came home about four o'clock and had a break until six, when they returned to the class rooms. I started from the first to have a cup of tea for the Boss, but soon, on account of the generosity of the neighbours, I was able to add a bit of toast, with real Somerset butter and honey, an egg salad, watercress sandwiches and other products of my imagination and aptitude.

Munn's man, Cludge, was a dull oaf. His activity ran as far as a cup of tea, which he made from the dregs of my pot. Of course, he had no "traders," for, as I forgot to tell you, my Boss had brought with him half a dozen unopened parcels from home. Hence the chocolate bars, the soap, and, finally, the sardines.

The Honourable Basil had brought his car with him. How he got the gasoline coupons was a matter between him and the Lord. We knew when our lads were on the way to tea because, over the noise of the wheezy engine, the voice of Col. Munn rang out: "Cludge, you lazy so-and-so, where are you?" This, I'm sure, about two miles away.

Cludge was always on hand with a pair of carpet slippers, which he tenderly placed on the Honourable's feet after peeling off the high field boots which the Master wore. By the time the de-booting was over, I had the table set up in the garden, beside the goldfish pool, and down-wind from the rose bower. Artistic, that's me, fellows!

The Honourable Basil thought so much of his comfort that he evaded the niceties of inter-allied co-operation and, in time, he used to regard me as one of his own retainers. It was "Ritchie, more tea!" and "Ritchie, another egg sandwich!" and so on, entirely oblivious to the fact that the goodies came from my own—well, you might call it scrounging or from my Boss's cache of Canadian dainties.

Now, Colonel Basil was very fond of my special dish, SARDINES ON TOAST SLIVERS. "A few more sardines, Ritchie my lad," he would grunt, and the day was rapidly approaching when our stock was getting near zero. How to satisfy the ducal appetite of the Honourable Basil was one of my major problems.

Sardines! They swam up and down in front of my eyes at night. They jumped over hurdles like sheep. What were we going to do when the Boss's stock ran out?

Well, boys, you probably are guessing the tail-end of this yarn which is not intended as a pun but which is, as I now realize, a sordid story.

With the camouflage net from my tin helmet and the aid of a couple of twigs I made a landing net. Each morning I crept to the edge of the gold fish pond and snagged a couple of finny monsters from their home. You fellows may not realize that a skinned fish soaked in sardine oil, nestled on Somersetshire butter, garnished with parsley and sprinkled with salt and pepper makes a hell of a fine "SARDINE ON TOAST SLIVERS." ॐ

No Room at the Inn
Dave McIntosh

Freddie, who is still alive, praise be, says it didn't happen exactly this way, but I say it did. I can't remember what happened this morning but I can recall clearly everything that took place at Christmas 38 years ago. Anyway, Freddie's heart surgery has seriously reduced his drinking and therefore, according to the best medical advice I can get, affected his memory glands.

We navigators were at Cranwell, Lincolnshire, in 1943 learning to bat out 18 words a minute in Morse code, a talent that we, the instructors, RAF Cranwell and RCAF Headquarters in London all knew would never be put to use unless, perhaps, there happened to be a train wreck at the station and the telegrapher dropped dead. Cranwell was dreary. It was Stalag Luft III without the fence. We escaped to Lincoln whenever we could, or even Sleaford, and escape was particularly in demand at Christmas. A bunch of us reserved a few rooms at the Great Northern Hotel, which wasn't great, northern or much of a hotel. But there was a war on, y'know. However, that wouldn't be cutting in to the lobster-and-champagne breakfasts back in the messes in Toronto.

Shorty tried one of his loud rumors as we joined the long queue for the Lincoln bus: the Germans were about to attack a secret Cranwell H-hut where a system of doubling the speed of Morse students to 36 words a minute had just been devised. It didn't work of course, being so far-fetched (about getting up to 36 words a minute, I mean), and we had to stand all the way to Lincoln. This gave us a chance to survey the WAAFs with their hair rolled under and prim little overnight cases full of all kinds of birth-control devices. Some lucky buggers in our very bus probably had them all lined up.

It wasn't snowing and it wasn't raining when we reached Lincoln. It was a clever combination of the two and the dark was coming down. From the street I could barely make out the cathedral on the hill.

A couple of us had entertained a vague idea that we might go to church Christmas Day.

A tattered paper Christmas bell hung over the reception desk in the hotel. The blackout curtains were already drawn. We were pleasantly surprised not only that the hotel had our names but that our rooms were unoccupied. They were the usual English drab with no bathroom. I wasn't to get an English hotel room with can until well in to '44 when my pilot and I stayed at the Imperial in Torquay, and even there I think it was something special.

Freddie and I were tossing our greatcoats and haversacks on the two narrow beds when Freddie whirled around. He could hear a cat on a carpet. "Did you see that?" he asked. I thought he was practising his aircraft recognition, but our door was still open and the shadow of a figure had passed in the gloomy corridor. "A girl," Freddie breathed heavily and was down the hall like a shot. He came back in a few minutes. "Chambermaid," he reported. "Very busy. Maybe later." He sat on the bed. "Damnedest green eyes I ever saw," he said as if to himself. I saw her later because she was also a

Service personnel sign in at a Canadian Club in London.

waitress in the dining room and Freddie was right. He decided to call her Tiger, which whipped up my erotic imaginings into an even more fevered state. But Tiger disappeared (with Shorty, it was later claimed by Shorty) after she had helped clear away Christmas Eve high tea—dry bread with ersatz jam, a tasty scone and good tea out of an enormous samovar, the hotel's only claim to long-faded elegance.

"Well, off to the pubs," Freddie said after a final search of the upstairs corridors and two calls at the linen cupboard where he had originally chatted up Tiger.

"That'll be different," I said, laying on the sarcasm with a shovel. We always did a pub crawl in Lincoln.

"Can you suggest anything better?" Freddie asked.

He and I both knew I couldn't.

Out into the blackout, the sleet still stinging slant-ways, the damp going through our coats and tunics in seconds. We groped our way down the street, the noise and the smell guiding us to the first pub. It was packed, of course, mostly with young men in battledress. Non-belligerent Cranwell wasn't the only base around. There were dozens of bomber fields near Lincoln. Nearly every evening at dusk we could hear the Wimpys and Hallies forming up. Sometimes it was even clear enough for us to get a glimpse of their dark silhouettes heading east.

"There must be a better place than this," Freddie shouted in my ear.

"I doubt it," I roared back.

We pushed and shoved our way to the bar where the beer pump handles were going like things possessed. The innkeeper or his deputy finally stopped long enough (his arm was probably tired) to hear my imploring "two brown ales."

"No brown," he said. "No bottles. Just mild and bitter." My God, the evening had barely started.

"Two pints of mild and bitter," I said.

"No glasses left," he said.

Freddie and I had him there. We each produced

The interior of one of the rooms in the Canadian Legion Club in Belfast, Ireland, October 1944.

large tin cups that folded up in to something which looked like cookie cutters. After all, we weren't amateurs when it came to the wartime English taverns.

"Not regulation size," the pumper said.

"We'll pay regulation prices," Freddie said. The cups were smaller than the standard pint glasses.

"Right," the publican said.

The only trouble with the tin cup was that sometimes it folded up when it was full. We had learned to use thumb and forefinger like a vice around the top rim, supporting the stretched cup as if we were holding up a weak-kneed inebriate.

We worked our way from pub to pub, jostled outside in the blackout, jostled inside by drinking airmen who, because they were off Christmas Eve, likely would be flying Christmas night. Some pubs had red-and-green paper chains and bells but most hadn't bothered with decorations. In one pub, three Salvation Army carollers were drowned out by the high pitch of the conversation and the crashing of the glasses. In another, a drunk tried to sing "Away in a Manger" but was overwhelmed by a chorus of "Roll Me Over in the Clover."

"I wouldn't mind being rolled over even in a manger," Freddie said. He was the religious one.

It was obvious the pickings were going to be very, very slim—not even leftovers, in fact. The few WAAFs and other women were tightly guarded by their escorts. And I mean guarded. One guy built a little barricade of a table and two chairs around his girl when he went for drinks. And he backed all the way to the bar so that he could keep his eye on her and any possible raiders. I don't know what he did when he had to go to the can.

Inevitably came the landlord's bellowed "Time, gentlemen, please" and we scrambled to buy a last beer. By this time I didn't know how many pubs we'd been in. But I did know I had to hang on tight to my folding tin cup because two pilots and one observer had tried to grab it away from me. "Get your own cup," I shouted. "You can buy them anywhere in Toronto." I had had my sister send me several on the understanding they were the best thing for accurate measurement of the fluid in an aircraft compass, which wasn't so far off the mark because some guys tried to drink compass fluid.

Stumbling around a bit, excusing ourselves frequently for bumping in to clinching couples in doorways, we made our way back to the Great Northern. We fought our way through the blackout curtain at the door, punching back when it billowed inward on the cold draft from the street. "Mind the blackout," said the ancient clerk behind the desk.

"Hello," said Freddie.

I looked around and there was a WAAF who had come in from Cranwell with us on the bus. Beside her was a young man in battledress with an air gunner's wing on it.

"You can't stay here," the clerk was saying, obviously for the third or fourth time.

"Perhaps we could use one of those big chairs in the lounge," the air gunner said.

"No."

I could see Freddie was thinking what I was thinking: how do we get rid of this RAF air gunner but retain her? The WAAF could also see what we were thinking. "This is my husband," she said. "He just got in from Coningsby." Coningsby was a nearby bomber base.

This was going to be good, I thought. We were going to get the whole bit: a daring mission coming up the next night, this perhaps the last time they would be together, no meeting in weeks of strain.

But neither the WAAF nor the air gunner said anything like this because the next second Freddie handed the gunner our room key and the happy couple ran up the stairs.

"You can't do that," said the clerk. He had taken the words right out of my mouth.

Catching some zees at a Legion Club.

The interior of a room in the Canadian Legion Club, Belfast, Ireland, in October 1944.

"We'll replace any stolen towels," Freddie said. Guests had to supply their own towels and soap but the jibe went over the clerk's head. Freddie looked quite pleased with himself.

"C'mon," he said to me, "we'll go over to the King's Head." I knew what this meant because I'd done it before in Lincoln. The landlord of the King's Head was the only one in town who would let aircrew without rooms sleep on the floor of his dining room until the buses started running again in the morning to take them back to their fields and the briefings for the next target.

We were lucky to find any space on the floor. There was no room left near the walls and we were right in the path of all the guys who had to go to pee. All night long my legs and arms were walked on. "Jesus, Freddie," I whimpered every once in a while. Freddie slept on, or was playing possum.

At dawn, I demanded truculently: "How do you know she's married?"

"Oh, I checked on her some time ago," Freddie said. "I had a friend look up her file in the records office."

"Well, how do you know that was her husband?"

"Some things you have to take on trust, especially on Christmas Eve."

He was suddenly all abustle.

"C'mon, let's go for a walk."

"A walk?" I nearly screamed. I was damp, cold, bruised and hung over.

"Clear the old cobwebs. Work up an appetite. Put lead in the old pencil." He had every cliché in the book at tongue-tip.

We walked slowly up the hill to Lincoln Cathedral. There was singing from inside, even at that ungodly hour.

"Shall we go in?" I said.

"I don't think so," Freddie said. "We've already practised Christianity today and I wouldn't want us to overdo it."

We walked back down the hill to the Great Northern where, I knew, Christmas breakfast was going to be sawdust sausages, cold toast, the same ersatz jam we'd had for high tea and execrable coffee. I only prayed the WAAF and the air gunner wouldn't be sitting near us, smiling to beat hell. ∽

The interior of a Canadian Club in the United Kingdom during the Second World War.

Service personnel sit in their room at a Canadian Legion Club in Paris.

GOODBYES
Ben Malkin

Leave-taking was unavoidable. A serviceman about to depart couldn't simply slip quietly away. Yet leave-taking battered the emotions; if some way could have been found to abolish it, that would have been a step forward. For example, the military authorities could have issued a diktat: "The practice of leave-taking will cease immediately," or words to that effect.

About the only point in favor of leave-taking was its intensely private nature—that is, when you said goodbye in private, which was usually the case. But sometimes it was done in public, on a train platform, with mothers pouring out tears, wives trying bravely to hold them back, fathers keeping a stiff upper lip, and sons and husbands in uniform wishing the train would leave soon.

Out of embarrassment for their comrades, the lucky servicemen whose families had remained at home rather than go to the station would turn away. Happily nothing is forever. Eventually the order to board would be shouted and with a sigh of relief and a last wave, the ordeal was over.

Servicemen who married overseas had to face two leave-takings: the first, with their families in Canada; the second, with their wives in England. I suppose the girls at home in Canada could say it served them right for having married overseas. But served right or wrong, the ordeal was nothing less than double jeopardy.

Each leave-taking was different, so I won't say mine was typical. My first was in Winnipeg, in the privacy of the home. I was tying my bootlaces, when my mother entered my room, sat down on the bed, started to say goodbye and look after yourself, then broke down in a Niagara of tears.

What was a guy to do? My mother almost never cried, though there were times when she did look bewildered. With six boys and a girl to do for, fetch for, and keep the peace among, she was always far too busy to cry. I put my arm around her shoulders, said not to worry, everything would be all right. That seemed to be helpful, and she composed herself.

My father put his hands over my head, placed the tips of his fingers together, and gave the traditional Hebrew benediction: "May the Lord bless you and keep you." I wasn't much of a believer, but it never hurts to count your blessings. Then a brother drove me to the station. An endurable leave-taking, done in private.

That was in the winter of 1939. In June, 1943, I had my second leave-taking.

Our regiment, the 3rd Field RCA, was at Airdrie, a suburb of Glasgow, waiting to embark for an unknown destination. All leaves had been cancelled. Bert Burgoygne, an officer in our outfit, asked me would I like to see my wife, she being in London. I said sure. He said I'd be included in a group going to Larkhill, site of the Royal Artillery school on Salisbury Plain, to take a four-day course on how to handle the German 88-mm anti-aircraft gun.

We left Friday night, and were to report at Larkhill Sunday evening, giving us a clear weekend in London. We had to take all our gear. (It turned out that we went directly from Larkhill to our ships.)

A Canadian soldier is greeted by a young child as troops march down a street in New Westminster, B.C.

Having all my stuff was what caused the trouble. I had my rifle and the new short bayonet. On previous visits to London, I'd brought nothing more lethal than my laundry. In going through my kit to see whether anything needed cleaning, my wife found tropical clothing: shorts, bush shirt, and the like.

By 1943, the British had become so security conscious that she didn't ask any questions. As for the tropical kit, as soon as it was issued the rumor spread in our regiment that we were heading for Norway, the tropical kit being issued to fool the enemy.

My wife and I went to Lyons Corner House that Saturday night. As we ate, the tears suddenly gushed. What the hell, I thought. Not here. Not now. What would the next table think? I tried to reassure her that nothing was in the wind—just more manoeuvres, like the dozens already held. For all I knew, this was true. She stopped crying.

We left for Salisbury the next afternoon. Salisbury on a Sunday afternoon was not, at that time anyway, a lively town. Not a tea shop was open. We tried the American Red Cross, which had a clubroom functioning, but were told only Americans could be served. For reasons of its own, the American Red Cross established that rule early in the war, although all other auxiliary services, whether American, British, Canadian or any other, opened their facilities to all Allied servicemen and women. Perhaps the Red Cross felt that Allied soldiers of different nationalities might, when brought together, enter into unseemly disputes.

No matter. Let's try the cathedral for a place to sit down. That turned out to be best. The great Salisbury Cathedral was almost empty. An organist was playing, very softly. We sat near the rear, holding hands. After a couple of hours, it was time for my wife to catch the London train, and this time she was doing the departing, not I. That seemed to make it much easier for her, and I was glad. ❧

GOD KNOWS
Rosemary Hutchinson

The year of our war 1944 finds me and my friend Charlie still driving cars in the RCAF, but Ottawa has lifted us out of Newfoundland and plunked us on a Yorkshire bomber station.

We are having supper in the mess. I jab at a piece of burnt toast covered with blobs of melted cheese, the whole surmounted by a piece of raw bacon. Only in the air force have they the ability to burn the bottom of something and leave the top raw.

"Hey Charlie, call the maitre d'. This bacon is still twitching, it's about to crawl off the plate."

Charlie flips her toast in the air with her fork to see if the other side looks better. "Very funny," she says, then changing the subject: "When are we going to ride the bikes down Sutton Bank?" Charlie has a one-track mind. When things are going OK she has to think up something dumb to make life more exciting.

"Never," I tell her, chomping on my burnt offering; it is amazing what you can eat if you are hungry enough. "I'd rather go down Sutton Bank on roller skates than those old wrecks."

These are our issue bicycles. When people are transferred out they are turned back to stores. Someone there gives them a shake; if anything rattles it is tied up with wire and they are reissued: "airmen for the use of!"

Sutton Bank has a chilling gradient of one in four. It joins the soft rolling Vale of York to the higher moors and dales that stretch away into the distance to Scarborough and the sea. The road ascending this mini-Mont Blanc borders its edge, so that any fool daring the descent stands a good chance of soaring into space and landing below in a horrible tangle of body and bicycle.

Charlie and I go up and down regularly in our little Hillman cars and I always treat this hill with great respect. In fog it is a brute. It is so steep that if I have someone fat like Floot-Loot Plopper in the car we simply don't make it. The Hillman stalls halfway up and

I push—figuratively, of course—the Floot-Loot on to the road where he trudges forlornly upward while I pass him, to await his arrival at the top. Plopper isn't a bad old duck, and a real tiger with the ladies. He must have addresses all over Yorkshire where he "stops for tea"—while his driver waits. We frown on such unmilitary behavior.

Charlie and I leave the mess and repair to the NAAFI to eat its stodgy tarts, drink its milky coffee and eat our chocolate ration in one glorious orgy. The initials stand for something, but I never can remember what. We just call it "naffi" with affection. It is a canteen, a great social spot for the other ranks, which certainly includes us.

The subject of the great suicide ride is dropped and might have lain forever buried had not Bussy Bodine's aircraft blown up practically on the end of the runway while Charlie was watching it take off.

This gave Charlie an acute case of shattered nerves quite unlike her usual stoic acceptance of sudden death among aircrews.

Bussy was our old cohort of laying-the-flare-path days in Newfoundland, when the three of us had worked together on the runways with the harsh sea wind howling about our ears and extinguishing flare-pots as fast as Bussy could light them. He had come up in the world, a pilot with his own crew, halfway through his tour, but was the same cheerful, chatty boy quite unchanged by promotion. We had been having great fun together through this hot English summer.

Apart from Bussy's death, I think Charlie was just fed up with life in general, the deaths, the food, the black-out driving, even the titanic struggle to bag a bathtub at the wash-house before the hot water ran out. It was about the only place you could be alone, though as you lay in the tepid water contemplating your toes someone was sure to bang on the door telling you to get the lead out.

So, to cheer up the poor girl, I gave in to the inevitable: "OK, I'll ride down Sutton Bank with you."

Our next 48-hour pass finds us staying with my Aunt Sophy in Thirsk, a town within biking distance of our project. Aunt Sophy is a pal of my grandmother, a remarkable old girl who still plays tennis wearing a voluminous ankle-length white skirt. She can smash a ball so accurately that your survival depends on leaping out of the way and, as Aunty likes her tennis appreciated, you must shout "Oh, well played" as you dive to safety. She should be commanding a gun site on the south coast: She could waste any enemy object in the Channel with one shot.

The next day is very hot and it is late afternoon before we struggle to the top of Sutton Bank and collapse exhausted in the grass bordering the road. Shirt, shorts and even my socks are wet with sweat. We lie in silence gazing down over the Vale of York. The green fields flow into the distance, dotted here and there by darker clumps of trees. The farm houses look like toys, and in the distance the Pennines frame the sky. The sun is low and the landscape shimmers in the heat, giving everything a golden glow.

Charlie gently touches the tiny flowers that grow among the grass. "Where do they go?" she says softly as though to herself. "Where do all those dead boys go?"

I stare up at the blue sky wondering if she expects an answer. Perhaps the Archbishop of Canterbury or the Pope know, but they are not handy. Then I think of my mother—in times of crisis I often think of her.

"Charlie," I say, "my mother is quite good-looking for her age. She's old now, of course, must be nearly 50. She likes parties, nice clothes and doesn't go to church much, but she has this awesome faith in God.

"If she were here now she'd give you a bit of a hug and say 'God knows,' and really mean it. Of course she'd weep for their short lives, but to her God knows everything. So why not let Him look after your boys. He knows where they are. What we must try to do is remember them always and what they did for us."

There is a long, long silence, Charlie and I not often dealing in subjects so profound. She gives me an intent

Coffee and sandwiches are served up to Canadian service personnel at a NAAFI (Navy, Army and Air Force Institutes) establishment in the United Kingdom during the Second World War.

look and finally says quietly: "You do me good," adding in an offhand way "Kid, you got depths I have not plumbed. Let's get down that hill."

We line up the bikes at the top. I nod at Charlie to go first. As I watch her gathering speed I fervently hope this is not one of the days the air vice-marshal decides to drive to Filey. Perhaps, at this very moment his big staff car is climbing the hill towards us. He won't take too kindly to us plastering ourselves all over his windshield. Neither will his driver, who has spent hours checking and polishing the Chrysler. If we are not dead on contact she may finish the job in a furious rage.

I push off, the hill grabs me and my clapped-out old bike and we start to fly. Charlie disappears around the first curve at a precarious angle. I follow and survive. The wind sings in my ears, the road edge flashes by in a green blur. Everything on my bike is vibrating,

there is an ominous flap-flap from one of the tires. I am paralysed with fright at the furious speed, but as the road straightens I am suddenly exhilarated. It's fun to be young, alive and doing silly, dangerous things like this. "Live for the moment," I shout at the wind. "There may be no tomorrow!"

We reach the foot in a ridiculously short time, considering the long struggle we had to get to the top. The road flattens out and I wobble to a stop beside Charlie. "Wasn't that great," she shouts. "If I weren't so pooped I'd do it again!"

"Yeah," I reply, "next time we'll try it in a fog. Let's go. Remember we're taking Aunt Sophy to the Red Lion. Do you suppose they'll have steak and kidney pie tonight?"

Charlie gives me a small, very apologetic smile. "God knows," she says. ∽

FACES OF WAR
Rosemary Hutchinson

My friend Charlie and I are cruising down the Strand in a Hillman. Now a Hillman, to the uninitiated, is a type of car spewed out to meet the emergency of wartime. It is extremely small, and much inclined to rattle at an early age, especially this one under Charlie's heavy hand.

A vitriolic mustard shade, it sports two orange blobs of special paint on the hood. In the event of a gas attack these blobs will change color. Charlie and I are at a loss as to the action necessary if this catastrophe occurs, because our gas masks are somewhere in the bedsitter we rent on Earlscourt Road.

At the moment I am more concerned with this girl's driving. Her approach might, at best, be termed nonchalant. "You are the most gawd-awful driver," I tell her as a traffic light stops us at full belt.

A taxi pulls up beside us. The driver, in a dusty cap and shapeless raincoat, leans across his steering wheel and shouts: "Hey Canada, where'd ya learn to drive, on one of them Rocky Mountains you have over there?"

Popping her head out the window, Charlie replies: "Na Guy, on one of them h'icebergs we have over there."

The cabby starts to laugh, I laugh and Charlie, overcome by her own wit, laughs hardest of all. The traffic light turns green and the taxi cuts us off neatly. "Serves you right," I remark, bracing my feet on the dashboard.

But the cabbies of wartime London are kind to the Canadian girls who drive here. They give us endless patient directions when we get lost in the maze of the city, sometimes holding up long streams of traffic to do so. I suppose that after years of blitz and blackout our remarkable driving habits are a source of amusement. The war is nearly over, soon we and our tacky cars will disappear. Perhaps they will even miss us.

This war has made Londoners of Charlie and me. We are the grateful recipients of a living-out allowance, 12 shillings a day, that enables us to rent the bed-sitter, a vast, shabby chamber with a permanent smell of cooking.

We also get civilian ration coupons for milk, margarine, cheese and endless tins of corned beef. We admire the British housewife, who manages for a week on this meagre supply; we devour ours in two days. However, we are lucky: The Sally Ann and the Knights of Columbus canteens fill in the void.

Food, any kind of food, interests us greatly, so we are pleased when some affluent boyfriend asks one of us out to dinner. A great gastronomic event is the arrival in town of Charlie's father, a big gun in the navy. He always finds time to take us to the Berkley, where he sits and frequently remarks: "I don't know how you kids can eat so much and stay so skinny!"

We are enjoying ourselves. Life is not as traumatic as at an operational station where people you know and like have a tendency to disappear—permanently. Each morning, we board the Underground at Earlscourt and eject near Russell Square, site of the RCAF motor-transport section. From this vast subterranean garage we are let loose on our daily ploys. We drive hither and thither about London with important people or documents, or both, and often make runs through the lovely countryside.

A wartime dance in Moncton, New Brunswick, draws a huge crowd.

We are on such a trip today, bound for the plastic-surgery hospital at East Grinstead. Charlie is delivering sealed documents and, on my day off, I am keeping her company—at great peril to my life, I think, as we wheel down the Mall at a great rate. We have planned this safari carefully. We will take the long route home with many stops to contemplate nature and refuel the inner man. The night shift, which tends to be more casual, will have taken over by the time we get back and we are hoping our tardy return will go unnoticed.

In due course Charlie delivers her papers, getting all the right signatures in the right places from the proper people, and we wheel down the drive towards the main road.

Two figures standing by the entrance have their thumbs out in the universal gesture. They are sergeants with pilots' wings. I know what is coming, so I turn to Charlie: "Are you ready for this?" She glares at me: "Of course I'm ready."

We stop. I lean out the window and shout cheerfully: "Are you bound for the Big Smoke?"

One of the sergeants leans in the window: "Can we get a lift then?"

I smile, determined he will not guess that I am shattered by his face. It is a patchwork of pink and white skin crisscrossed with surgical stitches. His nose is a queer shape and he has no eyebrows. But his brown eyes are cheerful and when he smiles his teeth are white and even. But then, I think, teeth don't burn. His pal, an Australian, has fared somewhat better facially but his hands are like claws and he tries to hide them behind his back.

"Hop in," I cry. "We run a super taxi service here!" They laugh and squeeze into the narrow back seat.

As we drive along we learn they are going on leave, but must return to the hospital for further surgery. They hope to reach the one lad's Yorkshire home by catching the night train north.

Conversation languishes, but Charlie saves the day by shouting "Pub time" and wheeling down a leafy

A 1943 Christmas Day dance in progress at the Canadian Legion Club at Cartwright Gardens in the United Kingdom.

lane to a drinking place she knows. We sit in its little garden quaffing beer and things improve dramatically. By the time we cross Putney Bridge we are all chirping like little birds in the spring.

Charlie debates hanging on to the car for the evening and suffering the inevitable wrath tomorrow, but caution prevails. We dump the Hillman back at the section and take our new friends to Soho where we eat spaghetti in an Italian restaurant.

This is augmented by beans on toast, a couple of fried black-market eggs, chips and a slice of spicy chicken that Charlie claims is really "London alley cat." It says much for the quality of the wine that nobody finds this remark upsetting. We finish with spumoni—water ice streaked with violent colors of red, green and yellow.

Our pals have three hours before train time, so I suggest we go dancing. This idea is met with shouts of approbation, so we take a cab to Hammersmith, where the mighty beat of the band surges out to engulf you before you can even see the Palais de Danse.

We join the rocking humanity on its enormous floor. They are playing our music—Glenn Miller, the panacea of wartime youth. Gone are thoughts of ruined faces and clawed hands. We jitter and jive to "Chattanooga Choo-Choo," "Jersey Bounce" and "The Boogie-Woogie Bugle Boy." I am so hot I tear off my jacket, then pull off my tie and wave it round my head. I would take off my shirt too were I not afraid of being thrown out. We dance in twos, we dance as a foursome, soon we are dancing with people we have never seen before. We dance away the dreary sadness of the war.

We barely get our 'outpatients' to their train on time. At Kings Cross we push them past the irate guard at the barrier, but when he sees their faces he becomes kind and gets them on board. We wave frantically as the train slides away from the platform.

Charlie and I walk to the station entrance. It is wet and dark and the euphoria is beginning to wear off.

"Do you think too much drink, too much food and too much exercise is good for plastic-surgery patients?" Charlie asks anxiously.

"Dunno," I reply. "It's too late to worry about it now, but they had a good time, and you know so did I."

Charlie looks surprised. "Me too, and you know we never even found out their last names."

Coat collars turned up, we plod through the rain to the Underground to take the long trip back to the bed-sitter. ☙

SURVIVING THE SLAUGHTER
Jean Margaret Crowe

There is no mistake: There has been no mistake. There shall be no mistake.

– Arthur Wellesley, Duke of Wellington

"They shall not grow old as we who are left grow old." Those words have always angered me. It is as if somehow by being killed our men had gotten the best of it. When all they really wanted was just to come home and grow old as the rest of us have done.

Last year I went to the anniversary convention of the Hong Kong Veterans of Canada. They are my generation and our faces are beginning to belie the spirit within us. But as I waited and watched and listened, the faces around me changed and they were once again the young soldiers whose world would come to a sudden end in an Asian country on Christmas Day almost 40 years ago.

The words no longer angered me. There was love in the middle aged voices that spoke them. Through the fighting, through the years of imprisonment, through the years of living in spite of haunting bitter memories, through the years of struggle, these men have been as family to each other. It could not but be that way.

The British Colony of Hong Kong in 1941 was a strange mixture of opulence and stifling poverty. Rickshaws were the common mode of transportation. In the harbor was a floating population of 100,000 Chinese who seldom ventured ashore. In the exclusive Jockey Club the English ruling class dined and danced. Sir Mark Young, the governor-general, Sir Athol MacGregor, chief justice of the colony, his wife Lady MacGregor and their friends had brought their own kind of England to the island. Each box in the club was a complete room with a large cocktail lounge and dining area at the back. The opulence would end with the siege. Later they would have barely enough to eat to keep alive.

Canadian soldiers shortly after arriving in Hong Kong, November 1941.

As early as 1937 the defence of Hong Kong had been discussed by the chiefs of staff in London. They regarded Hong Kong as important, useful, but not vital. The general officer commanding (GOC) Hong Kong until 1938 said he had no confidence in any plan of defence. The area favored the attacker. The decision was taken against reinforcement.

In the spring of 1941 it appeared to Churchill that war with Japan was inevitable. As the Japanese army moved deeper and deeper in to China he advocated that the isolated garrison be reduced to a symbolic scale. "We must avoid frittering away our resources on untenable positions. If Japan goes to war with us there is not the slightest chance of holding Hong Kong or of relieving it. I wish we had fewer troops there."

Nevertheless, on the advice of a new GOC, considered by many to be too easy going, the chiefs of staff changed their collective mind. It was proposed to Churchill that Canada be asked to send one or two battalions. On September 15, 1941, he made an astonishing decision. "There is no objection to the approach being made...."

To the cabinet in Ottawa, the request was not unwelcome. Since the declaration of war on the German Reich two years before not a single Canadian

army unit had met the Germans in battle. Australian, New Zealand and South African troops were heavily engaged. The Canadian brigades in England, restless and unhappy, continued their unending training exercises. The Second Front was a long way off. The government wanted action.

Col. J.K. Lawson, director of military training, was asked to prepare a list of infantry battalions in order of their state of combat readiness. He relegated nine battalions to list C—insufficiently trained and not recommended for operational consideration. The Royal Rifles of Canada and the Winnipeg Grenadiers were on list C. They were distinguished regiments but for the previous two years they had stagnated on garrison duty in Newfoundland and Jamaica.

Within a week of presenting the list Col. Lawson was promoted to command the Canadian Brigade and ironically it was composed of a small HQ, the Royal Rifles of Canada, and the Winnipeg Grenadiers. They provided a 'nice mix' of French- and English-speaking Canadians and of East and West said official Ottawa.

The decision had been made in haste. There was not even a map of Hong Kong in defence headquarters. Nor did Canada have its own information-gathering agency in the Far East. There was little at hand on which to formulate plans. Col. J.L. Ralston, minister of defence, who was holidaying in Los Angeles, spoke to Gen. H.D.G. Crerar, our chief of general staff, on the telephone, Churchill was again consulted and the die was cast. It was cast for men from Fork River and Birtle, from Melita and Estevan, from Swift Current and Coquitlam, from Aroostook Junction and Chomedey-Ville de Laval, and many many more.

Great Britain was serving notice to the world that she intended to defend her furthermost outpost against all aggression.

On October 9 precise details of the request reached Ottawa and the battalions were warned of service.

The journey to Hong Kong began by train in locked cars as the troops moved from the east to the west coast. One Grenadier recruit who had lingered a little too long saying his goodbyes almost missed the train. "I thought of that often as I starved in prison camp," he said. "If I had only stumbled, just been delayed for two or three seconds."

Two days before the regiments sailed, a brief reached Gen. Crerar from the War Office: "The Japanese are established on the mainland, are carrying out operations in the vicinity of the frontier and are in possession of a number of air bases within easy reach of the colony. They also hold command of the sea and are therefore in a position to occupy the surrounding islands at will."

There was no turning back.

The regiments departed from the port of Vancouver aboard the *Awatea* on October 27. The New Zealand ship was designed to carry 500 passengers. There were 1,973 troops. They had not been told where they were going, though some had heard in the bars and restaurants of Vancouver's Chinatown that their destination was Hong Kong.

The *Awatea* was crowded and uncomfortable. The upper deck, formerly a recreation area, was empty and out of bounds to the men. The whole ship stank of

boiling mutton tripe and onions. About 50 men forced their way off the gangway and in to the shed. In the words of officialdom, "They were persuaded by their officers to return in a matter of about two minutes." Actually they returned at gun point and under threat of court martial for desertion. The captain moved his craft in to harbor for the night to prevent any more attempts to go ashore.

There was insufficient cargo space. The mechanical transport alone required 125,000 cubic feet. The total space was only 45,000 and inexplicably 12,000 cubic feet was left empty when the ship sailed. A second vessel was dispatched on November 4 carrying the equipment but the contents were turned over to the Americans in the Philippines. War had been declared on Japan. Hong Kong was in jeopardy.

Hong Kong island is just a 10-minute ferry ride from mainland China. In 1898 the British decided they needed a protective buffer so they moved suddenly on

Lt. Cdr. Fred Day and officers of HMCS *Prince Rupert* with Canadian prisoners of war at Shamshuipo Camp, Hong Kong, August 1945.

to the mainland. They took a strip 26 miles deep. This area was henceforth called the New Territories and was leased to the British government by the Chinese in 1898. It was an undefended space of hills, old villages, small vegetable gardens and fir trees. On November 16 the Canadians landed in Kowloon, the principal city of the New Territories, and took up residence in the military barracks of Sham Shui Po on the peninsula.

The 1st Middlesex Regt. had been enjoying itself there for three years and for three weeks the Canadians had never had it so good. The beer was cold and the girls were friendly. There was a profusion of restaurants and bars, shops laden with jade and silk, and everything was dirt cheap. After Jamaica and cold Newfoundland it seemed ideal.

But the 10,000 British and Indian troops on the island were armed mainly with rifles and bayonets. There was no ammunition for the 2-inch mortars and each battalion had only 70 rounds of 3-inch mortar ammunition, enough for approximately a 3-minute barrage. Some of the troops had been there since 1937. The alarms of war had come and gone with regularity. The possibility of war was considered as philosophically as one considers ordinary death and taxes.

Eighteen miles away on the mainland was Gen. Ito Takae, infantry commander of three divisions of the Japanese Imperial Army numbering 60,000 battle-seasoned combat troops. The Japanese Navy commanded the sea. The Japanese Air Force commanded the sky.

Sunday morning, December 7 in Hong Kong (December 6 in the Western Hemisphere) was, as always, a festive day at the Jockey Club. Gala breakfasts, lunches, riding, whisky and soda continued until 5 a.m. It was the Gibraltar of the Far East and elegance of living was the 'official British' commonplace. After all the Japanese Ambassador Karuso had left from Kai Tak airport only a few weeks earlier on the giant Hong Kong clipper to take his peace plans to Washington. All was serene.

But early Monday morning, a lovely sunny Monday morning, a formation of high-flying planes was seen making its way toward that same airport. As they swooped down, if one had time to look, they bore the 'Red Circle' of Japan. The bombs began to fall. Eight hundred Chinese were killed in the market in the first minutes of the war. Pearl Harbor had become Hong Kong.

The code word for the Japanese attack on Hong Kong was *hana-saku*—flowers abloom! The red and fiery flowers of war; as red as the poppies of Flanders fields.

The Japanese commander had received his orders three months before. His intelligence was good, his troops were trained, equipped and cruel. He would begin with the destruction of the reservoirs, the water supply of the colony; the few old Vildbeeste and Walrus aircraft would be destroyed on the tarmac, depriving the British commander of air reconnaissance. Troops would drive through to the southern shore of Hong Kong mainland preventing any escape to the island. The navy would pound the coast.

Gen. Maltby had been summoned from church parade on Sunday morning. It was rumored the Japanese were mustering near the border. Against opposition he had ordered the Canadian troops to trenches along the mountain ranges. By 5 p.m. they were all in position. Among them was one private who said: "I only had 20 days training. I learned to salute. I learned how to turn right, turn left, but I never fired a shot before I got here."

Far away in England Winston Churchill was dining at Chequers with the American Averill Harriman who had just come from Washington to see him. A portable radio was carried in to the dining room by the butler. A program of music was suddenly interrupted by the announcement that Pearl Harbor had been attacked.

On December 13, Churchill sent his first message to the Hong Kong garrison: "We are watching day by day and hour by hour your stubborn defence....Every day of your resistance brings nearer our certain victory."

Brig. Lawson had noted in his diary on the 12th: "Find I am in command of all troops on the island. Quite impossible with staff and facilities available." On December 19 the Japanese overran his headquarters. He got on the phone to Gen. Maltby. He reported that hand-to-hand combat was going on all around him. "I'm going outside to fight it out," he said. And he did, a spectacled brigadier with a revolver in each hand firing point blank until he died. The old soldier who had been awarded the Military Cross at Passchendaele fighting with the Canadians had given a good account of himself again.

The same day, A Co. of the Grenadiers was ordered to recapture Mount Butler on the island. After the company commander was killed, CSM John R. Osborn took charge of the 65 raw soldiers. He drove them up the slope in the face of withering fire that cut their strength to 30. Then they held their position as counter-attacks came from all sides. Osborn directed a fierce resistance, picking up grenades before they exploded and throwing them back at the advancing Japanese.

When there were at least six Grenadiers left a grenade fell where the sergeant major couldn't reach it. He shouted a warning and threw himself on it as it exploded.

He was awarded the Victoria Cross posthumously.

Later on Pte. T.S. Forsyth of Reston, Man., was to write in his diary at the prison camp in Sham Shui Po: "Heard this morning that Col. Sutcliffe died last night of malaria, dysentery and anemia. I think myself he died of a broken heart."

Churchill wired again: "There must be no thought of surrender. Every part of the island must be fought and the enemy resisted with the utmost stubbornness...."

The situation was hopeless but those instructions were obeyed to the letter.

D Co. under Capt. Allan Bowman, a Winnipeg school teacher, had been ordered to the mainland to hold the line while the Royal Scots evacuated the island. He did so stubbornly and cleverly and waited the order that would send him back to the island too. It never came. On December 10 he ordered his men to the ferry dock. He got word back to the Grenadiers but the Grenadiers knew the ferry had stopped running on the island side. So transport officer Lieut. Wilfred Queen-Hughes went to the dock, pulled his revolver, and ordered the captain to sail for D Co.

Capt. Njál Bardal, also of the Grenadiers, remembered that the last time he saw Bowman he was so tired he was "talking gibberish." But he was ordered out again. He was last seen charging the Japanese with a blazing Tommy gun.

The Royal Rifles were engaged in hopeless murderous fighting at Repulse Bay. They were so tired they would fall down on the roadway and yet they fought. They not only defended themselves against the Japanese but they launched counter-attacks again and again and continued to fight as a unit.

Rfmn. Sydney Skelton of the Royal Rifles, a gangling, freckled 20-year-old, had recorded events from the time he left Canada in a diary he wrote for his sweetheart. It was found behind a picture in the makeshift hospital at St. Stephens College after the Japanese had surrendered.

"The first thing we heard this morning," he wrote on November 3, "was the news we had been waiting to hear. Our officers announced that we were going to China—Hong Kong to be exact. The Japanese are expected to declare war on the 15th and we are expected to arrive on the 14th."

On November 10 he wrote, "The brigade major gave us a very stern talk. This is no pleasure cruise. It might be another Dunkirk."

Later he had a grandstand view of the dive bombing from Tytam Gap high above the reservoir. "From where I am sitting I can see Japanese planes bombing Hong Kong. They are playing hell. Hundreds of Chinks have been killed already. Our plans have been wrecked. There must be at least 50 planes dropping bombs. Japs are raising Cain over on our barracks.

On the 9th we headed up the hills and camouflaged ourselves with grass."

Later, out of touch with all but his immediate area, lost, his leg badly injured, his only food in five days a few biscuits, he wrote: "Our heavy guns can be heard now. They are firing at Japanese ships. With us are the fellows from Middlesex regiments....Two of our boys have lost their minds, gone crazy in the head....Some have been machine-gunned from the diving Japanese planes."

By December 18, "This day has been the worst yet. My nerves are on edge. I could eat a horse. Shell landed 30 feet from where I was standing. One fellow got shrapnel in the side. My head swam and my nerves seem to be all gone." A day later he scribbled in his diary: "This is one day I shall never forget. Tomorrow will tell another story." There was only one more bleak entry on December 19: "Today was the worst of all. We were awakened at 3 a.m. and were told to...." Here the diary ends.

In Hong Kong the fight was over. The New Territories had fallen in five days, the fortress of Hong Kong in 12½. Four years of imprisonment lay ahead.

Canadian soldiers arrive at Hong Kong in November 1941.

"I cannot bring myself to write about what happened between the 18th and 25th," recorded Pte. T.S. Forsyth. "All I can say is I saw too many brave men die. Some were my best friends and they died beside me. It is hard to put in to words our feelings when the governor of the colony surrendered to the enemy. I saw some break down and cry like children. 'What? Surrender?' they sobbed, 'after all the good men we've lost?' Others cursed and raved as though delirious. Others like myself were stunned, dazed, apathetic. Ah well, there's one Lee Enfield that no Jap will ever use against us. I released the bolt, slipped it out and flung it in to a rocky ravine 200 feet deep."

Pte. H.A. Atkinson wrote: "They took us, ripped off our insignia, took our shoes, belts, pictures, and wrist watches. We walked with our hands up and they nicked us in the back with bayonets. They took out De Laurier and two or three others and used them for bayonet practice all night long. We could hear them."

One-quarter of the garrison, 3,000 men, were dead; 290 of those were Canadians.

The people at home were stunned by the suddenness of defeat. Little word of the fighting had reached them. Senselessly, the communiques had continued to say: "Our position holds. The enemy has made no advances." And now it was over. They ate Christmas dinner, if they ate at all, in silence as they listened to the bits of news that came waveringly over the battery-powered Rogers Majestic and De Forest Crosley radios that sat in most homes across Canada.

To some, the news came as a relief. They believed that once the fighting was over the loss of life was past. The fact that Japan was not a signatory to the Hague and Geneva conventions regarding the treatment of prisoners of war was known to the government. The possible implication of this for the treatment of the troops in Japan was not generally known to the public.

But time went on too long. The casualty lists remained incomplete. There were few letters. During the whole four years many families, wives and sweethearts received none at all. They survived on hope and memory and by the end there was not much of either left.

In the camps men starved and died. Their mail was not given to them. They did not know what was happening at home or what their families knew of them. Njál Bardal was allowed to send a brief card to his wife. "We are well treated and I am in good health," he wrote. And then cryptically he added: "I can sympathize with the boys at Stony Mountain." (Stony Mountain is a federal penitentiary.)

The barrack complex at Sham Shui Po was turned into a prison for the Grenadiers. It was not the comfortable place the Middlesex Regt. had enjoyed for three years. Furniture, windows, doors, toilet fixtures had all been removed. Only the bare walls and the cement floor remained, a floor on which men later choked to death from diphtheria.

The Royal Rifles were at North Point camp, a collection of wooden huts that had been used to house Chinese deserters. The Japanese had stabled their horses there and they were full of rotting manure, dead horses, flies, garbage, rats and disease. Fifty men died in that charnel-house in the first three months. The Canadian doctors had little to work with but aspirin. Malaria, diphtheria, dysentery were epidemic. Operations were performed with a razor blade. Anesthetic was given with cotton batten soaked in chloroform.

Each morning the men were given a small mug of unsalted rice with a few potato tops added to it or, if they were lucky, a few pieces of carrot. Sometimes the vegetable was just plain grass. "Green horror" they called that dish. At noon they got nothing. At night the same rice mixture.

A makeshift hospital was set up. The beds for patients with dysentery had a hole through the wooden base so a man could defecate without moving. Men were alive in the morning and dead by evening. The Last Post was no longer played because it was too depressing. Later an entry

Stanley Peninsula, Hong Kong.

in Forsyth's diary reads: "All the buglers are dead now."

Nutritional diseases were severe. Men began to go blind or develop a painful foot ailment, symptoms of beriberi and pellagra. Many were delirious from the burning pain of what they called "Hong Kong foot." By day they would sit on the sea-wall and cool their feet in the ocean. By night they sat with their little stick legs in buckets of water.

"I dreamed I was home last night kissing Isabel," one veteran wrote in his diary. "I wish now I had kissed her oftener when I had the chance."

There was some brightness. There were about 2,000 books in the camp. Men, all sorts of men, when they go to war carry a book with them. They set up a library. Forsyth recorded his reading: "Sons of Others—Phillip Gibbs, A Modern Chronicle—W.S. Churchill, The Good Earth—P.S. Buck, The House of Four Winds—J. Buchan...." But finally an entry in his diary reads: "I'll have to give up reading—my eyes are giving me a lot of trouble and I have a queer rash on my legs called pellagra."

The human spirit seems unquenchable. Those who could formed an orchestra. Capt. Bardal, a good musician, made a guitar. He even wrote a "how to play" book for the others. It was added to their library. Later the Pope gave the Japanese some money to buy food for the prisoners. The Japanese did not want to admit food was needed so they bought instruments for the orchestra instead. The prisoners gave concerts that even the Japanese enjoyed.

The men made radios, calendars and maps, and plotted the war as best they could. They were reasonably accurate.

Beginning in 1943 the healthiest of the prisoners were sent to Japan to work in the mines and on the docks. They worked 12 hours a day on an 800-calorie diet. In all, 1,184 Canadians worked in Japan and 135 died there.

Finally the bombing of Hiroshima and Nagasaki ended the long ordeal.

But in the words of Njál Bardal again, "The funniest thing, when we finally left that buggy old place and I said 'Bardal, we're going now, we'll get out of here,' I felt a hell of a wrench. Honest to God I didn't want to go. I felt I had to stay there, my roots were down deep. I had to tear myself away. You can get roots even in a prison camp. You get attached, even to a hell hole. It's hard to understand. I went back to Hong Kong to a reunion in 1968 but I just couldn't go to the camp. I saw North Point by accident and it made me sick just looking at it. The memories come flooding back. I said: 'No, you go to the camp. I'm going to a bar someplace to get drunk.'"

After 1,300 days of starvation, sickness and death, the veterans came home. But somehow home was not as they expected it to be. The roots of North Point and Sham Shui Po were long indeed. Nobody really understood them. Nobody appreciated the eroding effects physically and mentally of the long starvation, the beatings, the sickness and the dying. Government policies were adequate, perhaps even generous, towards its World War II veterans. But they did not fit the needs of the men who came back from Hong Kong.

They formed the Hong Kong Veterans Association and once again they fought together for what was their due. In 1976, 35 years after they sailed on the *Awatea*, the Parliament of Canada passed Bill C-92. They had won their battle. We will remember them.

MYSTIC MUNDA
H. Layton Bray

All Air Force boys remember lectures. Lectures on armament, lectures on navigation, lectures on the more personal aspects of health, lectures on mess conduct, lectures, lectures, and more lectures. But there was one that the R.C.A.F. forgot—or was I asleep through that one? The one on how to cope with a native bearer.

After a 50-day delay (something to do with the Navy) we were landed in India full of information on jungle survival, malaria and the muzzle velocity of the 50 calibre, but not one word on the likes of Munda.

On my arrival at the Squadron (356 Salboni, India) the mess sergeant trotted out a line of dark humanity for inspection, particularly recommending a small, grinning lad, Munda by name, who claimed to be thirteen. To cancel objections to his size (he was all of four feet) he seized my 120-lb. trunk, hoisted it to his head with the help of the sergeant and wobbled off in the general direction of the quarters. I had been chosen.

Munda commenced my training the first afternoon at *char* time. Promptly at four he entered the *bhasha* with a borrowed tea service and the ever-present grin. I hate tea. I told Munda so with sufficient colour and enthusiasm to send him scurrying for cover. Four thirty bath-time, five o'clock dressing, seven thirty dinner, brought no return. The following noon he appeared silently from nowhere, shifted from foot to foot alternately, looked at the floor and announced his intention of visiting relatives on the other side of India. He had lost face; all *sahibs* drank tea; all bearers carried tea to their *sahibs*; he must visit his sick uncle immediately and at my expense.

I capitulated quickly and ordered tea. Munda's uncle had a miraculous recovery!

Munda proved worth saving. Though he padded the laundry and fuel account to the maximum of my patience, his easy grin and eagerness to please won him pardon. It was his effort to excel that made me, or rather my *bhasha*, famous.

On a multi-coloured cotton square nailed to one wall, I had pinned the current maps of the Eastern and Western fronts surrounded by the choicest pin-ups I had been able to gather. This educational display fascinated Munda. Whether it was the fighting fronts or the female figures that he studied, it was impossible to tell. His later selection gave no clue to his preference. My enquiries brought only a grin.

Our day-long flights often left Munda in complete control of the *bhasha*, my pen, razor and other things dear to his inquisitive mind. For some time previous to the day on which I became famous I felt that he had been using some of my equipment, but all efforts failed to catch him.

We had flown all night and most of the morning. By the end of the usual session with the debriefing crew it was *char* time before we returned to the *bhashas*. The C.O. was quite pleased with our day's work and in an expansive mood, so I invited him for tea. He chatted pleasantly as we walked towards my quarters, complimenting me on the high morale of the flight, the way the boys were holding up under the strain. On reaching the door I stepped back to let him enter first. He took one step, then stopped rigid.

Walls, furniture and thatch were covered with every conceivable form of pin-up. Maps, girls and advertisements crowded each other in ragged rows. Several large placards extolling the virtues of toilet tissue had found prominent spots. On the foot of my bed in the most choice location was a blonde testifying to the comfort of some highly personal feminine needs.

The C.O. retired hastily, mumbling about an appointment with the medical officer and some of the boys cracking up.

I took a moment to gain strength, then bellowed for Munda. ᘓ

The staff at Canada House in Calcutta.

WAITING FOR THE CHARWALLAH
Ed Pearson

It was unusually hot on the northeast coast of India during July, 1943. The Air Ministry, in its wisdom, had chosen the district of Cuttack as a likely site for an airfield. The non-commissioned aircrew of D for Donald lived in a straw basha on the east side of the station. This particular afternoon they were seated on the veranda, moving as little as possible, waiting for the charwallah.

The sun beat fiercely and the air was filled with a low hum as a myriad of insects fulfilled their life's purpose. The buzz was similar to the drone of distant traffic. Not that one would mistake one for the other because the nearest traffic was in Calcutta, 240 kilometres to the north.

The view from the veranda included the distant runway and the central control tower, windowless and rudely capped with a straw roof. The aircraft around the perimeter seemed to crouch low, the shimmering sun bouncing off the ground distorting them so they appeared to pant in the heat of the Indian summer.

Beneath the wing of each huge bomber stood a solitary figure, who, even from a distance, suggested vigilance. These soldiers formed the airfield defence. Members of one of the famous Baluchistan regiments recruited from among the wild hillmen of Afghanistan and the sturdy farmers of the fertile Punjab, they were splendid warriors.

Casually dressed aircrew members would self-consciously straighten their backs and fasten shirt buttons in the presence of these soldiers who stood proudly, boots burnished to a glassy finish, khaki drill pressed with precision, while the sun glinted off silver regimental badges set in blue turbans. A good three inches taller than local coastal Indians, they felt more akin to the alien English than their own countrymen.

Assigned to guard an aircraft, they positioned themselves so that as the sun moved across the heavens the aircraft wing shaded the place where they happened to be standing. The rifle butt would be surreptitiously lifted a fraction from the ground and with tiny, scarcely discernible movements of the boots, the sepoy trooper would travel perhaps 18 inches towards the rear of the aircraft during his four-hour tour of duty.

From the veranda the aircrew watched a relieving detail of soldiers march smartly from aircraft to aircraft. The voice of the Jemedar floated on the still air as he orchestrated the exchange of guards for His Majesty's aircraft.

High in the afternoon sky the group could see an ominous, black bird hovering effortlessly in the still air. Small of body with an enormous wingspan, it could hover then drop like a landlocked gannet to scoop up its small prey. The great Indian kitehawk had adapted to wartime conditions by haunting military establishments and choosing targets adjacent to the cookhouse. Kitehawks had become so familiar the troops had christened them less elegantly but more aptly by substituting an H for the K and adding an S to the front of the name.

Reggie Pelling, the second dickie, watched the bird with envy. He was a competent pilot but afflicted with a lack in height perception. On the rare occasions the skipper allowed him to land an aircraft he usually performed a perfect landing 20 feet from the ground. As well as the thud when he finally connected with *terra firma*, he frequently came perilously close to using more runway than was available.

Reggie was reflecting on the bird's diving capability when Fewly Rice broke into his thoughts remarking "marvelous how that bleeding hawk can keep his arse in the air like that without actually flying." Fewly was the navigator and used mild profanity naturally, with panache. It was not the Queen's English, but would have been if she had been born in Waga-Waga. Two people could hardly have been less alike than Reggie and Fewly. Though dressed alike they presented totally different pictures. Australians seem born to wear shorts, appearing both smart and manly. Englishmen like Reggie appear uncomfortable and resemble overgrown schoolboys. Photographs, viewed in later years, show Reggie in shorts with his hands clasped in front of him, coyly shielding his genitalia. Perhaps it had to do with the solemn English ritual of changing the boy into long trousers at age 14.

Pugwash Shannon, the front gunner, told of the pelican he had observed back home in Nova Scotia, and how that pelican could outdive that kitehawk any day. The other members of the crew were patient when Pugwash extolled the virtues of his home province; he was eternally cheerful and pleasant.

Ted Parsons was the most ordinary member of the crew. The rear gunner, he had been born on the outskirts of London. Leaving school at age 14 he had appeared destined to spend his life confined to the drab existence usually reserved for his education and station in life. The war may have been a holocaust to some, but to Ted it was a reprieve from the grinding monotony of a factory job. He didn't feel guilty about it; he was enjoying it too much.

Ted was amazed at the sudden stature he seemed to acquire when he joined the RAF. It became even more noticeable when he graduated from air-gunnery school and a kindly WAAF sewed his wing on his tunic. In cosy country pubs affluent men would send over drinks, then nod gravely when he raised his glass to them. He would sip their beer and think to himself that the toffee-nosed sod would have walked a mile to avoid him if he had been in his factory clothes. Ted was careful not to engage these benefactors in conversation for fear that his accent would betray his class background. He enjoyed flying with a Commonwealth squadron, where nobody attached importance to background.

His life in the air force had also been made more pleasurable by hearing himself addressed as Ted. It had such a manly ring to it. On leave he told his relatives and friends that he preferred Ted to Teddy but all seemed unable to break the habit. All through his early service life he revelled in the shorter name. When he joined his present crew at operational training unit

Fewly tagged him Cockle. It stuck. Otherwise Ted Parsons was the happiest man in Southeast Asia.

Ken Spencer completed the quintet. He was the wireless operator. Ken seemed to be disliked by the other Canadians in the squadron for the sole reason that he came from Toronto. He was highly regarded by his own crew but not the kind of person you gave a nickname to. Ken dealt with people coldly and efficiently. He was not only a very good wireless operator but organized everyone with whom he came in contact. Because of Ken the crew's basha was better equipped than any other on the station. The YMCA, the Salvation Army and other organizations clamored to send him parcels from Canada. Many feasts were enjoyed by oil lamp during long Indian nights. Ken always managed to find an empty railway compartment for the crew when leave time came around. Unless the reader has travelled on the Indian railway he would not appreciate this minor miracle.

"Charwallah, charwallah!" the cry was muffled on the warm moist air. He came into view from behind the neighboring *basha*. The tycoon of the local business community, he carried on his head a tin cabin trunk that bore the legend, "Not wanted on voyage." This green trunk had been repainted a hundred times and the information faithfully reproduced each time. Within the trunk reposed the charwallah's entire inventory of pastries. The lid was essential to defeat the scavenger kitehawk circling hungrily above. While his left hand steadied the trunk his right hand carried the tea urn.

He wore the Sikh's white turban and his clear blue eyes, which he had inherited either from the Germanic hordes that had swept through India a thousand years before or from a British soldier of later vintage, were set wide over high cheek bones. His jet black beard was worn proudly and an ear-ring hung from his left ear. A brass bangle circled his right wrist while the common white collarless shirt peeked from beneath the even more common brown waistcoat. The right side of the waistcoat was connected to the left side by a brass watch chain. This affectation was evidence of the wearer's social status, but it was uncertain whether the fob contained a watch.

The phenomenon of the waistcoat in India has always been a cause of wonder. It is integral to the dress of most of India's 200 million males. But what happens to the brown trousers and jacket that accompany the waistcoat? Those two other elements are rarely seen on the streets of India. Perhaps it has been the practice to purloin waistcoats from brown suits that were then sold to unsuspecting Englishmen as natty two-piece outfits. Is it possible that gullible Englishmen, in their grimy cities, have been deprived in order to sheathe the brown ribs of Asia's teeming millions? Or has some hard-working Manchester lad had to endure his long apprenticeship being slowly driven to madness by being forced to make only waistcoats?

The charwallah wore white dhoti trousers, wide fitting and gathered at the ankle. His highly polished brown field boots showed extreme care and devotion. It was evident that the boots had found a far better home than when originally purchased by some weak-chinned subaltern with his mother in Harrods in 1928. His ankles, unembellished by hose, gleamed dully through the mahogany skin.

On reaching the veranda the charwallah laid the cake box on the floor carefully so as not to disturb the contents. When the urn had been placed beside it he turned to the group. Placing the palms of his hands together and bowing from the waist he said: "Salam, Sahibs." It was more of an honor bestowed than an expression of servility.

"Good-aye, mate," said Fewly. The others grunted or grinned.

Squatting between the implements of his trade the charwallah collected the men's tin mugs. Placing the mugs beneath the tap he watched as the rich brown liquid flowed. Sweetened with honey and flavored with cinnamon it gave off a fragrant aroma. The copper clad urn, heated by charcoal in a tray at the base, was a thing of beauty. Of course Ken Spencer was served first.

When the tea had been dispensed, the charwallah addressed himself to the cake box. Nervously looking skyward for the kitehawk, he opened the lid. Revealed were all manner of confection, including gaily iced buns of many colors. Ken chose a virgin white fairy cake, tastefully topped with pink icing. While the others were still selecting he took a large bite and emitted a strangled cry.

"Charwallah," he croaked, holding up the remainder of his cake. Exposed for all to see in the uneaten portion was a beetle, quite dead. There was a pregnant silence as they looked towards the charwallah. He looked stricken as he rose from his haunches. His career was falling around his ears.

"Let me see, Sahib," he said gravely. Holding the offending object up to the light, he suddenly opened his mouth and gulped down the small black fragment. He struggled to maintain his composure, then said with great dignity: "No, Sahib, it was a currant."

They looked to Ken; he knew how to deal with people. He contemplated the situation, then said: "Fair enough, charwallah."

The charwallah beamed his gratitude, opened the box again and breathed again. "Perhaps the Sahib would choose another cake, what kind do you desire, master." Ken thoughtfully surveyed the stock. "Do you have any without currants?" he asked without visible trace of sarcasm.

When the lid had been replaced the charwallah turned to the crew and with an expansive gesture said: "Sahibs, today the refreshments are from me to you, without charge, to honor our great friendship."

They accepted the gesture in the manner in which it was intended. He left them drinking their brew and eating their cakes with a little more care than usual, to be sure, but with a feeling that honor had been satisfied. ➷

A BLOODY MIRACLE

Eswyn Lyster

The men of 3 Platoon of the Calgary Highlanders had been away from their unit for several weeks competing with mortar platoons of the Black Watch and Maisonneuve Regt. Battle schools; schemes and exercises were so much a part of the Canadian infantryman's life in England that nobody thought it particularly significant when the Calgarians chalked up the best score. Everyone's mind was on the scarcity of leave.

Wearing good battledress, the men boarded a transport one afternoon. As usual, Pte. Red Anderson carried a base plate and sights. When Lieut. Jack Reynolds passed out special tags, Pte. Dusty Rhodes spoke up: "Hey, you guys, we had these same tags on the Isle of Wight. I'll bet we're going to Dieppe." But nobody else had been on that May exercise for an assault that was cancelled because of weather conditions, so they said, "Pull the other leg, Rhodes."

The truck headed south on the quiet Hampshire lanes. It was a warm summer's day, Aug. 18, 1942.

Near Portsmouth, progress was slowed by dozens of military vehicles, all converging on the dockyards, where 3 Platoon marched on to a flat-bottomed craft with a large 6 painted on its side. Officially it was landing craft tank (LCT) 163, commanded by Thomas Andrew Cook, RNR. Already it was crowded with three tanks, a bulldozer and Canadian servicemen, including Calgary Regt. tank crews. Reynolds led his men to a space between a tank and one side of the craft. Sergeants Bert Pittaway and Bill Lyster, buddies since training camp in Shilo, Man., noticed that two tanks bore their Christian names. Almost immediately LCT 6 began to pull away from the dock. Everyone had the feeling of being inside an overcrowded box because the steel sides of the craft only allowed a clear view of the sky.

Back at Halnaker Camp, near Petworth, Sussex, Capt. John Bright, adjutant of the Calgary Highlanders, was writing in the regimental diary: "No. 3 Platoon (Mortars) was reported to be coming back to camp but did not turn up. Further messages revealed that they were putting on a demonstration for the RAF."

Anderson climbed up a narrow walkway on the LCT to get a better view. As they cleared the harbor he saw that other landing craft, equally crowded, were ahead of them. Reynolds assembled his men and announced: "We're on our way to France."

"I knew it!" said Rhodes. This time nobody argued, but Reynolds could tell they were still skeptical. Too much phoney war, he thought. Too many schemes. His face serious, he read out the orders. Then he unfolded a map.

"This is the town of Dieppe," he said. "We'll be landing on this section of the beach, codenamed Red, just before sunrise. We're to set up at the tobacco factory, here, and give covering fire. At 11:00 hours we're to rendezvous here, at the church, and make our way back to the landing craft. Anyone who can't rendezvous or get off the beach is on his own."

Then he distributed escape kits containing waterproof maps and packets of French francs. Fingering the notes, Pte. Bill Simpson said: "This can't be a scheme. The army doesn't give money away unless it absolutely has to!"

But with the clear, blue sky overhead and the leisurely progress it felt the same as all those other exercises, even when the order came that steel helmets be worn.

Eventually one man began writing a letter. Others followed suit and Pittaway wondered how this mail would get to its destination.

"Here, Red, I owe you." Someone pushed £6 in to Anderson's hand. Always a soft touch for a loan and a good poker player to boot, he stood amazed as debt after debt was paid. "Well I'll be a hairless Highlander," he said. "They should put on more raids like this."

The long twilight faded in to a warm and cloudless evening. After a haversack lunch the men tried to settle down for the long night. Anderson leaned against some sacks almost as uncomfortable as the steel deck. By the earthy smell he guessed they held potatoes.

Bodies of Canadian soldiers lie among damaged tanks on the beach at Dieppe, France, August 1942.

LCT 6 had been riding steadily in a calm sea, but about 23:30 it swayed slightly. More ships were joining the small convoy and they jockeyed for position as they passed in line astern through the swept section of a minefield. Unaware of the hazards mere yards away, Reynolds and his men shifted uneasily, cussing the army brass that in its wisdom had decided blankets weren't necessary for this short voyage.

At 02:00 the moon set and in the darkness the men dozed fitfully. Only the even throbbing of the engines broke the silence. They were travelling slowly, keeping pace with the slowest vessels. They were not due in to Dieppe until first light.

At 03:47 a star shell burst overhead, illuminating the interior of LCT 6 like sudden daylight. Up ahead ships were exchanging fire and the convoy broke formation. As the star shell faded, a tremendous explosion lit the sky

and in the confusion another craft came partly across their bow. The jolt skidded Anderson across the deck. "I can't swim," he shouted. "What the hell do we do now? Jump overboard?"

"We can't," yelled Pittaway above the din. "No bloody lifebelts. It's against marine regulations or something." He was laughing nervously, but he was thinking "By God, we've had it."

But as suddenly as the firing began it was over. Eyes strained by the sudden glare of star shells and gunfire became accustomed once more to the darkness. Only the stars shone brilliantly from the black, cloudless sky. But sleep didn't come. In every mind was the dreadful thought that by now the French coast must be on full alert. The men had no way of knowing that the eight-vessel German convoy they'd encountered was steaming to Dieppe quite unaware it had been in the midst of a raiding force.

Just before 05:00 Allied light bombers and fighters came out of the north flying low, almost at mast level. Flashes of light and faint whomps showed that the Dieppe garrison was under attack and was retaliating with anti-aircraft fire.

With each mile the noise grew louder and almost imperceptibly the sky began to lighten in the east. Eventually Lyster scrambled up the side, but he could see little more than the dark silhouettes of the other craft and a false dawn reddening the sky over Dieppe. With an ear-splitting roar the four-inch guns on several escorting destroyers opened fire on the coast. Billows of white smoke rose from the shoreline ahead, signalling that the forward assault landing craft were almost at touchdown. With a curious, sick excitement Lyster called down: "Mortar platoon, load rifles!" The craft was picking up speed and someone set his rifle butt down heavily on the deck, perhaps to steady himself. A shot whistled past Lyster, missing him by inches.

"Gees, did I hit you, Bill?" The man was almost in tears.

Lyster was shaken. "You just missed my ass. Save your bloody ammunition for the beach!" he said, sliding down to the comparative safety of the deck.

Pieces of shrapnel began clanging against the craft. Suddenly Reynolds, who was squatting beside Anderson, said "My God, man, you just got hit!" Anderson looked down at a long tear in his battledress trousers and a piece of metal that lay on the deck between them. He thought shock must have numbed his leg, but found his skin wasn't even cut. He dropped the piece of shrapnel in his pocket.

Now shells were exploding inside the LCT and Pittaway called to some of his men who had been passing time by helping the galley crew peel potatoes. They'd scarcely joined the rest when the galley received a direct hit that killed most of its crew. Then a mortar bomb exploded nearby and blew an army service corps man into Anderson. They writhed on the deck, covered with a wet, sticky substance, the man shouting in a French Canadian accent that he'd been killed. "No you haven't, you fool….It's those God damned potatoes!"

Another explosion, this time in the engine-room, sent thick, acrid smoke in all directions. Shouts of "Gas!" went up. Pittaway, his throat searing, thought for the second time that morning: "We've had it! This time we've really had it!" Their respirators were with their blankets back at the battle school, but it was a smoke canister that had been kicked loose by the explosion. The craft swung wildly to port as the helmsman, overcome by fumes, lost control. Then the engine-room burst into flames.

Anderson and a few others manned a hose, but it had been shot so full of holes they doused themselves instead of the fire. Others had better luck and a new helmsman took over. Now, only 70 yards from the beach, the canister smoke mingled with the white smoke-screen drifting over them. Still, the wheelhouse took a direct hit that killed the second helmsman.

Again the craft swung hard to port. A medic, who was climbing up to reach a stretcher, lost his hold. Below him stood an infantryman, his old-fashioned, long style bayonet fixed. The medic crashed down, driving the bayonet through his thigh. Pittaway, who helped two others pull the blade out, saw that it had pierced far enough to lift the skin on the other side.

A new man took the wheel and within minutes he too was killed. A fourth man brought the craft under control and they approached the beach from a different angle. With yards still to go, they came out of the smoke-screen in to brilliant morning sunshine and a storm of gunfire. LCT 1—officially 145—was lying out of action broadside to the beach. Using it as partial cover, they crossed the last stretch of water. The men swayed as LCT 6 finally touched down on the shale. The gates creaked open, the ramp fell and they saw Red Beach.

Rough shingle sloped up to a huge roll of barbed wire parallel to the shore. Beyond it, more beach ended at a sea-wall and promenade. Well back from the promenade a row of buildings was dominated by the twin chimneys of the tobacco factory. From his limited viewpoint, Reynolds could see dozens of dead and wounded crumpled on the stones. "Red Beach," he thought bitterly. "It's well named."

With the ramp down, their last bit of protection was gone. A shell hit the nearest tank and ricocheted through Reynolds' men, just catching Pittaway's shoulder patch. He had dodged instinctively to the left, which saved his life. The Calgarians watched in horror as the shell struck a man crouched nearby. The force lifted his steel helmet and knocked him to the deck with part of his head torn away.

The tanks were ready to move, but the bulldozer was the first to trundle down the ramp. Reynolds watched the operator with awe, thinking: "He's up there with nothing around him but his tin hat and he's not batting an eyelid." The bulldozer travelled only a few yards before the man was dead.

Two tanks followed, turning left and right. The first went about 10 yards, hit a mine and lost its tracks. The second went a little farther before being stopped by heavy gunfire. A third, the one called Bert, went straight ahead

A disabled landing craft on the beach at Dieppe, France, in August 1942.

and over the wire. As it lumbered on, the wire sprang back in to place, halting the progress of the troops who were pouring out of the LCT. Caught in the murderous fire that seemed to come from all directions, they were adding their bodies to those already strewn in front of the craft.

Aboard LCT 6 the situation was chaotic. Medics, under heavy fire and often injured, strove to comfort the wounded and dying. On the bridge skipper Cook was still in command, but most of his crew were dead or badly injured, including the gunners at the exposed port and starboard anti-aircraft pom-pom guns. The 30 or so infantrymen still aboard fought the fires and assisted the medics.

The skipper was calling "All ashore!" but Reynolds felt he would lose every man on the beach. He ordered that the mortars be set up on deck. Anderson began the drill, but found his base plate wouldn't grip on the sloping deck. "I can't make the damn thing secure," he reported. Reynolds swore. "Why the hell didn't they give us a few sandbags?…"

The tide was rapidly going out. In a few minutes the LCT would be stranded.

"No more ashore!" the skipper ordered. "Up ramp!" But the ramp chains had been damaged and the struggling men could get it only part way up, so that the doors would not swing shut. Slewing badly, the craft pulled off the beach and came alongside LCT 1, which seemed about to sink. A line thrown to the stricken craft was shot away in a hail of gunfire. Abandoning the idea of taking it in tow, skipper Cook signalled to the few survivors. They swam across to LCT 6, machine-gun fire dimpling the water around them. Four ratings came aboard, followed by a young RNVR sub-lieutenant, his wet, red hair gleaming darkly in the sunshine. "My 22nd Channel crossing," he grumbled, "and the worst one yet!"

The intensity of fire lessened as LCT 6 moved in to deeper water and headed for the main anchorage where the larger ships directing operations were under aerial attack. The red-haired officer asked for men to handle the pom-poms and Reynolds detailed Lyster, Pittaway and Anderson and other groups to take turns. It was difficult at first, requiring two men to coordinate the traverse and elevation mechanisms and a third to handle the clips of ammunition, but despite their exposed positions these new gun crews felt a surge of energy and a profound relief to be fighting back at last, even if their accuracy left something to be desired.

Most casualties, including the man with the bayonet wound, were transferred to the hospital ship. Only the most critically injured were kept on board for fear they would not survive being moved. Among them, miraculously, was the man with the head wound.

New British naval crews came aboard and worked on the steering mechanism. There was constant harassment from enemy aircraft and those below were amazed to see the red-headed officer above decks, coolly shaving off his day's growth of beard. Reynolds and his men became aware of their itching chins and their hunger. By Anderson's count it was 16 hours since they had last eaten.

Word came that they were going back in. Men were already awaiting rescue on Red Beach under cover of a thick smoke-screen laid down by Allied planes. Those on LCT 6 shrank from the idea, but the craft swung round and joined a group of small assault boats heading in. The enemy were firing blindly in to the smoke. The small boats, travelling faster than the LCT, ran in to the fierce barrage with devastating results. Within minutes many were holed or blown apart, the remains of their crews struggling in the water. Up on the guns Lyster and Pittaway fired in to the tobacco factory. They little realized that the fires started that day would deprive Frenchmen, already suffering enemy occupation, of several weeks' tobacco rations.

A bearded individual was standing in one of the surviving boats waving them in. "He must be drunk," said Anderson, trying to account for the man's disregard for his own safety. But drunk or not, he had a boatload of Canadians and there were more in the water around him.

In later years, Lyster, Pittaway and the rest couldn't remember how many times they travelled between the beach and the anchorage, picking up men from the boats and the water. They could only remember the fear that gripped their empty stomachs and made breathing difficult—and the bearded man who always seemed to be waving them in.

On the last run to the anchorage, a Messerschmitt came through the smog that hung thickly over the battle area and dived straight towards them. Lyster and Pittaway got it in to their sights and saw their tracers plunging in to its belly. Suddenly the plane seemed to shudder. Pouring smoke and flame, it passed over their heads and crashed in to the sea. An almost-hysterical cheer went up from the dirty, weary men aboard LCT 6.

At last the order came to head home. For most of the mortar platoon the journey was a blank and there was only a mild stir when they stopped to pick up a downed RAF pilot.

It was dusk when they arrived back in England. They'd been away just over 24 hours. The wounded were taken off first, the man with the head wound still living, although death was surely only hours away. Anderson slipped on the gangplank and hung from the guardrail, his feet dangling in space. 'My God!' he thought. 'I get this far and now I'm gonna drown in a friendly port!' But strong hands soon pulled him to safety.

After interrogation the men were given a stiff rum. On the journey back to Halnaker Camp, Anderson couldn't stop talking. "Imagine," he marvelled, "they kept asking me, what did I see? I said 'I saw a helluva lot!' and they said did I see any dead guys? I said 'I saw lots of dead guys,' and they said did I see any planes and I said 'I saw hundreds of planes.' Where the hell did they think I'd been?"

Pte. Simpson leaned towards Lyster. In the dim light of the truck he looked anxious. "Sergeant, I've lost my rifle." Under normal circumstances this was a cardinal offence. "Well, if that's all you've lost," Lyster assured him, "you're damned lucky."

At Halnaker they had something less than a hero's welcome. It was necessary to rouse Cpl. Barnes, the assistant quartermaster.

"What the hell did you do with your blankets?" he wanted to know. The strong smell of rum didn't ease his suspicions.

Pittaway grabbed him. "Look, we've been to Dieppe and we're cold, tired and none too friendly." After that everyone wanted to help. They'd heard radio reports of the raid and how the Canadians had suffered almost 3,500 casualties in a force of 5,000. The men at Halnaker wanted to know every detail.

"Never mind that," said Anderson, "how about something to eat."

When Lyster and Pittaway finally reached their quarters, Lyster said: "Bert, did you ever imagine we'd be back here all in one piece? We're damned lucky, all of us."

"Lucky?" said Pittaway. "Luck be damned. It's a bloody miracle."

Lyster laughed. "Old Barney was sure we'd flogged those blankets. For a second there I thought you were going to hit him." But Pittaway was sound asleep.

Epilogue

Next day the entire mortar platoon went on leave. When Anderson put his pass in his pocket he felt the piece of shrapnel, and said: "I wonder what they'll expect us to do to get the next leave?"

Lieut. Reynolds discovered, quite accidentally, that he'd been officially reported missing. He cabled his wife: "Disregard any rumors. I'm OK."

Several weeks later he learned, again quite by accident, that a man who returned from Dieppe with a deep bayonet wound to his thigh was in an English hospital facing a self-inflicted wound charge. Reynolds gave evidence that resulted in dismissal of the charge.

Skipper T.A. Cook was awarded the DSO for his courage under fire. Two of the ratings who manned the wheel were mentioned in dispatches, as were sergeants W.L. Lyster and B. Pittaway for downing the Messerschmitt.

The war histories sum up the events on LCT 6 by stating that after some initial difficulties the craft reached the beach; that 30 men failed to disembark and, after 15 minutes, the craft withdrew. ❧

THIS TOO THEY ENDURED
Ben Malkin

It all came together off Sicily on the night of July 9–10, 1943: Our convoy of troopships, which had sailed from the Clyde; the convoy of slower landing ships carrying our guns and vehicles, which had left ahead of us from Liverpool; ships from Malta and North Africa carrying the remainder of the British 8th Army, which would land on our right, and the U.S. 7th Army, which would be landing on our left. They all assembled accompanied by warships to support the landing. Considering the distances travelled by vessels of varying speeds from widely separated ports in Scotland, England and North Africa, the orchestration was masterly.

There had been a storm on the 9th and in the pre-dawn hours of the 10th the waves still ran high. We sat below decks leaving the ship's upper reaches clear for action. Each group waited for its number to be called. There was no seasickness, and almost no conversation. Most of us appeared relaxed where one would have expected tension. Many grinned at the loudspeaker's banal public relations messages from generals Eisenhower and Montgomery informing us we were about to make history. It was still dark when my number was called and I harnessed on all my gear—the standard 60 pounds or so—and joined the file going on deck.

Instead of stepping dryshod in to a small landing craft to be lowered into the water by steel cables and to sail dramatically to the beach, which in the conventional phrase we would then storm, we were to embark on a landing craft, infantry (LCI). The landing craft, assault (LCA), in which we had trained and been promised a ride, was a much smaller boat, carrying only 35 men and able to sail in very shallow waters. It could be hoisted level with the ship's deck, like a lifeboat. The much larger LCI carried more than 100 men and we'd have to reach ours by clambering down rope nets along the ship's side. In a quiet sea that wouldn't have mattered. But the high waves made the leap from the troopship to the LCI a tricky manoeuvre, one for which we hadn't been prepared in training. Storms weren't included in the military manuals.

I got down the rope to about the level of the LCI deck without much trouble, but every time I put my foot out to step on the LCI the troopship seemed to go down in a wave's trough and the LCI seemed to go up. The two vessels were only about a foot apart, so perhaps this inability to synchronize on the same wave was only the result of an imagination rapidly becoming overwrought. A nearby monitor, firing its 15-inch guns inland, was a distraction.

A sailor on the LCI was trying to help by reaching his hand to grasp mine whenever the LCI heaved upward. Unfortunately, he kept adding to the commotion by steadily shouting advice to me. I needed advice like I needed a hole in the head. The sailor would have done a lot more good if he had kept his boat still, or so I thought. But he finally reached me and yelled: "Now jump, mate!" I did and landed on the LCI's deck. Other sailors and soldiers were repeating this untidy procedure along the length of the LCI. It worked: There were no losses.

It was daylight by the time the LCI travelled the few miles to the vicinity of our beach. I had dozed off but now emerged to find us stuck on a sandbar about 100 feet from shore, with a rope already strung to the beach. The idea was to grasp the rope, step down the ship's ramp, plunge in to six feet of water, walk on the bottom until your head rose above the water, then take a deep breath and, still grasping the rope because of the post-storm turbulence, keep walking to the beach.

We had been assured during a briefing session aboard the troopship that three sandbars would be blown apart by the engineers before the first assault craft reached them. Either the engineers got lost and blew up the wrong ones or their explosives were faulty, because the three barriers were intact. Only the lighter landing craft had managed to sail over them.

Well, then, we're stuck. Let's go. Down the ramp in single file to disappear for a few moments, the only sign of life in the man ahead being his rifle held high in his left hand and his right hand grasping the rope. Besides the rifle and the tin of hard rations good for 24 hours, matches and cigarettes also had to be kept dry. This was done by storing them in army-issue contraceptives, guaranteed not to leak.

Once you walked the few yards necessary to bring your head above water it wasn't too bad. The waves tended to knock you off your feet, but if you kept a good grip on the rope each step made the next, shallower one easier.

But about halfway to the beach the man behind me started yelling "Help!" He was losing his balance. The poor guy was even shorter than I am and I'm only five foot six. I let go the rope, turned around, held out my hand, which he grasped and we began to walk, myself backward and he forward, toward the beach. After only a few steps he said he was okay and I turned around to confront a tall youth wearing the green beret of the British commandos. He had spotted trouble and rushed out to help. A fast worker, there when needed.

On the beach were several men from our battery who had landed earlier, dryshod, from smaller craft. One of them helped me off with my pack and I gratefully lay down on the sand to dry out and rest in the hot Sicilian sun. When all our group had disembarked we moved inland to our rendezvous, recognizing hedges and roads we had seen on sand-tables of our landing area in pre-invasion briefings.

The farm where we were to meet had a small hut that the family shared with a mule and several pigs. It was our first contact with Mediterranean poverty. In Western Canada during the Depression, there was profound hardship, destitution intensified by years of drought, but it was considered abnormal. It would pass. Here in Sicily, we soon found out, utter poverty was normal. No one could see it passing unless a lot of

People are evacuated from the Sangro River front near San Pietro, Italy, in December 1943.

things changed besides the weather and the market for farm produce.

We gathered about 100 yards from the house and two of the men went there to get water from the well so we could wash. They ended up handing most of their soap to the peasant family, who were supposed to be enemies, but these fellows weren't very good conquerors. The rest of us stacked our rifles and sat around, waiting for the remainder of the regiment and the guns.

The head of the family walked over and eyed us silently. We stood up and eyed him back. It was hard to know whether he, or we for that matter, should feel hostile or friendly. We had just landed in a country that was at war with us, but if this peasant and his family were representative of the enemy we had to feel more pity than hostility. He was small, raggedly dressed and had something wrong with one leg, which he dragged, and one arm, which he carried stiffly.

Even in these circumstances to stare is rude. That much you feel instinctively. It's an affront to a person's dignity to stare at him. To break the spell one of our group said quietly: "Viva Churchill." That opened the flood-gates.

The Sicilian unloosed a diatribe but we could distinguish only the words "porco Mussolini." Before leaving Scotland, we had been taught a few simple German commands in case we had to march a group of prisoners away: *Achtung! Eingetreten! Still gestandt! Links um! Rechts um!* and the like. We had been told to snarl when barking these commands and had great fun practising. But we had been taught no Italian.

Fortunately, one of our number, whose parents had emigrated from Italy, understood well enough to translate. Apart from an impassioned assault on Mussolini's parentage and his fascism and on absentee landlords, the man wanted to know whether he could kill three chickens to feed his family and report to the bailiff that we had looted the missing fowl.

A modest request, and fair enough. We were delighted to accommodate him as soon as we understood that he was a tenant farmer who owned nothing. Expansively, we told him to use what he wanted and blame us. He appeared satisfied with the arrangement.

Finally our guns arrived and we moved inland to overtake the infantry. The division had been inordinately lucky. There had been no enemy soldiers to contest the landing, except a few elderly home guards who hadn't been alert, believing the previous day's storm would preclude an invasion. Indeed, on our beach the first troops to land found the home guards asleep.

An English yeomanry regiment of self-propelled guns had managed to land its heavy equipment early, but the British self-propelled 25-pounder had a relatively short range, only about 4,000 yards, and that was the only support—apart from naval artillery—the infantry would have had if they'd encountered heavy resistance.

We remained lucky. It was more than a week before we met serious opposition. That gave us ample time to get organized and to build up supplies of the three essentials: food, ammunition, gasoline.

Our enemies were the oppressive heat in the valleys and plains and the fine white dust churned up by the thousands of trucks, guns and tanks that moved north to invest the whole eastern sector of the island. The dust covered everything and everybody, the just and unjust alike. The infantry plodded through it in that highly specialized shuffle foot soldiers develop to conserve energy, barely lifting each foot above ground. Tankmen and gunners added to the foot soldiers' misery by raising clouds of dust as they wheeled past, themselves swallowing the billows from the vehicle ahead.

Strangely, there was far less complaining than there had been in England. There was a feeling of victory in the air, of momentum, almost gaiety. I saw a long column of the Royal 22e Regt., or Van Doos, shuffle steadily past a stalled tank of the Calgary Regt., and the grinning dust-caked tankman poked his head out of the hatch to shout: "I can just see the headlines back home!"

How about Canadians in Swift Advance or Canadians Pursue Retreating Enemy? What we were actually doing was just shuffling along and trying to keep the dust to a minimum while searching for an enemy that we seemed to have lost. What the communiques and newspapers reported us as doing were not always precisely the same.

During this early period some of our most exhilarating moments were experienced in the villages where we were greeted as liberators rather than conquerors. We quickly and quite happily tried to adjust to this unexpected role, though at first with some reservations. It took a little while to become convinced of the people's sincerity, to separate the fascists and opportunists from those who genuinely welcomed us.

They would line a street and yell "Viva Churchill! Viva Roosevelt!" Occasionally we heard a "Viva Stalin!" That was acceptable, though even at this late date in the Russian campaign opinion among us was divided, with what I believe was a minority still favoring no truck or trade with the Soviet dictator and convinced we would have to fight the Russians when this was over. But such views were rare and diminishing in number.

Once, I also heard a couple of voices shout "Viva Abromson!" so as soon as possible I asked Maxie Abromson, our survey sergeant, to explain. Easy, he said. Since his jeep led the regiment in convoy, he had gotten some distance ahead of the formation and, upon entering this particular village, in response to the usual "Vivas!" had risen in his jeep and yelled "Viva Abromson!" a number of times. Some of the people evidently deduced that this exuberant north Winnipeg youth, before the war a post office employee with whom I had gone to high school, was another eminent world statesman, deserving an occasional "Viva!" And so he did and, he insisted, so did we all. Maybe he was right.

During this period all the artillery regiments took a day off to be paraded in a hollow square and greeted by Gen. Montgomery, who welcomed us personally to his command. He was persuaded that soldiers' morale was lifted when they saw their leader face to face and heard him speak, although competent generalship and the right equipment and training were usually more useful. He spoke a few words, consisting mainly of "My, you do look fit." and "Keep your heads covered; the sun's hot here, you know."

Canadians enjoy an attractive anti-hero mentality that was confirmed by the meeting. Ottawa's Parliament Hill is decorated with heavy, soberly clad 19th- and 20th-century politicians, with not a dashing general in sight. The only concession is to Queen Victoria, who also rates a statue. A statue of a Galahad-like youth, erected at the request of Mackenzie King after a young friend of his gave his life in an attempted rescue of a drowning man, stands outside the grounds, as does a statue of Samuel de Champlain, reputedly the first European to reach the Ottawa site. And that's it for the heroes.

Italian troops in our sector were surrendering by regiments. We began to understand that the Italian people wanted no part of this war, whatever Mussolini's

A general view of the invasion beaches on Sicily after Canadians landed at Pachino, Italy, in July 1943.

exhortations. Hard-core fascists would still fight, but not the majority of the people, with whom we were soon engaged in brisk commerce, trading boots, blankets, underwear and cigarettes for wine. Not that we were wine drinkers. The common word for wine was 'goof' and there was a suspicion that it caused headaches, loose bowels and was generally a decadent and corrupting influence. But as we became accustomed to it, we began to see wine in a broader perspective.

We also began to suspect that, liberators or not, we were being had. A pair of boots or a blanket for a bottle of wine seemed excessive. There was no reason that we couldn't be as crafty as the Sicilians. Once, when our convoy stopped, the inevitable peasant appeared from the roadside and thrust a bottle of homemade wine in to the cab of our vehicle. "Scarpe," he said, wanting boots. I reached back, pulled out a packet of hard tack that was our staff of life but may well have been sitting in British military stores since Lord Nelson's day, said "Si, scarpe," took the bottle of wine and handed

him the biscuits. He behaved as though stabbed. "No biscotti!" he shouted. "Scarpe!" I smiled agreeably and pointed to the biscuits he held in his hand. "Si, si, scarpe. Multo bono scarpe." The convoy moved and as I looked back I saw the wine entrepreneur looking at his biscuits, looking at us, and shaking his head in disbelief. It was a minor triumph, yet gratifying to be ahead of the game for once.

A few days before, our guns were in position in a valley. They were silent and we had been told we would have no shooting to do for several hours. There was a house part way up the slope and another fellow—his first name was Bill—and I decided it would be fun to take our rifles, rush in to the house with guns pointing and snarl "Vino!" It would be just like in a movie. Anyway, we rationalized, why should conquerors, even if regarded as liberators, be subjected to continuous swindling?

We carried out the plan, but were horrified by the result. Here, living in two rooms, was a peasant family, with children ranging from 12 years down, and we must have made a monstrously frightening sight as we burst in on them. They all began to cry and to plead that there was neither wine nor food in the house. Bill and I looked uneasily at each other, our rifles lowered. It wasn't fun any more, and never really had been. I felt evil. Clearly, Bill felt as bad. We left, empty-handed.

When we returned to the gun site we filled a wooden compo box with whatever surplus army goods were handy: a pair of boots, a blanket, some tinned food. Used during the first few weeks of an invasion, a compo box held quite a lot, 48 hours' food for six men, the number in a gun crew. It was about 24 inches long, 12 inches deep and 12 inches wide, and when we brought it to the people we had just hurt so badly, so unthinkingly terrorizing them, they seemed surprised, incredulous; but they accepted the gift and smiled forgivingly. Then the father produced a bottle of wine that he had evidently forgotten in the earlier excitement.

We were learning that we just weren't cut out for a conqueror's role. Shortly after we moved forward and took up position in a field of winter wheat. The ripe grain was being harvested and stood in stooks. We covered our vehicles and ammunition limbers with stooks, camouflage against air attacks. Peasant women appeared immediately, convinced we intended to carry their wheat away, wailing bitterly. This was their bread. If we took it they would starve. We tried to explain we were only borrowing the grain, using it as camouflage. But we knew when we were defeated. We removed the sheaves and rebuilt the stooks. Mistrusting us, they carried away as much as they could. Not only the men from drought-devastated Prairie farms understood, but also those from the towns.

So little resistance was in our sector that it was almost a week before we first fired our guns. Then we shot off about 50 rounds per gun in support of a Van Doos action. My gun was in a little grove surrounded by olive trees. It had been occupied earlier by an Italian unit and the ground was littered with their hand grenades and correspondence from wives, sisters and mothers. I don't know why the Italian soldiers had left them behind. The letters were filled with complaints as well as passion and perhaps the officers feared they would be useful to Allied military intelligence.

As we started firing, a truck unloaded ammunition and I started to remove the shells from the steel boxes. Unfortunately, they had been unloaded in haste, and in line with the gun muzzle. Whenever the gun fired sheets of flame shot out horizontally from the muzzle singeing hair off my head and arms. At that 90-degree angle from the gun, the sound of every shot was like the crack of doom. We made sure that never again was ammunition unloaded in that position, no matter how impatient the truck drivers were to depart. Fair's fair and we felt that gunners had some rights, too.

The Americans on our left and British on our right had been doing most of the fighting because that's where the Germans were. But now, after a couple of weeks, the Americans were finding things easier as the Germans moved toward our sector. One result, of course, was that we began to take casualties.

We moved in to a long, narrow field that not long before had been occupied by a German battery. We admired the industriousness of people who, in 100-degree heat, had dug slit trenches with perfect precision in the dry, stone-hard ground. What we failed to realize in our inexperience, and possibly our unwarranted overconfidence, was that if the field had been a German gun site, they could shell it with great accuracy for they knew where every trench would be.

We soon learned the truth. We fired a couple of rounds in support of an infantry advance and a German battery immediately opened fire on us. We continued to shoot. Through his bull horn, the gun-position officer said only three men per crew need man the guns; the remainder could take cover in the German slit trenches. Not a man moved and the young subaltern said: "Thanks, fellows." Pride.

Soldiers enjoy a few moments of relaxation on Christmas Day in Ortona, Italy, December 1943.

With 11 killed and several gun shields looking like lace-work, we finally finished our assignment and moved on. Some ground had been won and the Germans had retreated to another hilltop. Once they began resisting from hilltop to hilltop, a little of the swing went out of our elan, and we settled down to a grim, grinding, apparently never-ending battle. That was to become much of the story of the Italian campaign.

We were beginning to assume the attributes of battlefield soldiers: numbed emotions, little conversation (though there was little enough before that), concentration on the crucial problems of keeping alive and well, respect for a strong opponent. Actions were informed by a spirit of sharing—food, work and, when necessary, life. That had been true before, but not as intensely. Men did risk their lives for their comrades, although most didn't think about it that way. They didn't think at all. They simply did it.

Numbed emotions were necessary. Without them, the cases of battle exhaustion would surely have been more numerous throughout the war. Nervous exhaustion stemmed basically from physical fatigue, but also took a psychological toll. Many people, including myself, start to build a wall around themselves in childhood to keep out the hurt. They are hurt by the direct insults of other children and by the indirect insults of condescending adults. They build this wall, which others find hard to breach, and they survive behind it. Soldiers living in such close contact strengthen their individual walls. A soldier would have one or two intimate friends, but even with them, he exorcises emotion. If they die, too bad. Otherwise, his heart would be torn too often.

Oddly, that numbness didn't extend to the suffering civilian population, perhaps because they were strangers—in a sense, an abstraction. I still feel deeply ashamed of the role I played in the two-man raid on a peasant's house. The face of the Sicilian "enemy" was the face of a hard-working, impoverished family that knew nothing of politics, that had no voice in its destiny, that had been the victim of petty tyranny throughout Mediterranean history. The emotion of pity was beginning to fill the vacuum of no emotion at all, but it was aimed at the defenceless.

Another emotion began to take hold—wonderment at some of the beauty and strangeness of the sub-tropical environment, a mixture of the harshly ugly and the softly, seductively beautiful. For almost all of us, experience of these latitudes was new. Few of us had ever seen a vineyard, or olive, lemon or orange grove, or the fruit on an almond or fig tree. The cactus was an exotic plant. We learned to handle the roadside cactus fruit without getting our fingers filled with prickles. Once the thick skin of the fruit was removed, the meat inside was cool and sweet, a little like cantaloupe.

If it was my turn to stand the last trick of the night on guard at the gun, from 4 to 6 a.m., and if it was in position on a hilltop, it was cool enough to require a greatcoat. Almost every night I would see a shooting star race in a great parabola from horizon to horizon. Here was a great wonder. In Winnipeg on a winter night, I had sometimes seen the Northern Lights, but I was lucky if they performed their dazzling dance of purples and reds and blues more than once in season, and in some winters not even that. The North is thrifty with its spectacles. The South is more profligate.

We came to understand that Sicily was the child of centuries of feudal exploitation and, therefore, neglect. It could have been a land of great fecundity and comfort for everyone who worked there, but they were robbed.

In the third week, after slowly fighting from mountain-top to mountain-top to the western slopes of Mount Etna, we were offered a pleasant change in

A woman hangs out her laundry in Ortona, Italy, after the town was cleared of enemies by Canadian forces.

creature comfort. The ships that had been wholly dedicated to the transport of food, ammunition and gasoline had finally found room for a cargo of beer, a pint of ale for each man. By the time the beer reached us it was hot and undrinkable, but that was no problem.

Enough of us remembered our high school physics and the theory of evaporation to set up primitive but effective refrigeration systems. You dug a small hole, set the bottle in and filled the hole with water, which of course was also warm. You shovelled the dirt back in the hole and as it formed mud, punched holes in it. As it dried you poured more water in. After two hours you dug up the bottle and had ice-cold beer, a great luxury.

That was an acceptable interlude as the advance continued, a collage of the dreary, the exhilarating, and the completely and mindlessly tragic.

In a creeping barrage to support an infantry advance one night, we fired 300 rounds per gun. The barrels became hot and each gun crew became a smoothly running machine. Whether such barrages lead to softening of the brain among gunners is a question long debated by infantrymen, but there is no evidence there are more addlepates among gunners and ex-gunners than among any other group of humans. The body is a sturdy plant. The time would come when a burst eardrum was considered a trivial injury to be treated within the regiment and the gunner returned to duty immediately.

For all the shattering effect of the barrage we found it exhilarating, for we knew we had done something that required endurance and fortitude. And we had done it right. The infantry sustained almost no casualties as they moved to their objective, overrunning the German positions before the defending soldiers had a chance to recover from the creeping barrage.

Regalbuto was different. The village had been marked for destruction by aerial bombs because it was assumed the Germans would defend it to the end. As it turned out, the Germans evacuated beforehand, but it was bombed anyway. By the time the bulldozers cleared a road through it, and we followed, the stink of bodies and the cries of survivors marked the spot where, shortly before, there had been a human habitation.

Why did it have to be bombed at all even if the Germans defended it? To bomb a town didn't destroy its defences, it strengthened them because the rubble became an almost impregnable fortification. That was proved a number of times, notably at Cassino. Yet the generals insisted on bombing towns no matter how little this accomplished. It was not the defending soldiers who paid, but the defenceless civilians.

But few people can be more long-enduring than the Sicilians and this they also endured. Regalbuto was near the end of our advance. The people didn't seem to hate us for what had been done to them. And there was the other side of the coin. As shipping improved, flour and other food had been transported by the Allied armies for civilian succor. This couldn't resurrect the dead, but it could persuade the living that we bore them no ill will.

We now believed them when they said we were their liberators. These peasants weren't responsible for the war. We weren't their enemies. The enemies were in Rome and Palermo, absentee owners of the Sicilian latifundia together with the kept politicians who had helped degrade the people and rob them of everything. These things we felt.

One day, we paused in convoy while moving to the rear to prepare for the Italian landing, our work in Sicily finished. A big man, broad-faced, with a countryman's thick hands and wearing earth-colored clothes, approached us. He carried a round loaf of dark bread. "You have liberated us!" he shouted, and thrust the loaf forward. We didn't talk. We passed the loaf around, each man in the gun crew breaking off a piece, and handed the rest back to him, and we were content to eat bread together.

Yet in the end, he was wrong. People have to liberate themselves. Outsiders can't do it for them. ✑

OPENINGS
Ben Malkin

After we joined the British 8th Army in Sicily, we found we could change our lifestyles in two particulars: dress and saluting.

In dress, we could express an individuality untasted since civilian days. To the two customary saluting styles, The Quaver and The Snap, we could now add The Pushaway and The Montgomery, or Throwaway. They provided a range of choices that, together with dress, opened up opportunities for personal selection unknown to most armies or even, perhaps, to any other organized military force.

We became aware of these openings within days after landing, and in the 3rd Field Regt. RCA, as in other formations, we showed a commendable aptitude for learning. Within a week, we displayed a variety of clothing that would have done credit to a church rummage sale. In the Sicilian heat, some men wore only shorts and gym shoes. Others wore shorts and boots. Still others wore bush shirts with shorts, while others, whose skins had proved especially attractive to the savage Sicilian mosquitoes, wore long pants with shirts. Finally, some wore their sleeves rolled up, some buttoned down.

The wedge, or field-service caps with which we were still outfitted weren't much protection against the Sicilian sun, and helmets were too heavy to wear except when being shot at. Old fedora hats, picked up from civilians in trade for cigarettes, boots, blankets or other merchandise, served admirably. A good idea was to cut away the brim except for the front. For added chic, a handkerchief pinned to the back of the hat gave a garment a dashing, French Foreign Legion appearance.

One innovative costume worn by a dispatch rider whom we passed while in convoy left him bare to the waist, except for a bandolier, of the kind worn by moving-picture guerrillas, anchored on one shoulder, a Tommy gun slung from the other, and a Daniel Boone-style fur hat on his head. Years later, he might have modelled at least part of the dress for the Davey Crockett television series, but he was ahead of his time.

Perhaps the most elegant habit was the one seen by a startled Gen. Montgomery, and later mentioned in his memoirs. Standing in the back of a truck was a shirtless Canadian soldier, wearing a plug hat. Montgomery happened to come by in a jeep and the soldier, observing what he must have felt was simple military courtesy, removed his hat, and bowed low as his general moved past the truck.

Montgomery subsequently issued the following order: "Top hats will not be worn in the 8th Army." In his memoirs, Montgomery noted that it was the only dress order he promulgated. He, of course, was known for his unusual uniform: suede shoes, corduroy trousers, a turtleneck sweater and a black armored corps beret festooned with regimental badges. He must have been the despair of his fellow generals, especially George Patton, commander of the U.S. 7th Army in Sicily, a stern disciplinarian who insisted on a West Point, martial appearance among all his men, all the time.

A formal parade was, of course, another matter. After the action ended, and before we sailed for Italy, we performed a ceremonial guard with each man dressed impeccably in regulation style. And winter compelled us to wear our warm battle dress and greatcoats, and as often as not our balaclavas, folded into woolen caps, so that once again we looked like soldiers rather than irregulars. But the freedom to choose among a variety of clothing had been great while it lasted.

As a salute, The Quaver was generally confined to warrant officers, especially when parading in to the orderly room some unfortunate charged with a misdeed. Accompanied by a resounding stamping of feet, it was calculated to impress the awesome authority of the army on everyone in the chamber, including the culprit awaiting an unknown fate—three extra guard duties, usually.

Pte. Stephen Wallace of the Princess Patricia's Canadian Light Infantry rests north of Val Guarnera, Italy, in July 1943. Note his attire, including short pants and a short-sleeved shirt, on account of the heat.

Gen. Bernard Montgomery stands on a DUKW amphibious vehicle to address Canadian troops at Pachino, Italy, in July 1943.

The right hand was brought in a wide gesture to the level of the head, the tip of the forefinger almost touching the temple. The hand then quivered rapidly sideways, a little like a metronome set to keep time to a rock beat. On approximately the count of three, the hand was brought sharply down.

The Snap was a variation of The Quaver, and probably more closely resembled what drill sergeants had in mind when teaching recruits to salute. It was simply the regulation salute—a wide sweep of the arm until the fingers touched the temple, count one two three and smartly down. No quaver. When in doubt, it was best to stick to it.

The Montgomery, or Throwaway, was an entirely different species. You brought your arm lazily up to the vicinity of your temple or, if you preferred, your face. Then you waved in the general direction of your right, your arm describing a gentle parabola until it rested more or less at your side. The Montgomery was much favored by senior officers after its introduction by the general.

This exotic form of salute had an interesting genesis. In his book *Alamein*, C.E. Lucas Phillips, a former officer in the 8th Army, describes Montgomery's early induction in to the ways of the desert:

"On his first visit to the New Zealanders, (Montgomery) said on arrival at Gen. Freyberg's headquarters, 'I notice your soldiers don't salute.' Freyberg replied: 'Wave to them, sir, and they'll wave back.'"

Montgomery did, and it worked. Thus was born The Throwaway.

The Pushaway was a variation of The Throwaway. You brought your arm up much as with The Throwaway, but instead of waving it down to your right, you pushed it forward, as though going through a revolving door. It could also be interpreted by the recipient as a signal to get lost. That made it a handy salute for a captain whose sixth sense warned him the sergeant clicking his heels and using The Snap was about to ask when the hell could he expect his turn for leave would come up, if ever. ᙣ

Personnel of 2nd Canadian Infantry Brigade Headquarters draw water from a well near Assoro, Italy, in July 1943.

JOY AND SORROW
Ben Malkin

While "the life of a soldier is terrible hard," as the old poem has a sympathetic Alice telling us, moments of pure joy emerge. Like the moments of sorrow, these are remembered, for though pleasure is fleeting, joy and sorrow tarry.

In November, 1943, the British 78th Div. was slowly bleeding to death as it tried to cross the Sangro River near its wide mouth at the Adriatic Sea, and then break through the winter line, an elaborate trench system established by the German Army to deny the Allies any more Italian territory that season.

Gen. Montgomery reckoned a diversion upstream might force the Germans to detach enough troops from the main sector to make life easier for the 78th. He used to describe this tactic as one of forcing the enemy to dance to his tune; often, it worked. Accordingly, he ordered the British 5th Div. to cross the river inland, in the mountains. And to divert attention from the 5th, the 3rd Canadian Infantry Bde. was also ordered upstream, to create a diversion to the diversion—something like a plot within a plot in a Shakespearean play.

The 3rd Field Regt. RCA went along to Castel del Sangro to supply artillery support. Two of the batteries—the 19th from Winnipeg, Man., and the 77th from Moose Jaw, Sask.—were forward. We in the 92nd from Edmonton were back, and sheltered from observation.

We were in a low-lying meadow, which insistent rain turned into a miniature Passchendaele during our few days there. Not that it was a genuine Passchendaele; to say so would dishonor the memories of the men of WW I. But though we were there only a relatively short time, it became a reasonable enough facsimile to give us a taste of the reality we had only read about.

Our steel gun platforms sank a little deeper with every shot and every recoil. The gun crew next to mine tried to solve the problem of swivelling their 25-pounder cannon on a mud-encased platform by detaching the gun from time to time, winching it out, winching out the platform and placing it on a new spot, then returning the gun to the platform. All this time the skies wept, wept for Italy, wept for the embattled armies, wept for us. Instead of the laborious winching process, which also kept a gun out of action if only for a short time, I tried drag ropes. They were attached to the trail, and with the six-man gun crew hauling, we swung the gun left or right, on the principle stated by Archimedes: "If I had a lever long enough, I could move the world."

When the six were insufficient, the neighboring gun crew helped, and we managed to keep the gun switched on line well enough and quickly enough.

That didn't matter too much. What mattered was that the two forward batteries were coming under heavy fire and sustained considerable casualties. It couldn't be helped, of course. But by the time the infantry and ourselves finished creating a diversion to a diversion, I at any rate was drained of emotion; I suppose we all were.

But not entirely. That night, we were billeted in a large villa in a small town not far from the coast. The four sergeants in our troop were sleeping heavily on the floor of one room. The next room, much bigger, was occupied by men from the gun crews. My sleep was interrupted by the tumult of raucous voices from the next room.

I dressed by pulling on my boots, and went on a patrol in to the next room. The men had just brought in a large jug of wine and were about to have a party. They looked at me inquiringly, but as long as the other sergeants snored on and didn't complain, I was game, provided I could join the revelry. They cordially agreed.

One, Buck Babkirk, had a guitar and another had a fiddle. Babkirk came from somewhere in Alberta. He wore a drooping, Hopalong Cassidy moustache, and his favorite song was something he called "The Calgary Stampede," which consisted largely of "yippees" and "yahoos" and stentorian shouts of "Here comes Buck Babkirk, comin' outa chute number five!" That's what he used to play at occasional sing-alongs.

Mud proved to be one of the worst obstacles to Canadian soldiers in Italy, including that found near San Pietro in November 1943.

Not that night. We drank, we danced and we stomped to "Turkey In The Straw" and "The Arkansas Traveller." We linked arms, we circled the room and we stormed the walls. We drank wine, we got the rain, the mud and the wounded out of our systems, and we inwardly said R.I.P. to the dead. And that was our moment of joy, the other side of the coin to the moment of sorrow, lingering hard and solid in the memory.

I remember another moment of joy, which one might represent as being more at the intellectual than the emotional level, for it constituted a victorious assault on the army's pedantic rules, rather than a release of deeply imbedded feeling.

During the Moro River engagement, on the road to Ortona, on a relatively quiet night, our battery was to harass the Germans by firing at intervals on a crossroad behind their lines. Each gun would fire 80 rounds within the hour, in turn. My turn was from 2 a.m. to 3 a.m.

We laid out our ammunition in advance, and I asked Billy Hines, who came from Owen Sound, Ont., and who would be on gun-guard duty at that hour, to wake me a few minutes beforehand (we all did a two-hour gun-guard trick each night, staggering the time so that no man would be on duty at the same time two nights in a row). Eighty rounds within the hour was presumed to mean one round fired every 45 seconds, and I saw no point in arousing a whole gun crew to do such a Mickey Mouse shoot.

A night-time artillery assault on the Gothic Line, August 1944.

As occasionally happened, we had a jug of wine at our disposal. Before our turn to fire came, Hines and I filled our cups, and we sipped as we waited, listening to the adjoining gun shooting its round every 45 seconds. Shortly before the hour, I said, "Let's get away 10 fast ones." Hines agreed, and while he laid the gun I loaded and yelled "Fire!" By the time our 10 rounds were gone we had saved up 8 minutes. We relaxed and sipped our wine, complacent in the knowledge that two well-trained men could fire a gun accurately at such speed.

Again we decided to fire—this time 6 quick rounds, saving up 5 minutes, and again we relaxed. We repeated the process during the hour—now 8 quick rounds, now 4, now 10 again, until 3 a.m. came and 80 rounds had been shot. The gun on my left took over, firing one round every 45 seconds.

The sergeant from the neighboring gun, who was a professional and had been in the regular army before the war, strolled over. His gun didn't need him at the moment, because he followed the book, and had awakened his entire crew to do the shoot.

Puzzled, he asked: "What interval were you following?" "No particular interval," I said. "No one said anything about intervals, just 80 rounds within the hour. Have a drink." He recoiled, being on duty, and left for his gun, shaking his head in disbelief.

Next morning, Tommy Montgomery, our troop commander, was equally perplexed. "What was your interval?" he asked. "No special interval," I said happily. "Just the 80 rounds."

Montgomery, who came from Montreal and would become a lawyer, looked thoughtful, then brightened.

"You know," he reflected, "that's not such a bad idea. If I'd been the German military policeman at the other end, trying to figure the interval so I could let traffic through between rounds, you'd have had me climbing right up the wall."

That, of course, was the point. To disregard ossified traditions dear to the military—or any other—bureaucrats, to find a better way, and to triumph, also brings a moment of joy. Who says you can't fight city hall? ॐ

DIVERSIONS
Ben Malkin

Some of the fellows said Gen. Montgomery's orders for the Ortona-Pescara drive reminded them of a coach exhorting his players during intermission. "We will hit the enemy a colossal crack," said Montgomery.

The high strategy was simple enough, like most high strategy. In November-December, 1943, the 8th Army's 78th Div. had crossed the mouth of the Sangro in a mile-wide waterborne operation and broken the Germans' winter line. They had advanced to the approaches of the Moro River, a few miles below Ortona. Having suffered grievously, they were now being withdrawn. The 1st Canadian Div. would take over.

After giving the enemy a colossal crack, we would take Pescara on the Adriatic coast. That would give the 8th Army control of the eastern end of the lateral highway linking Rome with the Adriatic. The 8th Army, presumably, would then swing a left hook aimed at Rome.

Standing in the way was the Moro River, Ortona, the Arielli Valley, the 90th Panzer Grenadiers, the 1st Paratroop Div., remnants of the infantry division mauled by the 78th during their northward drive, and the Italian winter mud, just beginning to cloy. Nevertheless, the plan sounded great, as most plans do.

The 3rd Field Regt. RCA was deployed a couple of hundred yards off the highway leading north. As part of the colossal crack, virtually unlimited use of ammunition was allowed. A subaltern or a captain on forward observation duty could order a shoot of 10, 20 or 30 rounds from all 24 guns of the regiment on any target he deemed essential. For the younger subalterns, some opportunities were too seductive to overlook. We heard of one case where a forward observation officer, his binoculars sweeping the enemy front, spotted a German soldier emerge from a slit trench, shovel in hand, and, finding a suitable spot nearby, let his pants down. Our officer ordered 10 rapid-fire rounds from the regiment, and saw the poor struggler on the other side make a sensational, Olympic-class dive for his slit trench, which he reached safely.

Officially, the story was never either confirmed or denied. But the very fact that tales of this kind gained currency suggests how lavishly supplied with ammunition we were. Somebody said each 25-pounder round cost the Canadian taxpayer $12.50. We didn't care. We fired our guns when our infantry needed our support, and when they didn't need it during a pause in the action, we fired anyway, generally at night, on German infantry, artillery, machine-gun positions and road intersections.

Why? The reason was explained by a staff officer from divisional headquarters who, several days after Ortona fell, came around to the guns to brief us. He spoke to small groups in turn. As staff officers are wont to do, he told us where we had been, and where the authorities hoped we would get to. In passing, he mentioned that in the drive from the Moro River to Ortona, the divisional artillery had fired hundreds of thousands of rounds.

Being simple-minded, I asked: "Why are we doing so much shooting, sir?"—for we were still doing an inordinate amount of firing, though by now we had become bogged down in static warfare.

He looked at me pityingly, the way one of my gun crew, in a mood that I attributed to battle exhaustion, had looked at me several weeks before when he said: "Sarge, you're so stupid even the other sergeants think you're dumb." Then the staff officer expounded: "It's to keep the enemy awake, of course. Wears them down. They can't get a decent night's sleep because of the ammo you fellows are firing at them."

Little did he know the truth. Unless we were manning our guns when the Germans fired at us, we snuggled in to our slit trenches and slept quite soundly. We could assume the Germans did the same when we were shooting at them. But when we were shooting, it was we who couldn't get a decent night's sleep—and whose brains were being slowly, inexorably scrambled by the endless explosions from our guns.

There were some things staff officers just couldn't be expected to comprehend. Shortly after the Moro River campaign started, I got three reinforcements on my gun crew, giving me an extra man. I figured, why not let one man off gun duty each day, in rotation, except for myself. He could wash his underwear, take a bath by soaping himself out of a canvas bucket, then pouring another bucket of water over himself, or sleep, or do anything he wanted.

Tommy Montgomery, our troop commander, liked the idea. But he urged that we speak to no one about it, because if word of the scheme got back to the rear, there might be trouble. Days off? On the battlefield? Some staff officer might not understand.

Despite everything that's been said and written about the need for conscription to ensure an adequate number of reinforcements, I never saw a great problem in terms of bodies. There always seemed to be plenty of men available, sooner or later. The difficulty lay in the training, not in the numbers. Of those three particular reinforcements, one had been trained as a machine-gunner, one as an anti-aircraft gunner and one to push a broom around the barracks. Not one had trained on the 25-pounder gun.

That was the problem with infantry reinforcements as well—plenty of men, but not properly trained. I heard Gen. H.D.G. Crerar say at a press briefing in the winter of 1944–45 (I was a war correspondent by then) that there were some 140,000 general service men in Canada prepared to go overseas, but a shortage of trained men in Europe. He wanted to know why, but couldn't get an answer. The reinforcement crisis was always a training problem—and a lot of propaganda by barrack-room politicians.

As the Moro River and Ortona campaign progressed, week after desolate week, we became very gentle with one another. There's nothing like constant shooting, and being shot at, to reduce belligerence in a person. Not that we were very truculent to start with, certainly not nearly as macho as Ernest Hemingway, or as Hollywood stars doing a war movie. And not only were we gentle with each other. Animals got their portion of kindness. There came a day when the trucks could no longer plow through the mud to dump ammunition at the gun positions. They piled the ammunition cases at the side of the road, and left the rest up to us.

One youth tried to set an example by carrying a four-shell case, which weighed almost 100 pounds, to my gun. Some example. At the second step he lost his footing, fell forward in to six or eight inches of mud and came up looking like a hog emerging from a wallow. Obviously, that wouldn't be the solution.

The authorities produced a practical plan. They requisitioned some donkeys, and we organized a donkey train from the highway to the guns. One of the world's most highly mechanized armies was back to the days of Genghis Khan. Each animal carried two cases, one on each side. Our driver-mechanics were put in charge. It worked well.

Soldiers like pets since they've little else to lavish affection on, and some of the men felt so well disposed toward their newfound friends they decided that, like everyone else, the donkeys were entitled to an identity. Consequently, they gave the animals names: there was The General, The Admiral, The Air Marshal, and so on down the line. The penultimate donkey became The Rear Admiral and the rear, of course, was brought up by Der Fuehrer. The donkeys didn't seem to mind.

There weren't many such diversions, so those that came our way were doubly welcome. Such moments are like photographs that stay in the mind, to be looked at again and again, whenever a man opens his mental album.

One night our regiment was firing while the Germans were harassing us with a barrage of 88-mm shells. In the midst of this barbaric uproar, our guns became silent for a moment and, miraculously, the Germans stopped firing at the same time. From somewhere nearby, the wail of bagpipes was heard.

PART II: THE SECOND WORLD WAR

Music to hearten. The guns roared again, and the shells burst. The music was silenced. But in the flickering light of the gun flashes, we could see the shadowy figures of an infantry column moving forward through our lines. That would have been the Seaforth from Vancouver, or the 48th Highlanders from Toronto. Westerners or easterners, it was all the same. The picture remains.

The Moro River battle finally ended and the front surged toward Ortona. So did we. By this time, the front line was running north and south almost as much as east and west. We were already at about the latitude of Rome, while the troops on the west coast were still considerably to the south of the Italian capital. We were a salient; if the Germans had had enough strength, they could have tried to cut us off, as they themselves were cut off in the Stalingrad salient. Fortunately, they didn't have the strength.

Well, let's fight for Ortona anyway, even if it was beginning to register that a victory there would be a hollow triumph. Fight the thick-skinned paratroopers, who were yielding the city only room by room, house by house. Fight until the infantry battalions were bled. Fight until the Germans were decimated. That's what really counted.

For instead of a colossal crack with wide, sweeping movements and rapid advances, we were in a battle of attrition. The division may not have known it then, but it knew the following spring, when it moved in May, 1944, to the Cassino area, along with the 5th Armored Div. Ortona and its colossal crack and its left hook were forgotten, valueless.

But that was still to come. Meanwhile, there was Christmas at Ortona to celebrate, with roast pork and whatever wine could be obtained for our usual trade goods. Since the fighting continued that day, both the infantry and ourselves celebrated in relays, each shift returning to the fray as its meal was completed. However, men who weren't attached to a gun crew or a platoon could celebrate as individuals. One man in our troop, a dispatch rider, cheered us all up as he came swaying from gun to gun, cup in hand, wishing each of us a happy holiday. With wry smiles, we accepted his attentions with considerable grace. A dispatch rider's life was often an uncomfortable one, and he was more than entitled to his moment of pleasure.

The last of the German paratroopers finally withdrew from Ortona on New Year's Day. That night, to mark the occasion, we experienced a cloudburst, a type of contingency not provided for in the military training manuals.

I was heavily asleep in my pup tent; we had by now been issued enough of these lodgings to keep all sleeping men dry. Though by now I could sleep through shell bursts, unusual sounds, even a whisper, would awaken me. The downpour roused me, and I crawled out to see how the man on guard duty was making out.

There were three or four inches of water in the bottom of the gun pit by now. Fortunately, neither the rest of my crew nor myself were possessed of the sin of pride. None of us fancied our engineering qualities so much as to insist that our gun pit floor be absolutely

Privates W.H. Rose and R.M. Stuart walk with a mule loaded with mortars near Terreti, Italy, in September 1943.

Mules are used to carry supplies over mountains to forward troops in Italy, in July/August 1943.

level. Ours was at a slant of perhaps five degrees—not much, but enough for water to run downhill.

From the side of the gun pit we dug a narrow trench in to the field. It was done within a few minutes and the water simply poured out. In the dark, we could hear adjoining gun crews frantically bailing out with their canvas buckets, a laborious process that seemed never-ending as the downpour continued. Their efforts reminded me of the childhood story of the unhappy predicament in which the apothecary's apprentice found himself. In this manner, the colossal crack ended.

I have mentioned pup tents, and the ability to sleep through shell bursts, but to be awakened by a whisper.

The pup tent, properly speaking, should accommodate only one person; at most, in a pinch, two. Some weeks after the rains began, our gun crew was issued two pup tents. Three of us would share one tent. You developed a special technique under these circumstances, requiring considerable self-discipline.

When one man wanted to turn over, he would nudge his neighbor, who would pass it on, and all three would turn over at once. It worked fine once you got the hang of it. When one of the men was awakened to take his shift on gun-guard duty, he would ease himself out of the tent, head first, so as not to disturb his companions.

Returning after his two-hour shift, he would slide in, feet first. It was much better than resting under a small piece of tarpaulin we had found, and which had hitherto served us as a roof, the sides being open to the fresh country air.

As for sleeping through shell bursts, two of our recent reinforcements sharing a tent at Ortona (by now we were well equipped with shelter) dug themselves in about five feet. I had dug my own slit trench about eight inches, which I figured was enough for anything except a direct hit, and then it didn't matter how deep you were.

I had placed my tent over my trench. On the floor, I had laid bamboo sticks, and four blankets as a bed. Covering me were another four blankets. They had belonged to former members of the gun crew who had departed, after which I had forgotten to turn their blankets in. The extra blankets were equitably distributed among the gun crew.

On the first night, I heard a whisper. It was the younger of the reinforcements. I doubt that he was the required 18 years old, but I hadn't asked. You didn't ask personal questions of your comrades. He was the one who had been trained only to push a broom.

"Sarge," he whispered. "We're being shelled. Yuh wanna get down in our slit trench?"

"No, better get back, and thanks," I said. He had crawled out of his safe trench and over to where I slept, to warn me. I was touched. A funny thing, but that's my clearest memory of Ortona. ॐ

THE PAPER SHOOT
Ben Malkin

Psychological warfare had its triumphs and failures during WW II. At Anzio, the Germans probably enjoyed their finest psychological warfare hour in the early spring of 1944 when, on occasion, they broadcast to the Allied soldiers the daily Allied password almost as soon as it had filtered down to the Americans and British troops from official sources. The Germans must have had ears like rabbits.

This might have had an unsettling effect on the Allied troops in the beach-head except that beyond a few patrols, there was little action. On the other hand, it provided a conversation piece for the isolated men of Anzio, thus helping to reduce ennui. This is always good for morale. To that extent, the German triumph was probably diluted.

It was always difficult to place a value on psychological warfare. My own regiment was once involved, being required to fire leaflets from our 25-pounders near Ortona a few weeks after that city fell. Following the action, the gunners felt high explosive would likely have done more good. This opinion wasn't shared by the psychological warfare people.

The leaflets were packed in to smoke shells from which the canisters had been removed by the ordnance section. Possibly because these men didn't take psychological warfare seriously enough, the fuses on some of the shells weren't properly readjusted. Consequently, a number burst over our heads instead of the Germans', although they got their share of paper as well.

Before the shoot began, the psychological warfare men had distributed sample leaflets in the belief that if we knew what we were doing we would do it without grumbling. These samples were in English. The leaflets made no appeal to the Germans to desert, nor did they try to create alarm and despondency among the enemy—mainly the thick-skinned paratroopers who had finally been ejected from Ortona—by suggesting that while they were facing death at the front, their wives and girl-friends were facing seduction by civilians in Berlin and Stuttgart. Instead, the psychological warfare department played it straight. The leaflets gave the day's news.

The trouble was, the news was almost entirely devoted to Russian action on the Eastern front, with some attention

Members of the Seaforth Highlanders of Canada search prisoners near the Moro River front in Italy in December 1943.

Military vehicles head through Italy (near Cassino) in May 1944.

paid to American successes in the Pacific. Our own efforts in Italy were ignored. I'm not sure what the Germans were supposed to conclude from this, but we felt neglected and that made us unhappy which I don't think was exactly the purpose the psychologists had in mind.

A remarkable psychological warfare foul-up occurred at Cassino after the efforts of the New Zealand and Indian divisions in March, 1944, to take that town and its overhanging mountain.

After the dust had subsided, the Germans used their loudspeaker system to shout at the New Zealanders in impeccable, Sandhurst-accented English. The Germans' message was wholly negative, devoted to all the disadvantages of soldiering in Italy. The New Zealanders cadged a loudspeaker system of their own, and yelled back insults and defiance in Maori.

Thinking they were getting feedback from the Indian division that had by now been withdrawn, the Germans, after pause for careful preparation, mistakenly shouted back in Hindi, urging the soldiers to lay down their arms instead of fighting for British imperialism.

By this time the New Zealand position had been taken over by the Brigade of Guards, which responded

Personnel of the 14th Armoured Regiment (The Calgary Regiment) share a meal with personnel of the 8th Indian Infantry Division at Castelfrentano, Italy, in March 1944.

by hurling taunts and menaces at the Germans in Welsh. The Germans lapsed into a sullen silence. I suppose you could say the Allies won that round by a technical knockout. ♻

Tanks of the 1st Canadian Armoured Brigade move forward to support the 8th Canadian Division during an Allied barrage near Cassino, Italy, in May 1944.

A special combat force is briefed before setting out on patrol near Anzio, Italy, in April 1944.

THE LONGEST WAIT
Ralph Niessen

The Battle of Arnhem had been fought and lost and thousands of Dutch people were roaming the countryside in search of food and a place to sleep. I was one of them, and it wasn't long before the Germans found out about my underground activities. I was arrested, with my brother. The SS walked into the factory where we had taken shelter and pointed a gun at us. After five years of war, we had learned that one should raise one's hands, which is what we did. We wound up in Amersfoort concentration camp, a *durchgangslager* or assembly point for transshipment. The Allies were close by and there were no more transshipments, so we stayed there.

On arrival we were locked in one-person cells, four to each: not comfortable, but quiet, and we managed to have a fairly good sleep. Next morning, without breakfast, we were marched into the camp proper. The first thing we saw was an emaciated prisoner with a towel around his neck. Early spring in Holland can be chilly. While we watched, a German officer in immaculate uniform started screaming at the apparition, tore the towel from his neck and proceeded to kick him to death. We were told that it was against the rules to wear a towel or anything else that was not a uniform. One learns.

We were led into a long, weatherbeaten shack, ordered to strip and issued worn-out German panzer uniforms. They stank, but in the surroundings did not seem out of place. Next, I was presented to the "barber," a prisoner with a pair of hedge shears who performed a combined cutting and pulling operation on my head. Hills and valleys, it felt, when I ran my hand over it. There were no mirrors.

I still had trouble believing this was actually happening to me. I had been arrested twice before but had managed to get clear. Escape could not be attempted this time because I was not alone. If I disappeared it would be rough on my brother. We agreed not to go, or go together.

Destruction in the city of Arnhem, Holland, April 1945.

After the barber's shearing I was kicked out into the compound and told to report to a block number. My brother had also been exposed to tonsorial activities and we laughed till we were sore when we first saw each other.

Together we made our way to our block number and reported to a trusty. Crusty would have been a better name for him. We were assigned a bunk, brother in the middle, I on the bottom. The top bunk belonged to someone who was absent.

We were then shown the "washrooms" and "toilets." There was no water in the washrooms; the toilets were invisible. Where the porcelain bowl had been—or perhaps still was—there was simply a heap of human excrement at least two feet high. I expressed my doubt about being able to sit on the toilet. The trusty asked me whether I had dysentery yet. When I told him "No," he said, "You soon will have." He was right.

Dysentery was so common we tore the crotch out of our uniforms and released wastes constantly, once when lined up to be shot.

There was a clandestine radio receiver in the camp and we got news almost as soon as the Germans did, from the BBC. I never knew who had the receiver. Occasionally we could hear battle sounds to the south. Canadians! It was a constant prayer in the back of my mind: "Please, please cross the Rhine and get us out." Sometimes frustration made us express less than flattering thoughts about the Allies' fighting abilities. We could see the German tanks were immobilized because of lack of fuel and their third-rate troops lacked even proper nourishment. Surely they couldn't put up much resistance. What we didn't know was that the Germans had a hard, thick crust of good troops along the river.

One glorious morning, the apple trees in bloom just outside the barbed wire, my brother and I and 33 others were to be shot by a certain time unless some escaped prisoners returned. The time came, and no prisoners.

We were lined up against a concrete wall. The guard was doubled in the towers, all guns trained on the compound. Two good-looking young Germans set up a light machine-gun about 20 paces from us. They smoked and talked while they fed the belt into the gun, sighted it and sat down beside it. Two things bothered me. One was that my mother had only two children and it would be hard on her to learn we'd been shot. The other was that I was afraid they wouldn't shoot me dead but bury me alive. My brother and I shook hands. It was dead silent in the camp. We could hear the birds singing outside the compound. They couldn't have existed inside the wire because they would have been killed and eaten, except the feathers. We could hear some small arms fire, tanks and an occasional artillery round. Why did those Canadians not get here?

We stood a long time waiting for death. Finally, the officer arrived. He just had to give the word and we'd be dead. He said nothing, but the two soldiers had extinguished their smokes and taken up shooting positions behind the gun. More waiting. The commandant arrived with a woman. We learned later that she represented the Red Cross and had informed the Germans that the Allies had cut Holland off from Germany and they could not get away. Fresh graves would not help them. Apparently, they had negotiated all the time we were waiting. The commandant spoke to the officer, and the officer bellowed at the soldiers who leisurely folded up their guns and left. We were marched back to barracks.

A few days later, about midday, there was some ragged cheering in the compound. The Canadians had arrived! They had cameras and busily took pictures. I began talking to one of them—he seemed gigantic beside us scarecrows—and of all men in the Winnipeg Rifles, I had to pick the one who didn't have any cigarettes! ✌

Pte. H.E. Goddard of the Perth Regiment carries a Bren gun as he advances through a forest north of Arnhem, Holland.

THE NIGHT THE BIG PLANE FELL
Donald MacDonald

Most veterans carry a hope and a fear when they think of returning to the scene of their war. The hope is that they can recapture something of things as they once were; the fear is that the world they once knew lives only in their memory.

About ten years ago, a movie called *Twelve O'Clock High* drove this point home with dreadful effectiveness. In one scene a former American airman was visiting the airdrome in England from which his squadron had operated during the war. A somewhat pathetic figure, he stood alone in a field overgrown by weeds. Nearby, cows grazed at their ease. Gradually, one became aware of a swath amid the weeds—a swath which had once been a busy runway.

The camera roamed over the skeleton of what had been an operations building, moving to a limp, abandoned windsock which hung in shreds from a pole. This was the only forlorn clue as to what had gone on in this place which had once been a wartime airdrome.

This, I think, is the greatest fear facing anyone who has ever thought of going back. We dread the thought that perhaps in places where friends died time has erased all traces of their passing; that nobody remembers what went on there.

I had such fears when I returned to Belgium last summer. But I also had a special reason for wanting to visit the little village on the outskirts of Liege. On a night in April, 1944, our Halifax bomber exploded onto one of the fields there. Three members of our crew were killed, and four of us were saved by strangers who walked out of the night.

I knew that the four of us who survived the night of April 28th, and later spent five months in hiding with the Belgian underground, would always remember that night. But, after seventeen years, what did the people there remember about the night a bomber crashed into their lives? This was the nagging question which went back to Belgium with me last summer.

I was a wireless air-gunner attached to No. 432 Squadron of the R.C.A.F. We were stationed near York in 1944. On the night of April 28th, our seven-man crew trundled its gear into a flight bus for our 25th trip. Earlier, at briefing, a sigh of relief had run through the room when the target was announced. It looked easy. Our crew was approaching the magic 30 trips which meant our tour of operations would be complete. None of us were bucking for a gong, and the thought of an easy trip didn't damage our pride at all. After targets such as Berlin, Stuttgart, Frankfurt, Magdeburg and Schweinfurt, a little place called Montzen would be a piece of cake.

So by the time the flight bus dropped us off at our aircraft, we should have been making book. We were odds on favourites. But we didn't feel that way. We huddled together for a few minutes before climbing into the Halifax, all of us unusually silent. Perhaps, though, on looking back, there is a tendency to read into situations like this something which was not actually present at the time.

Yet I remember Philips, our flight-engineer, saying, "I've got a feeling about this one, chum."

Philips had a young wife in the village near the drome. At the moment, she was sitting alone in a room, waiting for the sound of our engines. Then she would wait the long hours away until the engines returned. It was a tough proposition for a wife; a tougher one for a young husband. But Philips had never let his private life interfere with the job which he did extremely well. We had gone from Wellingtons to Halifaxes together, and Philips had never betrayed any emotion before an op. That's why it sounded so strange to hear him speak this way before take-off.

Yet when he spoke I could sense that the others felt the same way about Montzen. I know I did.

We climbed into the bomber, stowed our gear. Then F/O Harvey Whaley, the pilot, started up the engines. We taxied out and became airborne at ten o'clock.

F/O Johnny Burrows, our navigator, called out a course. An engineering graduate of McGill, he was one of the top navigators on the squadron. Soon we were out over the English Channel.

The gunners, F/O Paul Driver, in the rear turret, and P/O Dan McCoy, in the mid-upper, tested their guns. The aircraft shuddered as the six Brownings arched tracer into the darkness. Then it droned onwards on an uneventful trip to the enemy coast.

From time to time Johnny Burrows quietly called out a position. Then, inside his blackout curtain, he hunched over his navigation table again. There were seven men in the aircraft. But each was isolated by his duties and his thoughts. It was a lonely quiet night.

The calm, deliberate moments marched on as our bomber droned across Belgium. Then—shortly after one o'clock—we approached the target area. P/O Kevin Doyle, the bomb-aimer, prepared to take over the aircraft. The gunners searched the blackness, already reporting bombers which were falling from the sky.

The raid on Montzen was a diversion, designed to draw enemy night fighters from the primary target of Friedrichshafen. The Canadian Six Group lost 10 of the 54 aircraft sent against Montzen. German night fighters engaged in the Montzen area were drawn from two fighter groups and part of a third. Compared with 10 losses for 54 aircraft, the main force of 144 aircraft which went against Friedrichshafen lost five aircraft.

Doyle had just started his bombing run when suddenly cannon shells ripped through the plane. It came with stunning swiftness out of the darkness. No warning! No sign of fighters! Yet suddenly the plane trembled under the impact, filling with dust and smoke, and the sound of breaking glass and metal ripping against metal. Driver and Burrows died in those seconds, and I vaguely felt something hit me in the legs.

Somewhere out in the night, a Messerschmitt 110 —equipped with radar and cannon—closed in for the kill. Because we were on the bombing run, we were unable to take evasive action. We were a sitting duck. In a split-second we—who had patiently sought out our target—had suddenly become the hunted. The interminable seconds ticked by, punctuated by explosions within the aircraft. Doyle called the bomb-run, precisely, soothingly. I thought of the bombs, already fused, ready to explode on impact. And the cannon shells which ripped through the bomb-bay.

Finally, Doyle shouted: "Bombs gone!"

Whaley and Philips threw the bomber into violent evasive action. After a series of murderous dives and climbs we shook our attacker.

We were safe in the darkness. But only until some enemy navigator was able to lock onto us again with his radar. This would be a matter of seconds. We beat out several small fires and grimly reported the casualties.

For a time it appeared that we might make it back. The aircraft was badly damaged, but Whaley could still get a response from the controls. But this hope died aborning. The night fighters struck again.

The enemy merely stood back out of range of McCoy's .303's and cut our aircraft to pieces. Cannon fire smashed through the Hallie, sending chunks of the big plane falling off into the night. Fire broke out again in at least three places inside the bomber, and a wing was also burning. The intercom was gone, the controls shot away and we were falling.

Through the smoke I saw Whaley beckon us to bail out. We were under our third attack now, burning and dropping completely out of control. Philips scrambled over to the rear escape hatch. He did not appear to be injured. He waved and dropped out into the night. It was the last I saw of him. Doyle and I went next.

When I fell away from the aircraft, it rolled over on its back—a gesture typical of a dying bomber. Whaley was still in the doomed aircraft as far as I knew. But somehow he managed to escape and was dropping down somewhere above me—a fact which I only discovered some months later.

The night of the Montzen diversion (April 28, 1944), the Canadian Six Group lost 10 of 54 Halifax bombers and fought off fighters from three Luftwaffe fighter groups.

I dropped, semi-conscious. There was no sensation of motion until I hit the ground. When I did hit, a surge of pain shot up from my legs and I blacked out.

After I came to, I tried to stand but couldn't. My flying boots were wet. For the first time I realized that my feet and legs had been riddled with shrapnel. Slowly I unsnapped my parachute harness. Crawling to a ditch, I stuffed it under some branches. The night was quiet and black. I had no idea how far we were from the target area, but as I lay there trying to plan my next move I knew that shock was setting in. I just wasn't thinking straight. So I lay there, waiting for something to happen.

It happened sooner than I expected. A twig snapped like a rifle shot. Then footsteps coming towards me. A lone figure emerged from the darkness. He must have been watching for some time, because he walked directly towards me. He stopped a short distance away, looking at me in silence. He was a farmer, and I indicated that my legs were injured. Without speaking, he took a final look, then turned and left.

I had started to crawl away when five peasants returned a few minutes later. They carried me to a farm house and dressed my wounds.

Gradually, I learned that they were members of the Belgian underground. None of them spoke any English. I spoke neither French nor Flemish. So for days it was impossible to communicate with anybody. Yet I understood when they took my uniform, burned it and gave me civilian clothing. They also provided me with a civilian identification card. I became Oscar Pardon, a tailor.

Then began a progression of moves at night. I was shunted from place to place, handed from group to group. Because I was unable to communicate with these constantly changing groups, to this day I have no idea of just where I was hidden. Neither am I sure of how many times I was handed from group to group, or how many people were involved in the daring chess-game with the Nazis. Shadowy, intense figures were replaced by other figures. I lost track of time, became irritable, and felt that I was starting to go around the bend.

Five weeks passed in this manner. I think I had been moved about ten times. The inability to talk to anybody and the uncertainty of the whole situation was getting me. It must have showed. Because that's when Louis Stassart came to see me.

Louis Stassart spoke English. His mission was simply to keep me company. He explained that it was dangerous for me to spend too long in one spot; therefore I was being passed from one underground unit to the other. The underground worked in small units, each more or less independent of the other. In this manner, he explained, if one unit was captured there would be less risk of the entire network being discovered.

Louis' theory proved true. About seven weeks after his first visit with me, he was captured. He had spent several years in Detroit as a boy, so even at first meeting we had lots to talk about. When Louis told me the invasion of Normandy had taken place, for the first time in over five weeks I found an objective, a reason to stay under cover.

By the end of July, Louis left me. I didn't know then what he had gone on to. But a few weeks afterwards, he ended up in a German concentration camp. He escaped and worked his way back to Holland.

In September, the Americans liberated Liege, and I came out of hiding.

Since 1945, Louis Stassart was my only link with the many courageous people who had risked everything to keep me out of enemy hands. Therefore, when I went back to Belgium last summer, he was the first person my wife and I looked up.

Louis immediately took time off from his printing business to help us locate other members of the underground who had helped me. It wasn't easy. But we did visit many of the places where I had hid, many of which I had never before seen in daylight. The people also emerged from the shadows. They were able to talk more freely now—and, while there still was a language barrier, Louis acted as interpreter.

There were parties, gatherings of excited *Belgiques* and touching, sincere little speeches. One of the most moving of such reunions was at the home of the Maegers. I had spent four weeks with the old couple in 1944. He is an 80 year-old former police chief at Beyne-Heusay.

After 17 years, I didn't think he would recognize me. We rang the doorbell at the Maeger home, and he strolled around from the back where he had been gardening. He glanced at me, gasped and immediately threw out his arms. Mrs. Maeger, in her late seventies, also greeted me like a son who had finally returned home.

The many acts of kindness by all these people made me feel extremely humble. I owed them so much. Yet—according to them—they were being honoured. At first I was moved by this, then embarrassed. As my visit spun itself out, the embarrassment became a gnawing doubt. Something was wrong. This wasn't why I had really come back. True, I wanted to see all these people again, to thank them. But somehow, I had been projected into the role of a returning hero, and this was very wrong.

Three members of our crew had been killed that night 17 years ago. Philips, whom I last saw going out the escape hatch, was later reported to have died of wounds. He must have been hit as he left the aircraft. Driver and Burrows had been killed in the first attack. But there were no graves. These were the men who should have been remembered by the people around Liege. But there were no graves, not even for Philips.

This is when the doubts I had been harbouring for 17 years became real fears. As my visit grew shorter, I searched frantically for some sign that somebody remembered.

Louis drove us around the area. We stopped people in villages, in farm yards and on the roads.

"Do you remember the night the big plane fell?" he'd ask. There would be a glimmer of hope as some of them nodded. Many remembered, but none knew where it came down. The hours of my visit dwindled, each became a bit more desperate than the last. I wasn't even sure what I was looking for. But it seemed important that we find the spot where the Halifax crashed.

It seemed incredible that a bomber could have crashed in the area, that so many people would remember the night and yet none know where it had come down. As the search continued, during the last hours of my last day in Belgium, I told Louis this. He reminded me of how the underground had operated.

I agreed that there were too many missing links between the farmer who had first walked out of the night and the day Louis first walked into the cellar where I was hiding. I had no way of knowing where I had been picked up, neither had Louis.

Our last hope was the burgomaster of a village called Fexheple-Haute Clocher. Yes, he remembered the night. He also knew where the plane had come down. He directed us to a spot on the outskirts of the village.

We drove out and found a lonely peasant in a field cutting hay with a scythe. He didn't even look up as Louis started talking. But when Louis asked about the night the plane fell—I could recognize the words—the farmer dropped the scythe. He stared at us curiously, a bit startled. Then he moved towards the road, pointing.

The farmer had been there that night. He helped remove the bodies from the wreckage. Then the Germans arrived and took the bodies away in a truck before the Belgians could bury them.

But at the edge of the field the farmer indicated a small memorial: a simple cross, protected by an arch of bricks. Flowers grew in the small bed which ran out from the foot of the cross. The memorial was erected by the underground.

A man of the soil tends his fields on the spot where three men died the night the big plane fell. But his eyes tell you that he remembers. And the white cross with its simple inscription, in poor but sincere English, tells passers-by that the memorial is:

IN GLORIOUS MEMORY
JOHNNY BURROWS
AND HIS TWO FRIENDS WHO
FALLED FOR GOD AND CANADA
28TH APRIL 1944

THE DANZIG CAPER
Kingsley Brown

This story is true in every detail. If any part of it should stir your disbelief, you may refer to Gwyn Martin, today a respectable dispensing chemist who lives in Aberystwyth, Wales. Gwyn is one of several happy memories I have from my three years as a prisoner of war in Germany. He was a big-boned typical Welsh highlander, strong like an ox and a terrifying figure on the football field. He had black eyes and black undisciplined shaggy hair and a ruddy skin like beefsteak. When he laughed he shook the barracks and when he sang, as every Welshman must as a matter of tribal instinct, it was like a cracked record of a Wagner overture.

Gwyn was a navigator in the RAF and part of the all-Welsh crew of a Wellington bomber. The pilot was Shag Rhys; he was shorter than Gwyn, but stockier and just as tough, and his friends said they were sure he was the reincarnation of a mad Druid priest.

One night early in 1942 they had raided a naval objective somewhere on the Norwegian coast. A few hours later, on what ought to have been the flight home, Shag asked his navigator where they were.

"Damned if I know," said Gwyn cheerfully, and he didn't.

The weather was zero-zero, and after they had drawn a blank of the RDF and had no more than fifteen minutes' fuel in the tanks, Rhys decided to let down slowly and ditch in the ocean. From his deadest kind of dead reckoning Gwyn had figured they were somewhere over the North Sea.

It was surprisingly flat and calm, and the Wellington hit the water nicely and sank in 45 seconds. Unfortunately the life raft failed to discharge automatically from the stowage, and the crew were left floundering around in darkness, with only Mae Wests to keep them afloat.

All, that is, except Gwyn Martin, for he had characteristically left his Mae West hanging dry and tidy in his locker back at base. He swam around in the dark for about 20 minutes, but in his heavy boots and flying clothes he quickly tired. The others heard his casual goodbye from out of the foggy blackness.

"So long, chaps. I'm done!"

But about five seconds later they heard him come back to life.

"Hey, fellows, I'm walking on the bottom!"

In a misty dawn they all walked ashore from a tiny lake, not much larger than a duck pond, deeply cradled in a narrow valley between towering Norwegian mountains.

The good Lord, who concerns himself equally with the safety of sparrows, small children, drunkards and Welshmen, had led them blindly through the mountains to the only spot within hundreds of miles where they could have put down without being smashed in to eternity.

The odds had been a million to one, but they had won.

They had also lost, for all this explains how Gwyn Martin came to join me in Stalag Luft III, a dismal sprawl of shabby huts, barbed wire and machine-gun posts where Hermann Goering played host to Allied flyers unlucky enough to fall into his hands. Spread over the even, sandy Silesian plain where the dust gagged you in summer and the blizzards knifed through the jerry-built barracks in winter, the stalag was divided into numerous compounds. The smallest, removed from the main camp by several miles, was Fort Belaria.

Its *kommandant* boasted Belaria was escape proof. So, when it opened for business early in 1944, its original complement was selected from those old prisoners in the main camp who had persistently snubbed the *reichsmarschall* by their efforts to excuse themselves from his hospitality. In this "purge to Belaria" Gwyn and myself were included.

Among prisoners of war there were, generally speaking, three principal topics of conversation: progress of the war, food, and women, in order of priority. At Belaria we found another topic, of peak priority: bedbugs, or as

they came to be known in the bitter voluminous correspondence with the Germans, *bettwanzen*.

They were small insects, and to begin with not very numerous, so that for several months they were even welcomed as something of a wryly humorous distraction from the sordid monotony of prison routine.

There were bedbug races, solemn bedbug executions, and contests to see who could slaughter the most bugs in a given time—activities of signal service in preserving camp morale and our pre-capture levels of sanity.

With the advent of warmer weather, however, the novelty wore off. A succession of protests flowing from the senior Allied officer to the *kommandant* were of increasingly indignant tone. When these failed to bring redress the Swiss Commission was advised, and a formal protest laid before the International Red Cross in Geneva.

The German action, when it came, took the form of an indifferent program of fumigation. But the big, ramshackle wooden barracks were impossible to seal airtight, and while the old-fashioned sulphur candles left the camp choking and coughing for days, they seemed only to give the bedbugs new zest for their nightly hunting in the bunks.

From that time forward the ascendancy was with the bugs. Their numbers increased in staggering geometric progression and where during the spring months they had attacked singly or in pairs they now invaded us each night by whole divisions. You could actually hear them on the march, hear the repulsive plop, plop, plop as new arrivals parachuted down to the bunks from the barrack ceilings where they bred.

There was only token defense. The darkness after lights out was broken by the sporadic flaring of matches, as one man after another sought to rout at least one of the marauders by flame. But it was useless, and the futility was emphasized by the profanity that punctuated the long, itching torment of summer nights. A good night's sleep had become a memory, sweet but faint.

No. 426 Squadron Wellington bombers on the ground at Dishforth, England, February 1943.

When our misery had reached its unbearable zenith Gwyn Martin was suddenly inspired. It was on a hot day in late August; I remember because our underground radio had only just brought the news that the Allies had liberated Paris.

Gwyn and I had a stroke of rare luck that day. We had cultivated the acquaintance of a young German guard named Horst Reuter, a kid of about 18. He was a nice boy who didn't drink. He had a girl-friend in the town nearby. She was fond of chocolate, of which the Third Reich had little or none. Since we had some Red Cross chocolate bars, and Horst had only that day received his monthly ration of a litre bottle of brandy, he thought that perhaps we would like to have his bottle in exchange for two chocolate bars.

We took the bottle to a moderately secluded spot in the corner of the *sportsplatz*, lay down in the sunshine and drank it. It was very pleasant taking turns at the bottle. On the other side of the barbed wire we could see girls in fresh and bright print dresses pedalling their bikes along the highway. German fighters from a nearby aerodrome circled lazily overhead. The sun was warm, the breeze cool and it was good to be alive.

"Do you know," said Gwyn, "I know a place where there aren't any bedbugs."

"Sure, home," I said.

"No. Right here in this camp. And I think we can get ourselves a bunk there."

"Go on," I said. I was watching a pretty blonde *dienstmädel* walking along the highway on the arm of a Luftwaffe man. I felt tenderly for them.

"Yeah. In the cooler," said Gwyn. "All we have to do is get there."

The cooler was the isolated block of concrete cells in the *kommandantur* where as punishment prisoners were put in solitary confinement. Fifteen days was the usual term. Rations in the cooler were scanty, and solitary confinement meant exactly what it said. On the other hand prisoners were allowed all the reading material they wished.

"I never did read Gibbon's *Decline and Fall of the Roman Empire*," I said. "How are we going to get in the cooler?"

"Easy," said Gwyn. "We'll fake an escape."

"We might get shot," I said.

"Anything's better than the bedbugs. Anyway, we can play this dead safe. We could fix it so that Paul will be the guy to catch us in the act."

Paul Reemt-Heeren was a special guard working for the German security section, a ferret. He was a kind of house dick in a prison camp. It was his duty to smell out subversive activities and stop escapes before they could happen.

Paul was a friend. He lives in Emden now and I occasionally hear from him. At Belaria he made life considerably more comfortable both for Gwyn and me and just incidentally for himself by engaging in black market operations in such innocent items as onions, garlic, wine, lighter fluid and coal bricks for our stove. He took in exchange Lucky Strike cigarettes, Borden's sweetened condensed milk, chocolate bars and other Red Cross issue that came our way.

We found Paul later that afternoon. He was dispiritedly poking about the camp incinerator with the long iron rod he used for exploring suspected areas. He was visibly depressed.

"I went to see the *kommandant* this morning," he told us. "I haven't had any leave since the invasion of France. My family was bombed out of their house in Emden and the wife and kids have been evacuated to Magdeburg. I want to see how they are fixed there. They're having a tough time....

"But the *kommandant* just says, 'No leave!' When is this *verdammte* war going to end, anyway?"

Three weeks, we told him cheerfully.

Paul regarded us sourly.

"Like hell, three weeks....

"It will take us longer than that to throw you bastards back in to the Channel again!"

"Sure," we said, good naturedly. It's a dirty trick to kick a guy when he's down. "Sure," we said, but we kept grinning and Paul knew what we were thinking and he looked away and gave a little laugh. Paul was too smart not to know what the war score was.

"If I could get only a day or two," he said. "Just long enough to see the wife and kids and what kind of joint they're living in. But that *kommandant*; all he can say is *nein*!"

I could hear all the gears grinding around beneath

A display of Red Cross parcels for prisoners of war, June 1944.

Gwyn's shaggy black scalp, and I'm sure he must have heard mine. If ever the moment were tactically ripe this was it.

"Paul," I said, "do you suppose the *kommandant* would listen if you were suddenly to find a tunnel, or a radio, or catch a couple of prisoners trying to escape?"

That was just about the only way you could get leave, said Paul. The *kommandant* was like that, kept his troops in line with incentives.

"Why? What do you mean?" Paul's eyes narrowed and he looked at us sharply.

We told him quickly. Once or twice he glanced nervously over his shoulder while he listened. He was a bit doubtful at first, then warmed up a bit, and then just as quickly showed puzzlement and suspicion.

"What are you going to get out of it?" he asked. Paul was a practical fellow. A security guard in a prison camp has to be.

We told him: 15 days in the cooler with no bedbugs and plenty of quiet reading time. Paul looked a little shocked at that. He had had no idea that the bedbugs were that bad. He said he had never known any bedbugs.

It all went according to plan.

Each evening at 9 o'clock the grounds of the camp were cleared of all prisoners and the barracks locked up. About 8:30 on the evening following our chat with Paul we sauntered over to the wash house, a brick structure standing close to the wire, and busied ourselves on the pretence of scrubbing our socks, until shortly before 9 when the few remaining prisoners had left for their barracks.

Once the wash house was deserted we shinnied up some pipes by the wall and pushed open a trap door that gave access to the low loft above. The trap door had been placed there so the overhead piping could be inspected or repaired. We pushed the trap door back in to place and settled down to wait for Paul to make his appointed round.

"Might as well eat some of our escape rations right now," laughed Gwyn. "In a few minutes they'll take it all away from us!"

We had equipped ourselves to present reasonable facsimiles of escape-bound prisoners. We had a few Red Cross chocolate bars, some hard biscuits and other assorted odds and ends of food stuffed in our pockets. We also had pocketed a dog-eared map of the German State Railways, as well as a plan of the Danzig dock area, an escape chart so common that almost every prisoner had one. A few German banknotes added to the authenticity of our venture.

Paul arrived on schedule, and we set up the pre-arranged stomping and scuffling that was to be his cue to investigate. We made such a racket, in fact, that we learned later it was heard in half the barracks around the compound.

Paul's acting was superb.

When we pushed aside the hatch and peered down from the trap he was standing below us with a flashlight in one hand and his automatic pistol in the other. His eyes were flashing and his face flushed with excitement.

"*Kommen Sie heraus!*" he roared.

There was a grim menace in the beckoning gesture of the automatic, and for several apprehensive seconds I trembled at the thought that Paul might try to make a fake escape look really genuine by strewing a couple of corpses around.

"*Komm', komm'....*"

We went quietly. He walked along behind us with the automatic pointed at our backs. We went through the centre of the compound, with hundreds of wondering eyes looking at us from the barrack windows, and then out through the main gate to the guardhouse.

At the guardhouse they stripped and searched us, and while they were doing that the *kommandant* arrived and Paul had to tell his story. Once I looked at him while he was talking but quickly looked away because, when he saw me looking at him, Paul for one brief moment stopped talking and seemed to bite his lip to keep from laughing.

But even if he had laughed I don't think it would have mattered much. The *kommandant* was so excited he was only catching every 14th word. He kept glancing at Gwyn and me, then back to Paul again, and his face was a glowing mask of boyish joy. He kept bringing his hands together so that the fingertips of one hand caressed those of the other, and his lips were pursed in a serene grimace of satisfaction.

After Paul had finished his story the *kommandant* went over to the table and fished around among the odds and ends they had taken from our pockets until he came across the map of the Danzig docks. He picked it up and chortled happily and turned on us with a smirk.

"You're a long, long way from Danzig, boys!" he jeered. He grinned benignly at the guards and they grinned back at him, and nobody seemed to mind that we were grinning too. It was all as pleasant as a Rotary Club luncheon back at home.

"Give 'em their clothes and lock 'em up!"

I woke up next morning on the hard plank in the

antiseptically spotless little concrete tank in the cooler. I yawned and stretched voluptuously and reflected how luxurious it was to live and sleep without bedbugs.

Very shortly, I knew, the guard would come with my breakfast of mint tea and a slice of black bread, and bring me a basin and a jug of water so that I could wash. I knew the routine because I had been through it several times before.

When he came I would ask for pencil and paper, so that I could write down a list of the books I would require for my 15 days. During my last spell in solitary I had gone through Macaulay's History of England complete in five volumes. This time I would ask for Gibbon's *Decline and Fall*. The prospect of undisturbed rest and quiet study in this pleasantly severe monastic setting gave me one of the most blissful moments I had known in years.

An RAF Wellington bomber flies over the English countryside, circa 1940.

The key turned in the lock and I jumped to my feet and readied myself to ask for the pencil and paper before the guard might get away.

The door opened. The guard was there, but he had no mint tea and bread.

"Put on your boots," he said.

I put on my boots and he beckoned me into the corridor of the cell block and marched me into the orderly room where the *feldwebel* in charge was listening to a glowing account of how Germany's new rocket weapons were cutting the feet from under Eisenhower's doomed assault on Fortress Europa.

Gwyn was already in the orderly room. The *feldwebel* turned down the radio and looked at us with a superior grin.

"Such luck, such luck," he murmured. "The *kommandant* is such a pleasant fellow....He is very pleased this morning. Nobody yet has escaped from his compound. He is pleased. He is so pleased, in fact, that he has sent word you are not to be punished....

"Schmidt!...Take these men back to their barracks!"

When we looked around the compound for Paul that morning we couldn't find him. Later, when the sentries changed watch, we ran across Horst Renter and asked him where was Paul?

"*Ach*. Some people have all the luck. He's gone on leave. Five days. Gone to see his family. Took the train to Magdeburg this morning."

That night, while we lay sweating and scratching in our bunks, Gwyn struck a match, pursued a bedbug across his pillow and destroyed it with a sizzle and a pop.

"Do you know," he said wistfully, "but this is the first time in my life I think I've ever had that feeling a boy scout is supposed to have when he has done his good deed for the day? Funny, isn't it?"

"I don't know," I said. "All I know is that the war is almost over and now I never shall have a chance to read Gibbon's *Decline and Fall*."

And I never have. ↄ

PIGSWILL AND PRESTIGE
Kingsley Brown

Allied aircrew prisoners in Stalag Luft III never realized until after the war just how incredibly lucky they were to have had a Prussian aristocrat instead of some Nazi bullyboy as their *kommandant*. Ours was a baron.

Oberst (colonel) Freiherr Franz von Lindeiner-Wildau was a little on the elderly side, a professional soldier and WW I veteran who carried himself with the dignified stance he might have worn at the old kaiser's court at Potsdam.

He was nearing retirement age and it was no secret that he nursed an ambition to retire with the rank—and pay—of a general. Our knowledge of that aspiration was one of the winning cards we held when the *kommandant* sent for our senior officers one morning and sought to make a deal. The other high card in our hands had to do with the pigswill.

The *kommandant* had a problem.

A serious complaint had been lodged with headquarters in Berlin. There had been a mysterious epidemic in the pig population in the farm area surrounding the prison camp. One farmer after another had reported his pigs dying from no readily apparent cause. Eventually the local veterinarians had come up with the answer: The pigs had been killed by ingesting pieces of broken razor blades in the swill they were fed. Investigation showed that the swill had been coming from Stalag Luft III.

The *kommandant*, of course, knew how and why the bits of razor blades had found their way into the swill. Being the man he was, he didn't shout and scream about it. He accepted the fact that the prisoners had been deriving some small satisfaction by continuing their war effort through such little acts of sabotage. Killing German hogs aggravated the already tight food situation in the Reich.

"But it has to stop," he said. The high command took a grave view of sabotage, and there could be brutal reprisals. He didn't want that to happen. Sometime in the next few weeks, he went on, the inspector general of prison camps was due to arrive at Stalag Luft III. The subject of the murdered pigs would be high on the agenda and the *kommandant* felt it imperative that the inspector general be informed the practice had stopped.

RAF Wing Cmdr. Harry Day was spokesman for the prisoners. He, too, was a professional soldier, scion of an aristocratic British family, a nephew of the white rajah of Borneo and, like the *kommandant*, a WW I veteran. As a 16-year-old boy marine at the Battle of Jutland, he had won the Albert Medal for bravery under fire. The two men understood each other.

Wings didn't bother to deny the allegation about the razor blades.

"But, you know, Oberst, there really isn't that much swill leaving the camp, just a few potato peelings, mostly. Now if we had a supply of good, fresh, green vegetables—you know, carrots and cabbage and beets and the like—well, there would be a lot more swill for the pigs. Just give us some issues of fresh vegetables, and there'll be no more blades in the swill."

The *kommandant* brightened.

"I'm glad you see it that way," he said. He would make arrangements at once with the commissary people to augment our meagre diet with fresh vegetables. He would start the trucks rolling right away.

"It will keep the inspector happy," he added, affecting a somewhat pained grimace. Then he smiled. They were both professional soldiers with careers to think about; the *kommandant* knew that Wings would share his concern about promotion.

"Perhaps your boys could put on a good parade for him," he said. He thought it would be nice if just for once the prisoners turned out in smart formation instead of straggling on parade like a mob of derelicts. It could make the difference between his retiring as a half-pay colonel, and getting a general's pension.

Wings frowned.

"That wouldn't be too easy, Oberst," he said. "The boys aren't exactly in the mood for spit and polish, haven't the gumption for any real heel-clicking. Some of them are so slack they can barely salute properly. What they need badly, Oberst, is some red meat in their diet. Give 'em some energy, put 'em on their feet, so to speak. Yes, indeed, Oberst, a little meat in the rations and you've got yourself a parade!"

The day the inspector general arrived we were drawn up in squadron formation on the parade ground. It looked like graduation day at RMC or West Point, and when 1,200 pairs of heels clicked in the most incredible unison the German general and his aides were visibly stunned. Our *kommandant*, for his part, did his best to convey the impression that, thanks to him, that's the way it went every day.

We ate better that summer of 1943 than at any other time during our long incarceration. You can make deals—even with the enemy—when you know how to talk to him. ✃

A group of RCAF and RAF flight sergeants imprisoned in Stalag VIII B in Germany, sometime between 1942 and 1944.

NAMENSTAUSCH
Kingsley Brown

One of the few disadvantages of living a respectable, secure and law-abiding life is that one will never know the curiously exciting tingle of having an alias, of going under a name and identity other than one's own. On the other hand, an alias may lead to some awkward complications.

My first alias was Goleb Plasov, a Bulgarian steelworker. I had been born in the little village of Latulia, north of Sofia. My father was Yakov Plasov, and my mother's given name was Natasha. I had responded to an advertisement in a Sofia newspaper seeking workers for the German war industry, and through the *Arbeitsdienst* had been brought to Germany to work in the *Vereinigte Stahlwerke* plant at Liegnitz.

That alias, supported by an impressive forged ausweis complete with passport photo, lasted me only four days, the period I was free on my first, and abortive, escape from Stalag Luft 3 in the spring of 1943. Six million foreign workers moved about in Germany, so broken German aroused no suspicion. A Bulgarian identity was also chosen because extremely few Germans spoke Bulgarian. Neither could I; it wasn't necessary. An abominable "immigrant" German was convincing enough.

My first alias was not very eventful. We were picked up during a railway check and returned to our camp at Sagan.

My second alias, however, was something quite different, and led to a bizarre and unexpected sequel. It had been assumed to cover a second escape attempt, in December 1943, and in the company of a Czech air force officer, Joe Rix.

Joe's family lived close to the old Czech-German border. We had learned that many prisoners from "other ranks" camps were employed on working parties in the forests, on farms and in factories in the border area. It was our game plan to exchange identities with two enlisted men, join a working party, then make a break for the Czech underground.

The only place such a switch could be made was the central German PoW hospital at Lamsdorf, adjacent to Stalag 8B, one of Germany's biggest camps for "other ranks" Allied PoWs. Through the connivance and good offices of our camp medical officer, Maj. Edward Monteuis, a Scot taken prisoner at Dunkirk, we were admitted to the hospital at Lamsdorf. (As any doctor knows, there are some purported ailments that upon more competent professional examination turn out to be false alarms!)

The switch was made.

I suddenly became Sgt. Alfred Taylor, a London Cockney and RAF air gunner, while Joe Rix had the good fortune to find his alias in a Czech compatriot. On discharge from hospital Joe and I were delivered without incident to Stalag 8B at Lamsdorf, while two instant flight lieutenants, miraculously fitting in to the uniforms of Brown and Rix, went off by train to the officers' camp at Stalag Luft 3, some 100 miles to the west.

"But what a tangled web we weave
When once we practise to deceive."

I never fully understood that old proverb until we arrived in Lamsdorf.

It started out so well. We were both elated. We had been so clever; we had deceived the enemy. Everything augured well for the success of our operation.

For several days we basked in our status as rather mysterious new-comers among the denizens of Stalag 8B. This dirty, depressing, sprawling metropolis was a far cry from Hermann Goering's guesthouse for Allied officer aircrew at Stalag Luft 3. The motley population included thousands of British from the summer of Dunkirk, Canadian boys, irons on their wrists, taken at Dieppe, and sulky Palestinians from the Jewish battalions Rommel had captured at Tobruk.

Then the blow fell.

It was about mid-morning, on the fourth day in Lamsdorf, when we had the shock of hearing our names broadcast over the elaborate public-address system that reached every corner of the camp.

"Attention! Flt. Lt. Brown and Flt. Lt. Rix! Report at once to the *abwehr* officer at the main gate! Attention! Flt. Lt. Brown and Flt. Lt. Rix! Report at once…."

At about 15-minute intervals throughout the morning the message echoed monotonously through the miles of dingy barracks. We were dumbfounded. We couldn't understand what had gone wrong. All four of us had spent long hours in the hospital learning each other's identity. We were sure we had attained perfection in the business of being people we were not.

Only much later did we learn what had gone wrong. We had overlooked one small detail—to tell our exchange pair the number of our barrack block back at Stalag Luft 3. The ersatz Brown and Rix had been tripped up the moment they entered the camp at Sagan.

What should we do?

In that vast camp of 50,000 we might easily have gone into hiding. But the camp's Man of Confidence, a Dutch-Canadian warrant officer, advised against it.

"No dice! You'll have to turn yourselves in…We just can't risk a mass search by the *abwehr*. Not at this time. We are already hiding two or three. One of them's a kid who tossed a piece of chain into the turbine at a power plant….If they find him they'll hang him. We can't risk it. You'll just have to surrender. Tough luck!"

We saw his point. We marched down to the main gate and asked the guard for the *abwehr* officer. A few minutes later a *Wehrmacht* major was peering at us through the barbed wire. He was laughing.

"You don't fool me….You're not Brown and Rix!"

We insisted we were, but the *abwehr* man kept on shaking his head and grinning.

"I'm not a fool," he said. "Look, there are two British officers loose in that camp. You want me to believe that after all the trouble they went through to get in to the camp they are going to surrender the minute we ask for them? *Nichts*!"

155

He turned his back while we were still talking, and for the rest of the day the loudspeakers at every intersection blasted their demand that Brown and Rix report to the main gate.

We returned to the gate the next morning. The Man of Confidence was urging haste upon us; he was terrified lest the Germans mount a mass search. This time we were successful; the *abwehr* man led us off to the "cooler"—the big brick-and-concrete block of solitary punishment cells.

The *abwehr* major was still unconvinced.

"*Verstehen sie.* I don't know who you are. I don't care much either....All I do know is that you are not Brown and Rix. They are still in the camp....And we'll find them—sooner or later!"

There ensued 11 days of the most grotesque comedy I have ever known. To begin, the punishment block at Stalag 8B was pure Alice in Wonderland. Back at Stalag Luft 3 the solitary confinement cells were precisely that: for solitary confinement. Here at Lamsdorf the punishment block had all the disorderly charm of a stevedores' poker club. The cell doors, except for the occasional routine inspection by the orderly officer, were always open. Inmates spent most of their time congregated in the furnace room presided over by a big, handsome, good natured Yorkshire coal miner who was the real major domo of the block.

He, too, had been captured at Dunkirk. He was now a permanent fixture in the punishment block. But for the indulgence of an understanding German officer he ought to have been doing 10 years at hard labor in the *Wehrmacht* military prison at Fort Zinna. He had been convicted of illicit sexual intercourse with a German girl while on a working party, contrary to the Nazi blue law.

"It was just that her boy-friend was jealous," he said. "Only thing that worries me is, will my old lady back in Yorkshire find out about it when the war's over?"

We told him not to worry; war concealed a multitude of sins. "Anyway, she'll be so happy to have you home she won't give a damn, even if she did find out!"

That first evening in the furnace room our own anxieties had birth. We had just finished explaining to our new comrades why we were here, when a lean, haunted-looking individual emerged from the group to confront us.

"That's *Namenstausch*!" he said. "You switched names—*namenstausch*. Well, you've gone and done it now, boys! You wait....Look at me. I've been here a year and gone, all for *namenstausch*. You'll be here for the rest of your life! You'll see!"

He was quite agitated.

"Once you start on that road there's no end to it. After a while you forget who you are. Look, I've been everything. I've been a Frenchman and I've been a Dane. I think originally I was a Cypriot. Then I was once a Romanian Jew. Now nobody knows who I am, not even the Germans, and they don't care. They just leave me here. So they got you for *namenstausch*, eh? You'll be sorry!"

It made us nervous.

On the orderly officer's next visit we asked to see the *abwehr* major, and a little later were paraded to his office. He was quite pleasant, smiling throughout the interview.

"Look, boys. I don't know what those...two officers are up to. But they wouldn't be likely to surrender as easily as you did. Nothing doing!"

Back in the furnace room our Cypriot friend nodded in gloomy sympathy. "What did I tell you, eh? You're going to be here with me forever. Say, either you fellows play chess?"

A couple of German guards dropped in to the furnace room that evening, and a big poker game was abandoned in favor of a spirited discussion about the authenticity of werewolves and the magic of *walpurgis nacht*. The Germans were solid, honest peasant types, and superstitious. They enjoyed a visit to the furnace room because the inmates invariably had good American cigarettes from their Red Cross parcels.

During the talk about werewolves I was suddenly inspired. Joe was back in his cell, and I interrupted him and the Cypriot in the middle of a chess game.

"Joe! Fingerprints! Remember? Back at Sagan they have our fingerprints. Why didn't somebody think of that?"

We couldn't wait for morning to see the *abwehr* major. For once he stopped smiling.

"*Bestimmt!… Fingerabdrucken!* Come with me!"

Ten minutes later we were back in the furnace room, washing the ink off our fingers and wondering how long it would take to get the prints to Sagan and win our release. Not long. The day after next we were marched out of the punishment block and paraded, not before the *abwehr* officer but this time before the *kommandant* himself. He was flanked by both the *abwehr* man and his adjutant. All three spoke close to perfect English.

We were formally on charge, we were told.

The offence: *namenstausch.* Did we have anything to say before judgment was passed? These Germans always made some considerable effort to appear "korrect."

Common sense dictated that we let the hearing take its course. But occasions of drama were so welcome a break in the tenor of a prisoner's life that the temptation to make the most of it, and perhaps too much of it, was irresistible. I fell for the temptation.

"You have no jurisdiction, *mein Herr.*" I was now no longer an air force pilot and prisoner of war. I was playing Clarence Darrow before the Supreme Court. The Walter Mitty in me was having a field day.

"No jurisdiction?" said the adjutant.

"No, *mein Herr.* We are air force personnel. We are under the personal protection of the *reichsmarschall,* Hermann Goering…the *Wehrmacht* has no jurisdiction to try us."

The *kommandant* looked perplexed, and turned to the adjutant. He in turn, a little flustered, grabbed at a big volume that looked very like our own *King's Rules and Regulations,* and sifted through the pages. He looked up in frustration.

"That doesn't seem to be covered here.…Gentlemen, we shall have to refer your case to the judge advocate

general in Berlin." The court was adjourned.

Back in the cooler Joe Rix turned on me in fury.

"You stupid, God damn smart-alec! What the hell did you do that for? Now we'll be here for weeks while they debate the case in Berlin. They would only have given us 15 days in any case.…You bloody idiot!" A Czech in the RAF picks up idiomatic English quickly!

I told him I was sorry. The time passed quickly enough, what with chess, poker and endless philosophy in the furnace room in a fog of tobacco smoke, and it was only days before we were summoned once more before the *kommandant.* The adjutant seemed smugly pleased.

"It has been determined by the judge advocate general that our military law applies to all branches of the armed forces, yours as well as ours.…You are within our jurisdiction."

This time we had nothing to say.

"The sentence is 15 days solitary confinement and hard arrest. But we are sending you back to your own camp. You will serve the sentence there."

That didn't seem quite fair. We had already spent time in the cells at Lamsdorf. The prospect of solitary at Stalag Luft 3, with no furnace room, no Yorkshire major domo, no chess, cigarettes or poker, was forbidding.

I couldn't help myself; I had to be Clarence Darrow again.

"But *mein Herr,* we have already served 11 days of solitary here in 8B."

The *kommandant* frowned, pursed his lips, looked at the adjutant, then shrugged his shoulders and smiled. He addressed his adjutant.

"Give him a receipt for 11 days!"

The receipt was honored at Stalag Luft 3, but I had already learned my lesson. Never again would I be guilty of *namenstausch.* Unlike so many others, I have found my identity and I'm happy with it. I don't want any other.

And I still have that receipt for 11 days, just to fortify my resolution. It is one of my most prized possessions! ☙

WAITING GAMES IN A POW CAMP
Kingsley Brown

"Hear the latest, old boy? Wow! Twenty-five nurses have just been taken prisoner. They're on their way here now!"

It was just one more of what we called in Stalag Luft III a "latrine rumor," the kind of phoney news dreamed up in the prison camp wash-house.

"Yeah, 25 of them, they say, right from the States. Shot down in North Africa in a Yank Dakota. Boy, things are looking up!"

There was not, of course, one grain of truth in it, something most of us knew the moment we heard it. In RAF vernacular, it was not "pukka gen." But it was the kind of latrine rumor we loved to hear, very definitely the stuff of which prison camp morale was made.

There were no women in German camps for Allied PoWs (unlike those that held Russia's female front-line fighters!), but by some mysterious sorcery woman's spell drifted through the barbed wire to become a vital component of the prisoner of war psyche. In one metaphysical form or another the other sex was always close to us.

News about women rated on a par with news about the war, which came to us mostly through our own underground radio link, plus the daily communique from the OKW (*Oberkommando der Wehrmacht*). News about women came from many sources, including the new prisoners fresh from home. The Germans thrust them at us every few weeks in groups we came to call "the purges."

The purges were mobbed the moment the gates had closed. Already somewhat disoriented and confused, they were invariably puzzled by their reception. They seemed to find some difficulty in understanding why the thing uppermost in the mind of "old prisoners" was "What happened to Jane?"

Jane, as overseas veterans may recall, was the heroine of a popular British newspaper comic strip. She was marvellously endowed with tantalizing legs that dissolved upwards into a torso of almost unbearable callipygian beauty. Jane's story was one exciting and hilarious adventure after another, all marked by the common denominator of Jane being stripped of most, if not all, of her clothing.

"Jane? Let's see now. Hey, Bill, what was that last episode of Jane? Oh, yeah! She was trapped by some Nazi spies but she escaped....jumped out a window—then her dress got snagged in some brambles and she got stripped down to her bra!...Sure, Jane's doing just fine!"

The adventures of Jane were but one of the many influences keeping alive the libido of thousands of PoWs during the long years of captivity. But where Jane was the brilliant creation of a cartoonist (who assuredly deserved a decoration!), a myriad of other Janes lived in the flesh, and in the minds of all those men without women.

There were, for instance, the Hollywood film stars, whose eight-by-ten glossies, courtesy of mail from home, brightened the dingy recesses of the three-tier bunks. There were Betty Grable and Lana Turner, Rita Hayworth and Veronica Lake and a score of other lovelies. Then there were the more personal pin-ups, as well, of the girls the boys had left behind.

I remember well one pin-up of a Halifax girl, a ravishing member of the Junior League set who had kindled a torch in the hearts of a never-ending succession of servicemen passing through that East Coast port on their way overseas. Her picture, sultry and inviting, was pinned to the wall next to the bunk of an RCAF navigator who had courted her furiously during his three weeks' embarkation stay at Y Depot in Halifax.

That pin-up provoked one of the few cases of personal violence in our camp. A new prisoner, with a much more recent Halifax romance fresh in his memory, was stunned to confront his inamorata staring at him from the shelter of another man's bunk. There was a fight, a split lip and a bloody nose, and then, in a matter of days, the pin-up discreetly disappeared.

Affairs of the heart were a welcome source of prison camp gossip and entertainment. Some were more sensational than others. Few could rival that of the Czech fighter pilot who arrived with the almost incredible accusation that he had been deliberately shot down by his own RAF flight commander.

The Czech had been flying the number two position covering the flight commander in a dogfight with Germans over the north coast of France. Quite suddenly, in the middle of the melee, he said, the flight commander had throttled back, positioned his Spitfire above and behind him, and opened fire. The Czech had baled out of his burning Spit and was lucky to survive.

He was a big, dark, handsome fellow.

"When I get back to England I'm going to kill that bastard," he raged. His explanation for the episode was quite straightforward.

"He was jealous….But just because I was taking his wife out was no reason to want to kill me, was it?"

The Czech was robbed of his threatened revenge; within a few weeks we had word that his flight commander had "gone for a Burton."

Then there was *Vorlager Fanny.*

We attached that alliterative handle to the rather pretty young German woman who worked as a secretary in what was known as the Vorlager, the block of administrative offices just the other side of the wire near the main gate.

It began innocently enough with Fanny occasionally coming to the office window, primping coyly and giving us a flirting wave of the hand. We gave her all the encouragement we could, and Fanny grew bolder. She enlisted the support of some of the younger administrative officers and staged an elaborate and provocative tableau at the office window. One of the Luftwaffe officers would grab her around the

An artist's rendition of Jane, the heroine of a popular overseas newspaper comic strip.

waist with one arm, kiss her in an ecstatically tight embrace, then with his free arm slowly pull down the window shade.

We applauded wildly. *Vorlager Fanny* is a fond and happy memory!

For those who could read German, the daily newspaper afforded yet another kind of romantic stimulus. The personal columns of German dailies sometimes filled whole pages in a single issue, and in a land where virtually every able-bodied man was at the front, or had already met the *Heldentod*, each day brought its plaintive quota of little notices, inserted by hopeful females looking for a man.

A long winter's evening would often find a huddle of three or four prisoners thumbing avidly through the heart-throb columns of the *Völkischer Beobachter* or the *Frankfurter Zeitung.*

"Here's just the one for you, Jim! Geli, it says, aged 20…blonde and slender, likes theatre and walking in the woods—and she wants an older man….That's you, Jim; you're 28!"

"And oh boy! listen to this! She's Annaliese… Box 51…warm, sympathetic nature…and lonely.…I'll think about that one. But will you get a load of this?… Marlene, 23.…

Stories in the apocryphal category, such as that of the shot-down nurses, included a whole repertory involving camps where Russian women prisoners were incarcerated. One of the most popular scenarios, which routinely went the rounds about every six months, followed an escaping Brit or Yank who had found refuge by wriggling through the wire in to a Russian women's camp. Three days and nights later, he surrendered to the Germans, more dead than alive, and was now recuperating in the camp lazarette.

The German guards, too, sometimes contributed to our *ersatz* sexuality. For those who had come to know one more than casually, a guard could be the channel for what might be termed "vicarious sex." There's a bit of Casanova in every man, and with a little prompting a guard would boast of his philandering, playing a surrogate role in our famished fantasies.

There was, for instance, Hans, who I had come to know well over the years. Hans is not his real name. Today he lives happily with his wife and family in Emden. His not unforgivable wartime indiscretions shall remain forever concealed.

His wife and four children had been bombed out of their home, and now dwelt in a refugee area where he saw them only seldom. But Hans had a mistress in the little town of Sagan, adjacent to Stalag Luft 3. Emmy also had four children, but her husband was serving in the *Wehrmacht* infantry on the Russian front.

Hans called Emmy's husband a bad man: "*Ein böse Mensch.*"

"Why, what's wrong with him?" I asked.

"He runs around with other women!"

Hans' affair with Emmy titillated us. After he had enjoyed a weekend leave we never neglected on Monday morning to wheedle out of him every detail of his rendezvous.

One such Monday morning romance report stands out. Hans had visited Emmy on a Sunday afternoon.

"*Ach*! It was no good. Nothing went right.…We sent the kids out to play and locked the door.…But they kept coming back and hammering at the door and saying '*Mutti, Mutti, was ist los?*' (Mummy, Mummy, what's the matter?). We had to let them in. The day was ruined!"

"Hans," I said. "You should do what we do back in Canada. Sunday afternoons we send the kids to Sunday school—then we're home free!"

Hans swore.

"That's what's wrong with Germany," he said, "No Sunday school anymore!"

There were periods, however, in which our interest in the opposite sex was diminished. When the Red Cross parcels failed to arrive and rations were short, hunger was an effective sedative. This was never illustrated better than in the last months of the war when a competition was held among the camp's artists for the best cartoon depicting a prisoner's homecoming.

The winning picture, thumbtacked to an honored space on the latrine wall, portrayed the freed PoW, dufflebag over his shoulder, hurrying up the garden path to greet his wife at the door of a typical English cottage. A diaphanous and clinging negligee revealed a gorgeous figure of such voluptuous charm as to drive a man wild.

The cartoon's caption?

"What have you got to eat, dear?"

A BIRTHDAY TO REMEMBER
Kingsley Brown

I celebrated my 32nd birthday in the little village of Gross Hartmannsdorf in German Saxony. I should never have known that such a place existed had it not been for an ill-starred attempt to escape from Stalag Luft 3, a German prison camp in Lower Silesia.

I was accompanied by a young British fighter pilot, Gordon Brettell, a typical British public school boy: Cheltenham through Cambridge to flying a Spitfire in the RAF. It was a first attempt for both us. Sadly, Gordon was one of the fifty Allied airmen shot by the Gestapo, exactly one year later, after what was titled The Great Escape.

We slipped through the wire on the night of March 27, 1943, tramped the woods and highways and rode the trains for three days until we were picked up by railway police while we were warming ourselves and drinking beer in the station waiting room in the city of Chemnitz.

The police turned us over to the Gestapo, and the long, detailed interrogation gave us more than a few anxious moments. But our interrogator turned out to be a rather rare sample of Gestapo boss. He was an old veteran of WW I who had his own memories of being a prisoner of war in France, and of making a successful escape. So what had begun as a rather harrowing interview ended, almost unbelievably, in joviality and good-natured banter.

But our Gestapo man must have been a little unclear on just how to get us back to camp and we soon found ourselves incarcerated in a tiny cell located under the eaves of a four-storey factory building in Gross Hartmannsdorf. The place had been converted into a kind of barracks to house French and Russian prisoner work gangs—Germany's slave laborers.

It was far from Waldorf luxury. The cell measured about eight by six feet, with a plank platform for a bed, a wooden block for a pillow and two rough, brown blankets. There was no other "furniture." It must have

Technical Sergeant F.S. Zink of the United States Army Air Force holds a home-made compass that he used in escaping from a German PoW camp.

served as some kind of punishment cell. The barbed wire over the tiny, narrow window was scarcely necessary. The window opened on a sheer four-storey drop to the street pavement below.

That first night we were uncomfortable and restless. But came the dawn and I suddenly remembered that it was April 1 and my birthday.

Around breakfast time a guard opened the door to bring us a ration of black bread and some mint tea. He was a middle-aged man probably considered too old for front-line service. He told us he came from Hamburg and wanted to know how long we thought the war was going to last. We had a pleasant chat; I told him this was one hell of a way for a man to spend his birthday, and he laughed at the joke.

Clearly, there was nothing anyone could do about it, but I just couldn't allow the day to pass without mentioning the fact. After all, one's birthday is something no one can take away from you. On that particular day in 1943, apart from the clothes I stood in, a birthday was all I had.

About an hour later things began to happen.

The door rattled open; it was our Hamburg guard again. He had with him two men whom we had seen briefly the day before, huddled in the Gestapo office in Chemnitz. Still in United States Army uniform, they had been captured in North Africa, but had jumped from a moving prison train in Germany in an abortive escape.

The guard, with a conspiratorial grin, explained that the Americans might join us in our cell and remain for the day. It was his birthday present for me, he said, and he appeared positively delighted in his role of host. He even shook my hand and wished me a *"glückliches Geburtstag!"*

The two Yanks were about as unlikely a couple as we had ever seen. One was an officer, scion of a patrician family in Scarsdale, Long Island, and a graduate of Princeton. He had a lanky grace and spoke good German. His buddy was an enlisted man, a former New York City policeman of Italian stock, who spoke only Brooklynese and Italian.

They were an entertaining pair, with an almost incredible story. At one point in their short-lived freedom, while walking a German highway in broad daylight flaunting their U.S. Army uniforms, they had been accosted by a German motorcycle cop. They had thought this the end of the line, then stood in dumbfounded amazement as the cop lectured them about the danger of walking on the wrong side of the road, and then took off.

But my birthday party was not over yet.

That evening, our Americans still with us, the guard rattled his keys again and brought more guests, four or five French prisoners from the floor below. Nor was that all; the Frenchmen came with cakes and cookies and cigarettes, and the guard brought extra rations of ersatz chicory coffee in big steaming jugs.

It was a night to remember. We were all squatted on the floor on our haunches, squeezed in to the tiny cell elbow to elbow, suffocating from the deadly Gauloise cigarettes our French guests had brought.

Every half-hour or so our Hamburg guard, sometimes with another smirking guard in tow, would drop in. Then for a spell we would all be joined—British, French, American and German alike—in a disdaining indifference to the war that divided us and by our common hearty dedication to squeezing a little joy out of life.

It was late that night when the guards took our guests to their respective cells. The heavy door clanged shut; Gordon and I stretched out on the wooden plank to sleep and dream it all over again. My 32nd birthday was over. It was, I think, the finest I have ever known. ✍

CHRISTEL'S KITCHEN
Kingsley Brown

We were midway through the Battle of Berlin when I met Christel Achtelik, and the day is crowded with memories. The first, one of the sharpest, focuses on two middle-aged women gathering spring flowers in a field flanking the main highway between Luckenwalde and Potsdam. It was a few days after the Russian breakthrough across the Oder, and about as long before the collapse of the third Reich.

Memory falters on the kind of flowers the women were picking. I think they were little yellow things. But I recall quite clearly the color of the machine-gun tracers etching a lazy trajectory over the women's shawled heads. It was orange red.

The Russians had mounted machine-guns and mortars in the ditch alongside the highway, and were firing at unseen targets in the pine woods on the other side of the field. Elements of Gen. Busse's 9th German Army were holding out in the woods, hoping desperately to break out for a dash to the Elbe and sanctuary in the West. There were about 12,000 of them, and they were making things difficult for the Russian armor and transport moving up the highway to the Berlin front.

We had an excellent view of it all from our prison camp, Stalag 3A, a mile or so north of the town of Luckenwalde. We had been liberated several days earlier by the 3rd Guards Tank Regt. of the 1st Ukrainian Army, but liberation was only a word. The battle now flowed around us, behind us and over us. We had no choice but to watch it, and listen to the noise of history.

It was while watching the women gathering the spring flowers that I was struck by the strange surrealism of the scene. It was all bizarrely beautiful, like a dream in slow motion. There was the sunshine and blue sky, and the moist warmth of the earth, and the fresh greenery of April. The mortars fired at spaced intervals, and there was a deep silence between the shots.

The two women were quite unmoved by the gunfire. A few seconds after each shot there was a detonation in the woods and a splintering of trees. The machine-guns chattered in the short, measured bursts that marked seasoned gunners, and the tracers drifted leisurely across the fields, arcing high over the women's heads and into the trees.

It was our first venture out of the prison camp. It had been the order of the senior Allied officer that the prisoners, for their own safety, remain within the camp boundary, a sanctuary from the dangerous and shifting battleground. There were Russian guards around the perimeter, but they were human; they were not insensitive to the yearning of long-imprisoned men for some small, limited taste of freedom. They looked the other way when some of us trickled through the wire to explore the exciting wonderland beyond.

Will Higgins shared my first breath of freedom that morning. We were both air force, with an itch to savor once more that unique and indefinable smell of aircraft, so we headed for the nearby Luftwaffe airfield. There was little left but wreckage. The hangars were a mass of collapsed roofing and twisted girders, and a lingering wisp of smoke trailed above the ashes of a barrack block. Dozens of shattered aircraft, including some gliders, littered the tarmac.

There was no one around but a group of schoolboys, applying their cheerful energy to dismantling some of the wrecked aircraft. One of them was busily removing the perspex canopy from the cockpit of a glider.

"A cab for my wagon," he explained. "I'll have the best wagon in Luckenwalde!"

We asked the boys why they weren't at school. With the guns hammering all around it must have seemed a stupid question. The boys stopped what they were doing, one of them giggled, then they all looked at each other and laughed.

"Russians shot the schoolmaster!"

We weren't shocked. So the schoolmaster was dead,

but it was a fine April morning, and the boys were free to pillage a military aerodrome with all its wonders. They were young and healthy and life was good. Somehow it was easy to forgive them for laughing.

We wandered away from the airfield, watched some hungry displaced slave laborers digging up a farmer's newly-planted seed potatoes, then strolled through the woods and came upon a big fish-pond in what seemed to have been a private estate. Some prisoners were trying for fish with threads and bent pins. They weren't having much luck until a Russian soldier happened along and lobbed a hand grenade in to the pond. In moments the water was silvered over with fish. There would be fresh fish with the beans that night.

A little later that morning we met Christel Achtelik. The Achteliks lived not far from the stalag, in the Weinberge, a little row of charming middle-class homes nestled on a wooded slope overlooking Luckenwalde.

A girl of about 18, she was out in front of the house, wearing a bright print apron, and fussing over some spring bulbs. We stopped, and in our best *kriegsgefangenen Deutsch* remarked what a pleasant spring day it was. The girl talked to us, her mother came to the door, and we brought out our Red Cross cigarettes, Lucky Strikes. After we had talked a little more the mother invited us in to the house.

When we sat down in the kitchen I suddenly found myself struggling to hold back tears. After all these years I was in a woman's kitchen, and it seemed more than I could bear. It was all there, just as it used to be when we were children. There was the kitchen and pans shining on the wall, pretty print curtains at the window, and the comfortably-worn cushions on the kitchen chairs.

But I think it was mostly the aprons, the vision of two women in aprons, that brought me so close to tears. Life had magically become warm and

wonderful. The mother put the kettle on the stove, and Christel brought out cups and saucers. They were real cups and saucers, with a pattern of flowers and little golden curlicues, not at all like the big, ugly earthenware *Reich* mugs we used in the camp.

We had mint tea, green and savory, and smoked more Lucky Strikes. Christel introduced her small sister, Barbara, who was only five, and told us about their father, Herr Achtelik. He was serving in the *Kriegsmarine*, in submarines. They had heard from him last from Kiel, but that had been six months ago.

Will and I told them where we came from, and about our families, and how we hoped we might be going home soon. We didn't talk much about the war, because it was all around us. There was nothing to say about it.

The stalag had never seemed so wretched and dreary as it did that afternoon when we arrived back from Christel's place. The stench of stale sweat and musty bedding, potatoes and sour bread was something we hadn't noticed before. But the food situation had improved. The Russians had given us access to an enormous *Wehrmacht* supply depot at Fort Zinna, about 20 miles south. The big white concrete warehouses were brimming with such staples as beans, barley and margarine and, for good measure, hundreds of cases of a cheering *vin ordinaire*.

There was actually a glut of a thick bean soup in camp the next day. We found a four-litre stone crock, filled it with soup, then carried it through the wire, across the fields and through the woods to Christel's place. We knew they had little to eat. The battle was not yet over, and there had been no time to organize food for the German civilian population.

And so it was that the Achtelik kitchen became an enchanting refuge for us. Each day we waited impatiently in the stalag for the noon issue of bean soup, then set off for the Weinberge with the big stone crock. In the meantime the battle had been slowly ebbing away from Luckenwalde. Only during the night did we hear a desultory rattle of machine-gun fire as little groups of German infantry made their gambling dash across the highway in the faint hope of reaching the Elbe. Some made it; others helped to fill the town hospital, or found a hiding place with townsfolk.

It was not until our fourth or fifth daily pilgrimage that I sensed a shadow over our visits. Twice Christel had not been at home when we arrived with the soup, and for some reason her mother had seemed disturbed and ill at ease. She chatted pleasantly enough, and welcomed us with as much maternal warmth as if we had been her sons. Yet there was no mistaking, barely beneath the surface, a measure of anxiety and disquiet. On those occasions when Christel blew in, I didn't miss that millisecond exchange of glances between the two women, nor could I fail to notice Christel's effort to mask some obvious embarrassment.

Higgins and I talked about it on our way back to camp that afternoon, and an explanation quickly came to mind. These people were good, solid, respectable German townsfolk, the kind of people who would not wish to be 'talked about' in their nice, middle-class community, war or no war. Repeated visits from two strange men might compromise their respectability. And so, reluctantly, for the sake of Christel and her mother, we determined not to visit the little house in the Weinberge anymore.

For me, it was a grievous decision, and hard to accept. The following day Higgins was drafted for truck-loading duty at Fort Zinna, and when the soup issue came at noon I was overwhelmed by the thought of Christel's kitchen. My resolve evaporated; I filled the stone crock once more and set out for the Weinberge.

Christel's mother was there, as usual, and little Barbara was playing outside. Frau Achtelik poured the bean soup into several smaller containers, we had a cigarette and she made a cup of mint tea.

She appeared even more agitated than before, made a brave stab at small talk and then, suddenly, with tears in her eyes, the truth came stumbling out.

"It's Christel," she said. "Christel....She is afraid you'll be angry with her...about the soup....It's the soup....Please don't be angry with her. We haven't had the soup....Christel takes it to the soldiers, the wounded....She's afraid you'll be angry...."

And so once again, in that kitchen, I came close to tears, as Christel appeared in a new and beautiful dimension. And I was suddenly reminded of that nocturnal machine-gun fire, as Gen. Busse's boys tried to make it across the highway. Some had made it; some had died; some had been wounded and were holed up wherever they found shelter in Luckenwalde.

And Christel had been playing Florence Nightingale for her fighting and wounded compatriots.

Many, many months later, back home in Canada and with the war only a memory, I received a letter from Christel. When I opened the envelope a photograph dropped out; it was a picture of Christel and her little sister Barbara. My wife was at my side. She picked up the photo, and with an arched glance and a feigned note of shock, said: "Is this your German family?"

She was only joking, of course, but somehow or other, that is the way I best remember them! ☙

ESCAPE
John Grogan

It was January, 1945, and bitterly cold. We were prisoners of war struggling along a snow-covered road in Czechoslovakia. Some had been in prison camps since the fall of France, others like myself since the Dieppe raid. Now the Germans had us on the move to keep us from being liberated by the fast-moving Russian army. Already we had crossed the Oder and Elbe rivers and the Sudeten mountains.

The nervous German guards, their faces dark under their helmets, herded us on with shouts, curses and blows.

Some were left along the road side; sick men who could not carry on. They lay where they fell, and that terrible winter reached out and embraced them. Stronger men, who had sworn they would stick it out, also lay there, their bodies riddled by bullets from Allied planes.

American bombers moved in this area in the light of day, Canadian and British by night, and Russian fighter-planes at anytime. The roar of propellers, the hammering of machine-guns, and the crash of exploding bombs sent prisoners and guards alike scrambling for cover in the ditches. Anything that moved was fair game.

The road ahead led unendingly into the night. I felt drowsy and my gait became mechanical. I thought of houses with people lying in warm beds not worrying about the snow falling outside. The man in front of me, one of the survivors of my regiment, walked with drooped shoulders. The snow fell on his head and on his bent back.

The column stretched for miles. Dead men lay on both sides of the road. The snow had settled over their uniforms making it impossible to see whether they were allies, Germans, or in the striped uniform of the Jew.

The thought of escape was never far from my mind. Artillery flashes and rumbling from the direction we had come told us the Russians were not far behind. Perhaps I could make my way back?

My chance came one evening after nearly two months of marching. It was now March 3rd, 1945.

The barn where we were to sleep this night was surrounded by a stone wall, eight feet high, inclining to twelve feet at the gate. Guards were posted, and a search light on the back of a truck made ready. Rumour had it we would get hot soup, the first hot food in three days. The men were excited by the prospect.

I made up my mind. This was the place, the time, during the confusion that always accompanied the soup issue. I thought of the hot soup, but consoled myself with a vision of the food I would get from the Czechoslovak people.

Someone shouted, "Soup up." Men ran in every direction. Some ran to hold a place in the line, others to the barn for mess tins. It was dark now. The sweeping ray of the search light moved back and forth along the wall. At intervals the beam played on the long line of hungry men, then back to the wall.

The light moved slowly, from left to right. I intended to go over the wall on the left, at its lowest point. I watched the beam of light on the wall. I would make my move when it reached the center. Now, I thought and I moved to the left. Then something went wrong. A guard came running straight at me, rifle thrust out in front. He went on by me, towards the soup line. A fight had started there. Because of the disturbance another guard was placed by the wall near where I had chosen to go over.

As I stood there thinking about it, a German soldier went by carrying over his right shoulder a huge fork full of hay. I fell in step on his right. The hay shielded me from the guards. I prayed he would not shift it to his other side. He didn't and I walked through the gate and around the end of the wall. I crouched close to the wall for a few minutes, then walked swiftly past the Germans in their wagons, on out of the area. If all went well, I would have seven or eight hours before being missed.

I kept to the road, walking fast, diving into the ditch when anything approached. Just before daylight I left the road and plodded through a muddy field patched with snow towards a clump of trees on a hill. From here,

Canadian prisoners of war are led through Dieppe, France, after they were captured on August 19, 1942.

through the grey dawn, I could see the outline of a small village. Exhausted and hungry, I picked a house off by itself, then curled up on the ground and waited. I dozed off, and perhaps an hour went by. When I looked at the house again there was a thin trickle of smoke coming from the chimney. I was startled to see, to the left of me and further along, a small airfield, and the shapes of planes huddled together, a sentry walking among them.

I made my way to the house and knocked at the back door. It was opened by a plump, middle-aged woman in a flowered apron. She did not seem surprised and, motioning me inside, shut and locked the door. From the depths of a huge cupboard she produced a bottle of schnapps, a loaf of bread, and a chunk of fat pork. She sat and watched as I ate, smiling happily and talking in her own language. I ate, drank, and I talked in a mixture of German and Polish. I could not stay long. This woman was putting herself in great danger should the Germans find out she had helped me.

When I was ready to go she became agitated, gesturing, pointing, and making signs with her hands, indicating airplanes. I had learned how to say thank you in many languages, and I used all of them now, as I tried to assure her that I knew there was an airfield close by, and that I had no intention of going in that direction. I left the house, moved to the right towards some thin pines, keeping to this cover for about a mile where the pine broke into a clearing. Just below in an open field was a straw stack. I would hole-up there until evening.

A sign was posted at the gate leading into the field. Several more like it were posted around the fence. Two words of the sign that I interpreted readily were, "forbidden and dangerous." Everything is forbidden and dangerous, I thought, as I burrowed well into the straw stack. It was warm and comfortable. I was soon asleep.

Several times I was awakened by the drone of airplanes. But I came wide awake when I heard the rattle of machine-gun fire. I crouched, trembling. A plane

German soldiers guard prisoners of war following the August 19, 1942, raid on Dieppe, France.

swooped low over the stack, spattering bullets in the straw. The first was followed by three more, then only the sound of their receding motors. I waited a moment, then ran out of the field, towards the woods beyond.

As I went through the fence I noticed the sign again. Then I understood what the woman in the house was trying to tell me. I was numb as I stood in the woods and watched the German planes circle and come back to the practice target. I headed back in the direction of some hills and some time later I made my way into a town that had been taken and held by the Russians.

The sun was shining. What was left of the winter snow was fast melting. A Russian officer with a big smile shook my hand. From his tunic pocket he took a silver cigarette case and offered it to me. He spoke in English.

"Take a cigarette, comrade."

My eyes filled with tears, as I puffed on the strong Russian cigarette. The war was finally over for me. ✍

Canadian prisoners captured during the August 19, 1942, raid on Dieppe, France.

THE GREAT FRIENDSHIP
Douglas How

He left school before graduating because his athletic talents got him a job when the Depression made them hard to find. For the next four years he worked in hard-rock gold mines and played softball and basketball in Northern Ontario. Then he spent a year riding the rods, hopping freight trains all over North America because "I figured there was going to be a war and this could be my last chance to see everything."

On the day war was declared in September, 1939, he was a 21-year-old cowpoke on a ranch near Empress, Alberta. Within 24 hours Clark Wallace (Wally) Floody planted his lanky, 6 ft. 4 in. frame on one more freight car and headed home to Toronto to enlist.

"It sounded," he says, "a lot more interesting than being a cowboy."

Floody had never heard of a millionaire shoe-manufacturer's son named George Rutherford Harsh who had, friends said, "commanded every avenue to happiness." Even if he had, he would have considered it entirely improbable that their paths would ever cross.

He was only 10 in 1928 when Harsh created a sensation by confessing, at 18, to the "thrill killing" of a store clerk in Atlanta, Ga.—the final, fateful act in a series of armed robberies by a gang of five wealthy college kids bent on proving they could commit the perfect crime.

Three lawyers, six psychiatrists and a $500,000 trust fund Harsh's father had left him failed to save him from a death sentence. When it was commuted to life imprisonment Harsh said this was because his family was "white, wealthy, and influential, for I was guilty as hell."

Harsh endured six brutal pick-and-shovel years in a chain gang, made friends among the convicts and finally helped in the escape of an alcoholic ex-priest who had tutored him. By 1939 he was a medical aide with no real hope of ever being free. Then, 13 months after Wally Floody hopped that freight, Harsh did something that changed everything. When an ice storm prevented his doctor-superior from reaching the prison hospital, he saved a fellow convict's life by removing his inflamed appendix. In November, 1940, Georgia's governor pardoned him.

"It was humbling to receive mercy," he wrote.

By then Floody had been given his missing school diploma by a sympathetic principal whose recommendation "made me sound like a potential air marshal," had married lively Betty Baxter and was enjoying his training as an RCAF fighter pilot.

Harsh tried newspaper reporting, but found people kept whispering about his past. He turned down an offer by ex-convicts to become a hired gun in the numbers racket. Instead he headed for Montreal and was accepted by the RCAF as a bomber-gunner. He was found to have exceptional night vision and led his class in training. He became an officer and, he'd note wryly, "a gentleman."

He got overseas about the time PO Floody's Spitfire squadron went out "looking for trouble" on a sweep over France. They got it. In a dogfight with Messerschmitts at noon on a day in October, 1941, Floody was shot down.

"I took to my parachute," he grins now, "and missed my lunch."

Instead, as German soldiers closed in, a little old lady came out of her house and poured him a glass of cognac, then scolded the soldiers for hurrying him. He ended up in Stalag Luft III, a prison camp for Allied airmen in a pine forest 130 km southeast of Berlin.

In the next year George Harsh flew numerous bombing raids. He recalled deadly duels with night fighters and "the insane sensation of feeling sorry for those mortals who would never witness the wild beauty" of enemy flak.

The night he was shot down he wasn't even supposed to be flying. When another gunner reported a broken gun-sight, Harsh took his place. He parachuted wounded into imprisonment in Stalag Luft III.

Floody liked Harsh from the start: "He was the perfect image of a Southern gentleman. Handsome. Six-feet-one. Distinction all over him. Grey hair. Grey moustache. I liked him."

Australian PoW Paul Brickhill, who related the exploits

of Floody and Harsh in his book *The Great Escape*, remembered Harsh as someone great to have around.

Harsh quickly settled into the routine he had learned in the Georgia prison: "Anybody can stand anything for 24 hours."

Asked how he got shot down, he joked: "I was sitting on a barn door over Berlin and some s.o.b. shot the hinges off."

In July 4 celebrations he wrapped himself in a blanket biblical style and announced he would walk on water in a fire pool used for swimming. Drenched, he mourned: "My faith gave out."

When his buddies joked that German Intelligence would deduce from his grey hair that the Allies were scraping the manpower barrel, he growled: "Next time I'll tell my right age."

Canadian journalist Kingsley Brown would call their years in Stalag Luft III "the finest of my life," a time when a man was judged "not by what he has or by his ability to get, but solely by the Christian yardstick of what he can give to the community around him." Floody summed it up: "George Harsh was great for morale."

Harsh would remember the gesture that started their friendship. Floody offered to use his monthly letter to ask his wife Betty to let Harsh's family know he was alive; they got the word weeks before it arrived through official channels.

One morning there came the whispered words that made them accomplices in what author Brickhill would make famous as The Great Escape.

Senior British officers had picked Floody to head underground operations on three tunnels. They hoped at least one would escape detection and allow a mass escape to tie up German energies. Floody now laughs at the choice: "They figured if I was an officer and had worked in a mine, I must be an engineer. But digging a 2 x 2-foot tunnel through sand had little to do with what I'd done in hard rock."

That morning he had gone straight to Harsh: "I want a man topside, protecting me. You, my friend, are going to be in charge of security."

While a prisoner of war, George Harsh helped build the tunnel used in The Great Escape from Stalag Luft III.

Harsh protested it was madness. "You crazy bastards are going to get the lot of us shot." But he took the job.

Harsh then told Floody of his past as a convict. Floody shrugged it off.

They made an excellent team day after day as Floody led men through cunningly-contrived entrances, down 30-foot ladders into the sand, into lengthening burrows equipped with electric lights on stolen wire, with wooden trolleys, boarded walls, a roof and improvised air bellows. Several times he was buried in sand. Once he was injured by a fallen metal jug. But he kept clawing the sand out, passing it back to a dispersal squad, who smuggled it into playing fields, gardens, Red Cross boxes, a theatre.

After a year one tunnel was discovered by the Germans and blown up. Remaining suspicious, the Germans kept searching, but prisoners kept on digging and making escape clothes and forged documents. They combed German newspapers and radio broadcasts for information to be passed back to Britain.

Harsh ran a 200-man, above-ground, security force keyed to a system of signals that told him where every ferret was.

Brickhill recalled that Harsh was a fanatical watchdog, glaring furiously at the Germans and mumbling ingenious American curses. Floody said: "He did one helluva job. He was on tenterhooks, pacing up and down, every minute we were underground. No Germans ever got near without me knowing it. We got so we could close a tunnel in 20 seconds."

As for Floody's own contribution, perhaps Brickhill said it best when he inscribed a copy of his book: "To Wally, without whom there would have been no tunnel and no book."

By March, 1944, the work was concentrated on the longest tunnel. Just as it was nearing its end in woods beyond the barbed wire the Germans banished Floody, Harsh, Brown and others they considered ringleaders to another compound. It may have saved their lives. Days after they left, the break was made. Some 80 men got out. Three made it to Britain.

Floody remembers a respected and distressed German security chief coming to his new camp saying he had terrible news: 50 escapers had been murdered by the Gestapo. When Toronto airman Bob Hamilton arrived at the camp he found the prisoners wearing black armbands.

The months ached on. In January, 1945, the Germans began to march thousands of PoWs west, away from the advancing Russians. The roads swarmed with prisoners, slave laborers, refugees. Floody, Harsh and Brown teamed up to survive what Harsh would remember "as a pastiche of cold, hunger, human misery and frostbite."

They finally got on a train and ended up in a filthy, overcrowded prison camp not far from Berlin. There the Russians freed them, then held them to ensure an exchange for Russian prisoners, but eventually the day came when they crossed the Elbe river to freedom.

"By God," exulted Floody, "we made it."

They went their separate ways once home in Canada. Floody went into business in Toronto, running trade associations and he became a driving force in an ex-PoW organization. When a movie was made from Brickhill's book, he was the technical adviser. Once a year he and Betty visited Harsh in the United States.

Harsh, predictably, had feared the challenges of civilian

Wally Floody was instrumental in the construction of the tunnel used in The Great Escape during the Second World War.

life after 15 prison years. He tried writing fiction, magazine articles, selling books, vacuum cleaners, furniture. He married and bought a small house in New Jersey. He worked for a neighbor and friend, Ray Berven, who ran a trucking business, then in the shipping office of a large plant nursery. He drank a lot. Soon his marriage broke up and he fell in love with another woman. He settled down to write his memoirs.

They came out in 1971, and the publishers called the book *Lonesome Road*. It was mistitled, said Harsh, who saw it as a tribute to "some magnificent men who made my life, if not enjoyable, at least bearable over all these years."

It threw light on his inner turmoil. He was losing no sleep over bombing Germany, but for the "ghastly reality" of the murder he committed as a youth there was no excuse or reason. No ex-convict could turn back the clock.

He quoted Dostoevski: "…crime is its own punishment and retributive justice can never be so severe as the penalty the human soul can impose on itself."

Arguments against capital punishment, says Berven, "became an obsession with him." Harsh once wrote: "It is a law zeroed in on the poor, the unprivileged, the friendless, the uneducated, the ignorant. How many rich men have ever been executed? With sufficient money, a capital case can be kept in the courts until the defendant dies of old age. You can't hang a million dollars. This is not cynicism. It is truth, and I am living proof. Capital punishment represents a sickness of the human spirit, drawn from the worst of human motives: revenge."

When his estranged wife fell ill with cancer, Harsh gave up the woman he loved to be with her until she died.

In 1973 he wrote the Floodys: "What a dreary, dismal world this would be without friends like you two. I am allowing myself to become terribly depressed, and then your letter arrived and once again life seems almost worth the effort."

Christmas Eve, 1974, he shot himself.

He survived but a stroke left him partially paralysed, unable to talk much, needing help to walk. At this dark moment, Harsh found refuge in the friendship born in Stalag Luft III.

The Floodys took him into their Toronto home to be near the help Canada would provide an ailing veteran. Ray Berven didn't think he'd last long, yet he lived another five years, and friends say it was the endless devotion of the Floodys that made it possible.

While Berven paid off Harsh's debts in the U.S. and sent him to Florida twice for winter weeks, the Floodys took over his social, medical and financial affairs.

Harsh was with them for a year and a half, then began to fret that he was too much of a burden. At his urging, they put him in a nursing home. When it depressed him, Floody arranged to get him into a veterans wing of Sunnybrook Medical Centre. The love, the caring went on as Floody kept hounding ex-PoWs to visit him and took him home on weekends.

His final visit lasted 10 days at Christmas, 1979. At 2 a.m. one day early in 1980 a doctor awakened Floody to give him the news that Harsh had died. He was the only logical one to call.

When you ask Wally Floody why he did what he did for George Harsh, he has a simple answer: "He was one helluva guy. I loved him." ↄ

HOME FOR CHRISTMAS
Joyce Turpin

The fog-horn boomed and the fussy little tugs shrieked an answer. For the first time that day the fog cleared a little and watery sun revealed Southampton, complete with its huge docks, and ships from all over the world. We were moving so slowly, it seemed as if the shore was receding instead of us, and suddenly I didn't want that to happen. I wanted to reach out and grab it and take it with me. Which was odd, when you come to think of it, because I had waited for this moment for years and now we were actually homeward bound. I didn't really want to go. I thought back over the last hectic weeks and wondered what I really did want.

"Home for Christmas," they had said. Home for Christmas! The very words made your heart pound with excitement. Back to snow and Christmas trees and bright sun. Back to all sorts of delightful food (to say nothing of the cooking!) and hockey matches and skiing down glistening mountain slopes. Back to lighted streets and gaily decorated stores and clothes without coupons. Back to plumbing you could count on, and warm houses. Back to long-unseen friends, and most of all, of course, back to family!

Family—even after three years overseas in the Service I could not get rid of that darned lump in my throat every time I thought of my mother and young sister and dad. Would they have changed, I kept wondering. My sister must have grown into quite a beauty, judging from the pictures mother was always sending me but I couldn't picture her as anything but a kid. As for mother, somehow you never think of mothers changing, they just go on being wonderful—ironing your clothes, listening to your troubles and solving your problems. And Dad, I wondered if he had aged much, for an older man he was working pretty hard these days....

When I heard I would be on the draft arriving in Canada in time for Christmas, I started on a round of good-byes to all the wonderful friends I had made in

Ice in Trafalgar Square, London, January 1963.

England. These people really do know the meaning of the word "friendship." If you were a guest and they only had one egg, you'd get it every time. And when the ration is only one egg in perhaps three to six weeks, you'll see what I mean. Everybody seemed very sorry to see me go but glad for my sake, and I was laden with good wishes for my family and promises to come out and visit us as soon as possible.

Then I had to say good-bye to London. Anyone who has been there will know how sad this was going to be—like saying good-bye to an old friend. I went to all my old haunts and found them good. Even the inevitable fog seemed benevolent. I stood in Trafalgar Square looking at Canada House and felt glad that our representatives in London were in the same place that had become so familiar and so dear to thousands of Canadians during the war. I saw two or three good shows and, on the last day, because my people had asked me so often to go, I went to the Tower. I was ashamed of not having gone before but had never seemed to have the time since it was re-opened to visitors.

I was waiting on a bleak platform in the suburbs of London, where we were to entrain for Southampton, when the lady who had always put me up on my London leaves (and treated me royally, I may say),

rushed into the station just as the train was drawing in. She had a parcel in her arms and thrust it into my hand. "For the train journey," she shouted, over the noise; and I thanked her with a smile and a nod as I was swept aboard. On the way down, I opened it and found a lovely cake, no doubt made with ingredients laboriously saved over a number of months from her rations, and a little note on top. The card read: "For giving me so much pleasure by staying with me, and helping to fill the place of my son, whom I miss so much." I shared the cake with the girls in my compartment, but I didn't trust myself to mention the note.

Our ship's siren blew and the deafening noise brought me back to the present and to the fact that I was leaving all this behind. The pull of home is very strong, but the pull of England is strong too, and I was torn between the two. The gap of steel-grey water widened, and just once I considered jumping overboard and swimming back, but I knew that wouldn't solve anything. The quavering notes of "Home, Sweet Home," played on an ancient concertina, wafted up from the deck below and, turning away from the rail, with another big lump in my throat, I went down to my bunk, fixing my thoughts firmly on Christmas at home in Canada. ॐ

TEN DAYS AND 7,000 MILES
Eswyn Lyster

The London billet
is cold
and filled with
triple bunks.
Goodbyes have
been said
and there's no looking back,
for the time being
we're the army's stepchildren.

We're all excited and talking too much
except for one
who, slight as a child herself,
sits quietly holding her younger
already expecting her third.

The girls bound for Toronto
and other points east
tend to stay together

War bride Freda Gannon with her son John Patrick Jr.

and be ever so slightly superior
making the rest of us wonder:
could it be right what those easterners say
that there's absolutely nothing
west of Winnipeg?

The childless wives draw their blankets high
and it's midnight
when the last infant gives in to sleep.
Then a tight-lipped corporal
who all evening
has been pleading for some kind of order
announces a last-minute medical examination
as if he's not absolutely sure we'll co-operate.

But we're a generation inured to broken sleep;
ten minutes later
we line a stone-floored corridor and wait
and wait....
My son who has cried himself dry
hiccups gently
his head warm against my chin.
We cling together
homesick
already.

Next day our train rolls north
passing tiny back gardens
sweet-pea trellises
Anderson shelters
old bomb craters
and roofs
pock-marked by
shrapnel.

At last we're alongside a ship
huge as a factory
and strong enough, we'd wager,
to quell any Atlantic uprising.

War brides bound for Canada's west coast in 1946.

There are five war brides, a war widow
and four war babies in our cabin.
Perce, our steward,
mentions a girl on A Deck
who threw up before we left port.
Small comfort for the rest of us
who waited 24 hours.

Children fretful
and Perce everywhere
warming bottles, offering crackers,
weak tea and advice
not all of it helpful.
Urging us to go to breakfast
if only for the kippers and the greasy bacon.
Like almost everything else
this ancient shipboard joke
is new to us.
We haven't seen our stewardess since the first day.

Perce tells us it isn't much of a storm
even when glasses smash overhead

and baggage goes adrift in the hold.
Next morning there are ropes in the passageways
to help us keep our feet
if we happen to be on them in the first place.

We're suspended in time
England light years behind

Mrs. Patrick Kyle and her children enjoy a bit to eat after arriving in Halifax along with other World War II brides and children.

the unknown still three long days ahead.
We wash in salt water
bet on the ship's progress
and begin to make it to the dining room.

Perce gives Canadian dollars
for our English pounds.
It's days before we catch on
that when it comes to money
he has all the instincts of a London spiv.

We don't know this when we collect for his tip.
Someone puts a farthing in an envelope
for the invisible stewardess.

It's rumored that some of the girls
have been found off-limits
in the crew's quarters.
'How could they,' we murmur.
'Yes,' someone agrees,
'and them all so seasick!'
They are not to disembark
until their husbands have been notified.
We joke about it.
In reverse circumstances

A war bride and her son arrive in Canada in 1946.

would we have been 'notified?'
Like most intriguing questions
this one remains unanswered.

Halifax.
Barren grey rock a-swirl with snow
and the floor of the dirty Customs shed
moving beneath our feet.

Aboard the train the Red Cross girls
play with my son.
I slide into sleep and wake in Maine
to piled snow and children
walking home from school.
No cowboys or movie stars?
Can this be that magic U.S. of A.?

Before we know it we're in Quebec.
At every stop
anxious brides are met by anxious strangers
in plush overcoats
broad-brimmed fedoras
and buckled overboots.
One girl bursts into tears.
I try to read her lips
can only think she's saying:
'Where's your uniform?'

Somewhere near Port Arthur
with the windows frosting over
our war widow says goodbye.
She'll go north by sled
share memories for a while
then go home to England.

My son is sick.
There's talk of a Winnipeg hospital
and the idea upsets me
almost more than his illness.

A young war bride and her children after arriving in Halifax following the Second World War.

To leave the train
will be to break a lifeline.
But his fever lessens
and we travel on
and on.
There really is something west of
Winnipeg.
Miles and miles of it.

A war bride and her child after arriving in Canada from
overseas after the Second World War.

Our stop is coming up.
Caught in the light
snowflakes fly sideways against the darkness
and my reflection stares back at me.
Bride
a silly term for a wife with a two-year-old son
and this feeling in the pit of her stomach.

The measured ringing of a bell
announces our arrival.
People are sliding past the window
and there
under the light
is a blessedly familiar face.
Arms are lifting us down
my foot crunches into snow
and for the first time
though England is ten days and seven thousand
miles away
this frozen land
begins to feel like home. ❧

PART III

KOREA

THE KEENER
Terry Meagher

I have no idea what the generals, historians and statisticians have said about that terrible spring night on Hill 187 in Korea. Frankly I'm not interested. My story is the one told in the barracks and canteens by the men who were there, in the forgotten war. It is the story of old friends, brave lieutenants and the men who stood guard on lonely hills.

Those of us in the ranks were mostly humble folk who came out of fishing villages, wheat fields and smokestack towns, away from the long unemployment lines and into the recruiting offices.

When I left home in the winter of 1952, my mother cried and told me to be careful. But I was too young to listen and in a few days her admonitions were forgotten. My sister's advice, though greeted with annoyance, lingered much longer: "Don't look up at the skyscrapers in the city or they'll think you're a hick."

The army sent me to Camp Wainwright to prepare for war. Our platoon commander, Lieut. Banton, was three or four years older than my 18 years. A student at Ottawa's Carleton University, he had joined the regular army hoping to lead a platoon in Korea.

Known as a "keener," Lieut. Banton always wanted our brass shined brighter and our boots polished better than the soldiers in other platoons. Though we hated spit and polish we seldom grumbled against him, probably because he didn't spare himself. Even during a break in a long, hot march he stood on top of the hill scanning the countryside through binoculars. He would know every move of every platoon in the battalion.

After what seemed like a long time, he walked down the hill and sat among us. He told us about his father who had been decorated in WW II. No longer the gung-ho lieutenant, he seemed more like a big brother. The older boy we all admired was taking us into his confidence. Suddenly he said: "I'm going to win the Victoria Cross in Korea."

We were surprised. You had to have dignity to make a statement like that, even if you were an officer. A private like me would have been hooted out of the wet canteen if he even hinted at dreams of glory. Nobody said anything until Lieut. Banton changed the subject.

In the late summer of '52, I left Camp Wainwright as a reinforcement for the 1st Bn., Royal Canadian Regt., in Korea. I didn't meet him again until the following March when the 3rd Bn. relieved the 1st. A member of Charlie Co., he still had the type of clean complexion my mother admired—as though he had spent a good deal of time in a barber's chair with hot compresses on his face. I think he had played football although he didn't have the bulk to grind people on the line; he was more likely a halfback or a wide receiver—trim and lithe at 80 kg.

"Do you want to transfer to Charlie Company?" he asked me. "It'll be the same platoon as in Wainwright."

I didn't know what to make of it but I suspected he was dreaming of glory. In me he saw the boy who had admired the United States Marines on their retreat from the Chosin Reservoir and he thought somehow I would figure in his Victoria Cross.

He saw me hesitate and said: "It'll be all right. I can arrange the transfer." But it wasn't that. I had made too many friends in Able Co., too much had happened.

"The offer's open," he said. "Anytime." I kicked the ridge of mud on the road, shifting the rifle on my shoulder to hide my discomfort.

"Thanks," I said.

Then I turned and ran to catch up with my platoon. That was the last time I spoke to him.

To pass the time in reserve, we played softball on the rice paddies. The games weren't much even by small-town standards, with sandbags for bases and a triangle of chewed-up wood for home plate. Stones abounded, and would sometimes send a well-hit grounder sharply into the face of a fielder.

My platoon had been baptized by fire—some of us on the Hook, a few on Hill 355. Cockier than we should have been, we treated the new men in one platoon shabbily. On the ball diamond we not only gleefully beat them, we rubbed their noses in their greenness.

"You've still got Canadian water in your water bottle," we'd shout across the field. When one of them argued a call with the umpire we cried: "Recruit! Recruit!"

One night our razzing almost got us charged with insubordination. Their lieutenant, G.B. Maynell, was the only man above the rank of corporal who ever played or even showed up and every night he was over by third base coaching them and needling us. One night while Lieut. Maynell was talking it up someone shouted demeaningly: "Hey, boy-san, where did you learn to coach?"

When our second baseman shouted: "Ninety-day wonder!" the game stopped. We had gone too far. In the eerie stillness we became aware suddenly of the ominous clatter of machine-guns on the front line several kilometres away. We watched him weigh the situation, struggle with it. Then to everyone's relief he looked at the batter and shouted: "C'mon hit one through the hole."

That night was the only time they beat us and afterwards we could hear them singing:

"A young Canuck soldier to Tokyo on leave
Was stopped by a provost, oh pardon me please,
There's blood on your tunic,
there's blood on your sleeve,
I'll just have to cancel your seven-day leave..."

They somehow didn't have the right to sing that song—not yet. But we knew their looie was just trying to make them into the best platoon in the battalion just as Lieut. Banton would be doing. Only there was a catch: They would never know until they came under fire who would hold and who would bug out. So we listened in our tent knowing and resenting. How petty we were and how tragic it all seems now.

Not long after, we loaded everything we had on to our backs, climbed into trucks and headed north to the front.

Soldiers use a candle to examine a document during the Korean War, June 1952.

I don't think we ever got tired of the same old clichés. Every once in a while someone would ask: "Is this trip necessary?"

I remember the moment we disembarked as clearly as yesterday. I remember soldiers from another company standing along the side of the road and in the ditches— dark, helmeted figures, disembodied, brooding. I remember the shadows of fear on their faces. Nobody asked if the trip was necessary any more. Someone made a wise-crack and someone else told him to shut up.

We moved up the road until we joined the rest of Able Co. Then the column stuttered forward, wound its way around the hills in close ack ack formation—a metre between each man.

Going up Hill 187, the march turned into a trot, then a scramble. Burdened by their equipment and unable to keep up several men fell behind and didn't find their way to our positions until morning. In the crawl trenches our fear of getting lost became greater than our fear of the Chinese. Helmets clanged against the steel pickets holding overhead camouflage netting in place. Ahead, a rifle tangled in it and a soldier stumbled and swore.

Tense, sweating and exhausted we staggered into the slit trenches and unbuckled our equipment.

While we leaned over the parapets catching our breaths large rats scurried through the bipods of the Bren guns. Occasionally the muffled noises of other platoons moving into position rose on the chilled night air. The clang of a shovel on rock rang clearly like an echo in an immense graveyard.

Hill 187 was shaped like a horseshoe with Able Co. at the heel. On our lower left Dog Co. was spread out on a ridge that turned like the crook of a finger. Farther to the front the main part of Baker could be reached by a road clearly visible by day to the Chinese.

Beyond Baker's command post was a long stretch of twisting crawl trench. Still further stood one of the most peculiar sights of the Korean War. On a point of land called the Songgok a lone tree draped with a tattered piece of camouflage netting stood bruised, burned, shell scarred and defiant.

Across the horseshoe valley from the Songgok Charlie Co. occupied a lowlying finger stretching into no man's land. Lieut. Banton held the sharp end, about 270 m from the Sami-ch'on River—gentle, meandering, easily fordable at about 15 m wide. Beyond the Sami-ch'on, hills seemed to rise endlessly back into the shadowy north.

On May 2, one platoon went on a fighting patrol down through Banton's position, along a narrow, dusty path, through a minefield gap—a place where the barbed wire appeared to meet but passed without touching. The patrol went left through the narrow gap, then jogged right and walked easily into the Sami-ch'on Valley.

At 2130 hours it walked into 400 Chinese assault troops and was cut to pieces with Russian burp guns.

Fire fights are brief encounters—30 seconds, a minute or two. The harsh sound of the Chinese guns was followed by the brief clatter of a slower Canadian Sten gun. A grenade exploded, muzzles flashed along the gentle Sami-ch'on.

In so short a time most of the young players had been shot and lay dead or wounded on the ground. Their brave lieutenant was no more. The ones left alive clutched their machine-guns, fingers on the triggers. They pressed their bodies against the ridge of a rice paddy, waiting. The wounded bit the pain, bit off the whimper that would give their lives away. In those moments, the glory of war, the elation of winning, all the firsts and lasts on all the roads leading nowhere became what they are— meaningless. They were alone, in the shadow of death, far from home.

The heavy machine-guns began firing, sending banks of tracers across the valley. The whine of artillery shells filled the night with terror. Mortars popped behind both lines. Their bombs rose high in the sky, paused and then began their deadly flutter to earth. Shells began exploding like bright, bursting stars, setting small grass fires all over the treeless valley.

In the midst of the terrible chaos Lieut. Banton's platoon left their position on the sharp end. Banton made his way to the gap in the minefield. The keener did what he had always done—he got there first. It was not spectacular, it was no way to win a Victoria Cross. But to those men caught between the Chinese and the minefield he was like a messenger sent by God. Once there, he stretched out his arms parallel to the barbed wire and began to wave, shouting: "Come through! Come through me!" It was all so odd and all so terrible. Some of the young ball players would find their way back to our lines, but the light to the way would quickly fade.

Lieut. Banton broke two rules of the battlefield: Never stand when you can sit and never sit when you can lie. Lieut. Banton was cut down in a minute and lay by the barbed wire.

I don't remember the name of the young Nova Scotian who went to get the lieutenant. Too big to look like a hero, he was almost fat, yet strong, and he lifted Lieut. Banton on to his shoulders and struggled through the cross-fire. Reaching his crawl trench he was about to drop in when a shell zippered open a piece of turf behind him. Shrapnel hit Lieut. Banton and they both rolled heavily into the trench. Lieut. Banton was dead.

At two minutes after midnight, Charlie Co. came under massive bombardment. For 20 minutes the hill shook, crackling and burning a brilliant, jagged yellow. When the artillery and mortar fire lifted, all the concertina wire on the forward slopes had been blown to bits and the protective minefield had been destroyed. The Chinese had fired 2,000 rounds.

Waves of their assault troops swept over the crumbled trenches, shining lights into collapsed bunkers and taking stunned Canadians prisoner. In desperation the remaining Canadians called artillery down on their own position. The skies turned a glorious orange and the valley and hills filled again with pretty death.

Later, the guns became almost quiet. Occasionally a machine-gun clattered and we heard the *carrr-ump* of distant shells.

Dog Co. counter-attacked at dawn. Khaki-clad figures

Serving in the Korean War, Private John Lewis *(centre)* of Colchester, N.S.—serving with the Royal Canadian Regiment—recounts his experience during the overwhelming attack by the Chinese on Little Gibraltar Hill in Korea. The photo is dated November 1952. Looking on are Pte. Murray Deadder *(left)* of Kentville, N.S., and Pte. Arthur MacDonald of Hampton Station, N.B.

moved like phantoms through the wisps of fog and cordite still hanging over the hill. But the Chinese had gone. It was one of those battles meant to put pressure on the United Nations negotiators at Panmunjom. The Chinese had never intended to hold the hill.

As the mist began to clear under the rising sun the last stretchers were loaded into ambulances. Small groups of soldiers, night reinforcements from Able Co. and remnants of Charlie, were drifting back to the rear, some of their faces blackened by gunpowder, some wounded, clothes torn, some without weapons, beaten, frightened, a few no longer fit for combat.

By my reckoning between 25–30 of us were killed that night, about 65 were wounded and 25 or so taken prisoner. My friend Eddie Nieckarz of Charlie Co. thinks my figures are too high. At the time he counted between 40–50 survivors.

Lt.-Col. Herbert Wood in *Strange Battleground*—the official Canadian history—using what he calls the best available figures, says 26 were killed, 27 were wounded and seven taken prisoner. Mr. Nieckarz says he can count at least 10 who were taken prisoner and the proportion of dead to wounded seems out of line.

None of the men I have written about ever received a decoration: Lieut. Banton, the brave young ball players, Lieut. Maynell, or the young Nova Scotian who carried Lieut. Banton back to our trenches.

A few years ago I went to a house party. When the hostess found out I had been to Korea she said she had gone to university with Doug Banton. "So young," she said. "One day he was here; it seemed the next we heard he was dead. Was it worth it?"

I stumbled over the answer. Should I say they were senseless men who had labored in vain a short way from the peace light at Panmunjom? They were hardly more than children. They played like children. They hurt like children and were hurt. In the end they became children of nobility, not by birth but by the spirit of their sacrifice. ৵

RUM ALONG THE IMJIN
Aralt Murphy

I was waving traffic across a one-way floating bridge on the Imjin River and hearing the distant crump of artillery for the first time in my life.

My partner—a big bear of a guy called Boucher—was still showing me the ropes when a Brit officer came across the bridge in a jeep. He wore a sweater with only two little brass crowns.

"Forget to salute an officer," Sgt. Wolfe had said, "and I'll see you in the digger in Seoul!" He meant I'd be made a guard, in his mind a horrible fate for an MP. But being green, I thought he meant I'd be put behind bars.

Boucher and I saluted.

"I'm the new assistant provost marshal (APM). Just out to see things. I'm responsible, you know, for 100 square miles of roads." His mouth was full of marbles. "Is this a busy bridge?"

"It has its moments, sir," said Boucher who had several months in Korea.

He caught Boucher's accent. "Oh, from Quebec, are you? I have a cousin in Montreal."

"New Brunswick, sir."

The APM frowned. "Ah, of course. The nights must get cold." He looked at me. "Are you getting your rum ration?"

I'd heard of sailors getting rum, but not soldiers, so I said: "I've never had any, sir."

"And you, uh, corporal?"

"L. Cpl. Emile Boucher, sir. No sir."

He seemed upset. Driving off, his last words were: "I'll check into that rum, lads."

"Why didn't you tell him you'd just got here?" Boucher said. "Now he's off half-cocked."

"Well, what about you?"

"I never drink."

"Hell, how was I supposed to know that? And what's this rum anyhow?"

"SRD—Service Rum Demerara. Wolfe keeps a gallon under his cot. We're supposed to get a shot when there's shooting, or when it's cold. He uses it for trading with the Yanks."

"And what's this APM to us?"

"I told you, we're part of the Commonwealth Div. He's the headquarters guy who gives orders on traffic control. Things like that. But our major runs company."

Late in the afternoon, Sgt. Wolfe's jeep stopped with a shower of gravel. Boucher was trying to sleep, but he woke him.

"Now you two deadheads, did you tell the APM you don't get a rum ration?"

"We told the truth," Boucher said.

"Did you tell him you don't drink?"

"He didn't ask."

"Deadheads! I was all set to buy new tents. Now I have to waste valuable SRD on you guys. There won't be enough left to buy anything."

He poured two-ounce shots in our tin mugs and barked: "Now drink it!"

The first taste was awful. Then I started warmin' all over.

Sgt. Wolfe drove to the next traffic post, a half-mile away.

"I think I'm going to puke," Boucher said. Instead he flopped on his bed. "Call me at midnight."

There wasn't much traffic and I was sitting on a post whistling when a Canadian lieutenant from company drove up.

"Howzit goin'?" he inquired.

"Fine, sir. Nice night."

"The word's out everyone's to have a tot of rum. Thought I'd just make sure. Brought along a bottle."

"Sgt. Wolfe gave me one."

"Good…but, seein' as how I've come this far, how'd you like another?"

"Well, it is gettin' cooler." I got out my mug again.

"Might as well have one with you," he said. We clanked mugs.

Rations are shared during a break in the action in Korea.

"What about your partner?"

"He hasn't had much sleep. But I could take a tot for him."

"Good idea," said the lieutenant, who seemed to want to use up the bottle.

"I'll use the same cup. Stuff's antiseptic as Lysol."

After he left, I got to thinking Boucher wouldn't want the rum anyway. It tasted better than the first two.

I was humming a few bars of "Ave Maria" when the Brit RSM came along.

"Evening, lad," he said. "The APM is out checking tonight. Wants to be sure everyone on duty has had his rum ration."

"Sir, my sergeant has already been around. But, of course, that's a while ago."

"I've a bottle here. Have you a cup?"

"Oh yes, sir. Yes, sir. Thank you. It hits the spot."

"Yes, it does cheer you up," he said while having one with me. "Well, good night, lad."

The flashing of artillery batteries was like the northern lights, but the sound was like far-away thunder. By yodelling between salvos, I produced echoes from the hills beside the river.

A Royal Military Police captain came along and insisted I have a short one. When he left, I got to wondering how many rounds from my SMG I'd need to sink one of the bridge's rubber pontoons.

I was relieving myself in the Imjin when the Canadian sergeant major appeared.

"Do up your fly," he ordered, smart like. "God, what a breath you've got!"

"Well," I said, "everybody and his brother has been givin' me my SRD ration, 'cept you."

"Half the pointsmen in the division are pissed as billy goats," he complained, but he pulled a gallon jug from the back of his jeep and said: "Still, if you can't lick 'em, you might as well join 'em." He poured a little into a glass, tossed it back and asked: "Is your partner sober?"

"He's a teetotalizer. I've been taking care of his ration for him."

"Murphy, you're a disgrace!" he joked, then poured me a good one.

"For a first day at the sharp end, it's been nice enough," I said, tossing it back.

He shook his head. "Here, have one for Boucher. Your punishment will come when you try to sober up."

Later I was on my hands and knees trying to pick up some ammo when Old Bristle Mouth, the Canadian company commander, drove up.

"Excuse me, sir, I was just cleaning my loyal SMG here when I spilled my bullets," I alibied.

He saw I was bombed, but instead of getting mad he chuckled. "I can see you've had your SRD. Care for the other half?"

"In for a dime, in for a dollar," I said, sticking out my trusty mug.

"I'd sure like the APM to see you before you change shifts," he said.

"Why's that, sir?"

"'Cause then he'd know what a stupid ass he is."

"I didn't know you and he held different opinions, sir."

"There are matters of principle that must be established between us," he said, glowering.

A little later, I was looking down at the crust of ice forming on a pontoon when my cap dropped into the river. It floated out of reach, so I stripped to swim after it and I was stark naked on the pontoon when the APM pulled up.

"Excuse me, sir, but I can't salute without my hat on. And it's floating down the river," I explained.

The 25th Canadian Reinforcement Group breaks down compo rations in July 1951 during the Korean War.

Soldiers of the 57th Independent Field Squadron, RCE, man a machine-gun near a pontoon bridge over the Hwachon River, Korea, May 20, 1951.

THE WAR THAT NEVER REALLY ENDED
D.A. Stickland

I guess he couldn't believe his eyes. He started out on the pontoon, then asked: "Are you supposed to be on duty?"

"Careful, sir, it's slippery," I warned.

"You've left your SMG here where any enemy soldier could seize it," he bellowed, pointing it at me. "You're helpless!"

"No he's not, sir!" said good old Boucher coming to the rescue and covering the major with a SMG.

You may be wondering if the APM slipped and fell in. He should have, but suddenly I did—and don't think that doesn't take your breath away.

By the time I caught up to my hat, the APM had driven away with a great gnashing of gears.

Boucher helped me into my sleeping bag and when I resurfaced it was daylight. Sgt. Wolfe was talking to Boucher and both were grinning.

"Murph," Wolfe said, "I don't know what you did—and you probably don't either—but the two majors have declared peace. Company is issuing extra jugs of rum to sections, and leaving its use to the discretion of section sergeants."

"It's rotten tasting stuff," I replied. "How about a new tent instead?"

"Murphy, if you so much as mention SRD again, I'll see you in the digger." 🙥

It seems incredible that 25 years have passed since the armistice in Korea halted Canada's last and probably strangest war. On the night of July 27, 1953, the guns fell silent along the battle lines that had split that mountainous land asunder.

The youngest of Canada's combat veterans are unlikely to pause very long to celebrate: It was scarcely a great victory to be commemorated like Nov. 11 or VE-Day. In fact many say that it really proved nothing and would best be forgotten.

It is hard to find much familiar ground in the scholarly dissertations of historians; personal memories are necessary to preserve a proper soldier's perspective. A recent visit to Korea added further insight.

There were many unusual things about the Korean war: It became a long, boring ordeal and the front-line troops were replaced not once, but three times.

In most cases troops can endure the dirty defensive warfare, the frustrating trench life and the mounting toll of casualties, but this conflict had a new and unnerving ingredient: Peace talks were initiated in early 1951 in the middle of the battlefield. For more than two years front-line commanders tried to conduct effective military operations without prejudicing the diplomatic activities at the ever-apparent tents of Panmunjom.

The effect on the troops was obvious: War-like acts seemed inappropriate and few wanted to become deeply involved in risky operations if the war could be over in a few days.

I left my hillside battle position to come back to Canada and when I returned almost two years later for a second tour of duty, I was astonished to be assigned to the same hill I had left. The trenches were deeper, the defences and the barbed wire seemed more permanent and the possibility of military victory was all but forgotten. We settled down to business as usual, with the lights from nearby Panmunjom still dimly illuminating our battlefield by night.

The armistice almost crept up unawares just as our unit, the 3rd Bn., Royal Canadian Regiment, was completing its third month of action. Following a first tour that featured a fierce battle with the Chinese in May, 1953, we enjoyed a short rest and participated in Dominion Day ceremonies, then went forward for another tour of front-line duties, taking over the battle positions of the 3rd Bn., Royal Australian Regiment, July 9.

Our new ridge was opposite Luke—the third in a series of Chinese-held hills called Matthew, Mark, Luke and John—and seemed much closer to an ominous enemy presence. To our right, across a deep gully, loomed the imposing bulk of Hill 355, looking much like its famous namesake, the fortress of Gibraltar. Its trench network was now manned by the Royal 22nd Regt.

It was soon obvious that we had fewer men on the ground than the Australians. My platoon was assigned a large isolated hill that could easily accommodate a full company. We covered the ground as best we could with only 28 men, of whom 6 or 7 were Korean soldiers, but the troops seemed a bit nervous.

The war continued for several weeks with most of the activity down in the B Co. area at the end of the ridge. There was mortaring and shelling by day with fierce fire-fights by night—both sides were competing to occupy a tiny pimple of ground halfway across the valley floor. Nothing really developed on our hill, although we took a salvo of shells early one morning.

We gradually sensed that something unusual was going on and one afternoon I was awakened (we slept by day and remained alert all night) and quietly summoned to the company commander's bunker on the main hill. Somehow the sunshine seemed unusual, a relic of our past life.

The platoon commanders and the company second-in-command were gathered for briefing and everyone seemed to be in a remarkably jovial mood. The major advised us that the war was all but over. The armistice would be signed at 10 a.m. July 27, but the actual ceasefire would not come into effect until 10 p.m. This news was to be kept secret and special instructions—such as removing all ammunition from the weapons, collecting the reserve holdings and guarding against accidental firings—would take effect when the official announcement was made.

Somehow the pressures and burdens of the past few years seemed to be lifted, and the relief of the officers must have been obvious to the troops. Rumors developed quickly and it was hard not to indicate how close they were to the truth.

On the actual day, the suspense was overpowering. The company commander arrived in mid-afternoon for an unscheduled visit and, clad only in trousers and an old airborne hat, sat among the platoon to confirm that the peace had just been signed. There was a loud cheer and he gave instructions on what we were to do when the armistice became effective.

Somehow the intensity of the historic occasion didn't quite sink in at first. It still didn't seem real because it would be a few more hours before the ceasefire. Skeptical soldiers remained cautious until the end—anything could happen, and did! It remained business as usual for the Chinese and B Co. took in a mortar bomb a minute throughout the late afternoon. A final casualty saddened the battalion.

Token standing patrols went out that night and we were still a bit uneasy that things might not go off as planned. Dusk was unusually dark, but as 2200 hours approached a full moon illuminated the hills in a ghostly splendor. Excitement rose and on the hour the sky behind us broke out in a blaze of glory: Everyone seemed to be firing off flares and illuminating rounds against instructions. Months of pent-up emotions were released and loud shouting echoed across the valleys.

There wasn't a peep or glimmer from the enemy hills, which seemed odd. We began to have misgivings about it all and wondered whether the Chinese were on a different time system or if they were merely waiting to test our sincerity. Then, sharp at 11 p.m., there was a flicker of light on one of the sombre hills and a new series of demonstrations started.

Canadian and British Army Provost personnel keep road traffic moving near the front lines of Korea.

Their reaction was similar to ours. Flares and illuminations went up in all directions. We heard a woman's voice through a tinny loudspeaker on the nearest hill, but couldn't make out what she was saying. I could hear what sounded like a tom-tom drum and the singing of a Chinese soldiers' choir. The music was unfamiliar and scarcely melodious, but somehow seemed happy.

There was little further activity that night. We unloaded our weapons, maintained the barest of vigilance and settled down for our first night's sleep in many weeks. The silence and inactivity seemed unnatural.

The first day of peace brought an unforgettable series of sights. We saw thousands of Chinese soldiers for the first time: Few of us had ever seen more than one or two before. On top of John, the highest hill, flew a large red flag that seemed to bear a white dove of peace. Winding around the crest just below the summit was a huge banner, about 10 feet high and 40 or 50 feet long, carrying the timely message, "Long live the peace."

There was activity everywhere. Hundreds of men were wandering all over. One big cluster sang more of the unfamiliar Chinese songs, led by college-type cheerleaders. Each wore new T-shirts in startling shades of red, blue, green, yellow and white. A scratchy old phonograph, which had previously entertained us by night from across the valley with My Old Kentucky Home, now presented beautiful but quite inappropriate classical music. The whole scene resembled a spectacular comic opera.

Fraternization had been specifically forbidden and a dangerous situation developed as the more adventurous got really curious, speculating on whether the Chinese might have pretty girls or beer.

About the same time, unexpected visitors began to arrive from the rear. Some were not aware of—or ignored—the orders to keep out of the valley and before long we had to control access to our position and block the paths to the valley. We became an unwilling tourist attraction to all manner of press and staff officers, along with the suddenly bold from the support units. There were too few of us to contain the stampede and some bypassed us.

Groups of very young, English-speaking Chinese soldiers dressed in immaculate uniforms ranged about the valley floor, giving out little plastic dove-of-peace badges and souvenir copies of quality glossy magazines with beautiful color pictures of life in the new China. The first day of peace proved more hectic than war.

Under the terms of the armistice we had 48 hours to vacate the forward lines and demilitarize the entire area. On the second day we started to fill up the trenches, pull out the steel stakes and demolish the bunkers, salvaging the timbers where possible. It was soon obvious we wouldn't get the tall order done on schedule. The exhausted troops became irritated because the Chinese, who were also busy demolishing their deeper defences, had sufficient manpower to post hundreds of soldiers on their hilltops to lounge around and watch our activities. However, we worked hard and at the agreed time moved back to new tented camps about four miles to the rear.

We didn't return home immediately, or for Christmas either. In fact, another Canadian battalion relieved us in April, 1954, as the armistice developed into a strange armed truce that hasn't really changed in 25 years.

The Korean experience was easily forgotten by most Canadian servicemen. Subsequent years have generated little further interest because little sense of accomplishment came from their military exploits. Few ever went back to assess the impact of the Canadian contribution on Korea's destiny.

My recent visit to Korea was a fascinating, enlightening experience: Our efforts were appreciated more than we realized. While all visitors are welcomed with a gracious, somewhat formal hospitality, Canadians seem singled out for preferential treatment. The place has changed considerably, but prominent among the new landmarks are imposing memorials to the individual United Nations contingents that fought alongside the Korean armies.

Great prosperity is everywhere and Seoul has become a sprawling modern city of more than six million people. The old haunts are hard to find: What used to be busy base camps, supply depots or rural rice paddies are now vast suburbs of fine homes, shopping centres and contemporary apartment complexes.

To the troops, Seoul was a deserted, bombed-out shell hardly worth visiting except for the primitive PX. It was eerie by night with hundreds of wretched little shelters lit by flickering oil lamps and visits by "bed-check Charlie" flying down from the north in his ancient airplane to alert the city's anti-aircraft defences.

Two aspects of life in Korea today strike a responsive chord with those who manned the battle lines during the 1950s.

Almost nothing has changed up by the 38th parallel, with a new generation of combat-ready Korean youth facing each other, like their fathers, across the ancient demilitarized zone. The Koreans have learned to live with it, but they are quick to alert visitors to the threat posed only 45 miles north of their capital. Somehow this continuing state of alert seems to have negated our efforts.

In strange contrast is the increasing talk of an early reunification of the two Koreas. Initial contacts have been made and cautious openings are appearing in the bamboo curtain. The old bonds of race and culture are strange and many would opt for a united Korea—to be achieved by Koreans, ideally without further war. Even the old soldier could concur if it eliminated the need for battle lines. However, most Koreans remain unconvinced. The conflicting ideologies and political systems, with their bitter harvest of diversity and civil war, have kept friends and relatives apart too long. Only blood relations remain in common between the north and south.

But our efforts had benefits: Next to the new Korean parliament buildings on the island of Yoi-do is a new, stadium-sized Christian church with 10,000 seats that are filled four or five times every Sunday morning.

The influence of a handful of earlier Canadian missionaries is evident, but this sight kindled a memory of 1951 when it was often necessary to halt our combat operations while hundreds of refugees from the north moved slowly through our battle positions to prepared camps in the south. We weren't aware of it, but many were Christian congregations migrating south in search of freedom of worship. My new glimpse of these people was a happy vision.

Yes, one could easily be disillusioned about the Korean conflict, but there are many worthwhile memories:

soldiering with the finest of comrades, balmy nights on leave in Japan, the forgotten words of Japanese once used so effectively and the personal friends left behind in the United Nations cemetery at Pusan.

And it has not been entirely in vain for those who considered it a grand crusade against aggression. No major war has broken out, nuclear weapons have remained inoperative and a new generation has grown to maturity in comparative peace. We like to think that our efforts helped make this possible, and that the armistice of 1953 is of some consequence in modern world history. ॐ

Capt. C.A.H. Kemsley of the Princess Patricia's Canadian Light Infantry informs his men of the truce signing in Korea. The men are occupying positions on top of the infamous Little Gibraltar where some of the heaviest action of the Korean War occurred.

PART IV

⤳

REMEMBERING

THE SURVIVORS GO BACK TO VIMY
Jane Dewar

All those damned graves. So many of them and I can't see the bloody sense of it. What was it for? I don't know.

"There were five different nationalities in that valley—dead—and we walked over them. We put lime on them, didn't we? We put lime on them."

"I couldn't make any sense out of anything."

"The glory to kill—it built up and it built up. When I saw that today it froze me."

"You know, before Kaiser Wilhelm declared that war, that ridge was just as beautiful—or maybe more so—than it is today. Why fertilize it with all those bodies?"

Struggling with the memories dredged up by an early April tour of memorials to the dead from the "war to end all wars" that climaxed in 60th anniversary ceremonies at Vimy Ridge, 29 survivors of the battle that became the symbol of Canada's true birth as a nation wondered again and again at the price that was paid.

"I don't want to think of the memories—they're all hard memories anyway. There are no pleasant ones."

"What a waste of energy...of manhood...of money. All for nothing."

But, in counterpoint to the terrible sense of what was lost and endured in those years in the lice-ridden, rat-infested, water-and-mud-filled trenches, was their recognition of the closeness they had developed with each other.

"When you spent three years in the trenches with those men you ended up loving them."

"You come out of it closer to them than your own family. You don't forget that in 10 minutes."

"There were certainly scalawags, but most of them were nice scalawags."

"No one felt the same way about their units in the second war. It was different. They didn't have the hardships that come from marching with a full pack—90 lbs., a rifle and a full water bottle—that's discipline."

And they understood that that closeness had changed their lives forever.

"I went into the city of Winnipeg and got my uniform off and they bought me a $36 suit and then I was away. It wasn't too bad until I got home then I missed all those boys."

"The old man said to me when are you going to settle down to farming. I said never. I'm going to go out on construction work because there's always a bunch around and that's what I stayed on all my life."

Bumping down narrow roads—some dating from Julius Caesar's time—built lower than ground level so marching troops could not be seen by the enemy, through clusters of soft pink, brown brick or pastel stucco shuttered houses with front doors opening right onto the road, brought back other memories and explanations.

"There's the Douai plain....Once we got over the ridge there was the Douai plain...."

"There's Mons—see where the two heaps of coal are... and there's Lens."

"There were three major engagements for the capture of Lens—Vimy Ridge, Arleux and Hill 70—and we never did get Lens. The idea was to encircle the hun...."

Moving from memorial to memorial through neat green fields and single lines of trees just coming into bud in the cool spring of northern France and Belgium, the bus passed cemetery after cemetery tucked into odd corners of the landscape. The simple crosses or headstones of the war graves were a stark contrast to the crowded, ornate, heavily statued regular burial grounds with their brightly colored wreaths of fresh flowers.

The Canadian memorials are all built on the same plan, each surrounded by dark green holly hedges and moss-covered trees. At each stop a simple ceremony with slight variations was performed.

The Royal Canadian Artillery Band from CFB Montreal played softly while the piper, sentries, wreath bearers and chaplains moved into position and the

Vimy survivors were seated. The bugler sounded Alert, the flag party moved onto the memorial base and the chaplains offered prayers. The Act of Remembrance was recited in French and in English. Silence followed the Last Post, the piper skirled his lament and Reveille was sounded. Wreaths were laid, the blessing was pronounced and the flag party moved off.

At Passchendaele, the Burgomaster in tricolor sash accepted a plaque.

At Tyne-Cot, a British military cemetery where the cross of sacrifice is built on one pillbox and the headstones surround others, the minister of veterans affairs bent down, scooped up a bit of earth and extracted several pieces of the shot that gravels the surrounding grounds.

"It was hard to see that pillbox and the graves all sitting right where my boys got killed. Just picture an officer on a white horse coming down that road, his whole battalion behind him. That's how they came after us and we were sitting on that hill. There were only 40 of us left out of about a thousand—and they were singing as they came, about a thousand of them. I think they thought they still had that ridge. They thought it couldn't be taken."

Waiting for the ceremony at Courcelette, France, to begin are *(from left)* seated front, Charles Lacroix, James Ellis, Joseph Vallee, Gordon Holder, Henry Royle, Brig.-Gen. James Melville, Frank Vandenbosch, Fred Claydon; seated in the second row, Lt.-Gen. E.L.M. Burns, John Stacey, Brig.-Gen. Milton Gregg; standing, J.Y. Lefebvre (Department of Veterans Affairs), John Hyde, Henry Hassall, Benjamin Howlett, Purcill Blain, Wilfred McPhee, J.U. Doucet (DVA), Gilford Holley, Walter Carver, Danny Lauzon (DVA), Joseph Berube, William Taylor, Murray Forman (DVA), Brig.-Gen. J.A. de Lalanne, Brig.-Gen. Pat Grieve. John Perry, Percy Hopkins, Albert Hensler, Charles Searle, Sidney Dix, Robert Dunsmore, William McMurray and Edward Forrest are not seen.

At the huge French memorial at Notre Dame de Lorette—high over the Zouave Valley—flags blew straight out in the chill winds as a flame was rekindled and a book presented to the French veterans with their tricolor arm bands. The French guard of honor, holding flags, lined the route as the bus pulled away, smiling and waving goodbye.

At Neuville-St. Vaast, down in the valley, the minister renamed the Grand Rue, Rue du Canada, after laying a wreath at their cenotaph. Then the townspeople and their visitors trooped into the town hall to drink champagne and nibble on ladyfingers. A 42-year-old French school teacher produced a Toronto newspaper, *The Sunday World*, dated March 11, 1917, that had been found with a cigarette package in caves near the town.

At Givenchy-en-Gohelle, Chemin des Canadiens was unveiled at the edge of town and La Marseillaise mixed with the Last Post, Reveille and O Valiant Hearts at the cenotaph in the square in front of the cream-shuttered, yellow town hall with red tile roof. The local populace rushed into the hall after the ceremony to help the officials in their sashes (this time with silver tassels) and the fire department resplendent in full uniform greet their guests with champagne and ladyfingers (for the second time that day).

"How else can these people express their gratitude. We tried to do our best in the trenches and they are trying to do their best for us."

And among the happy crew that boarded the bus later, one survivor, beret squashed straight on his head, face wreathed in a grin, cradled in his arms a paper bag that held a bottle of champagne and two boxes of the cookies.

"They're for my wife. I'm taking them home."

At Beaumont Hamel the caribou atop the rocky mound continued to point to the sky as the pipes whined and the wreaths were laid. Moved, but unable to find other words to express their feelings, it seemed every person there turned to the one next to him and said: "Impressive, isn't it, very impressive."

At Courcelette, the ceremony was repeated, but the bus drove slowly by Bourlon Wood, the Ulster Memorial and Thiepval Memorial to the Somme. The weather changed by the half-hour and the winds were cold for the survivors.

"Bloody country hasn't warmed up yet."

At Ypres after a vin d'honneur at the town hall and dinner, the Last Post was sounded by Belgian buglers at the Menin Gate as they do every evening at 8 o'clock. Police stop traffic for one minute.

The names of more than 55,000 Commonwealth dead (6,994 Canadian) are carved in the stone of this 17th-century gate.

The numbers piled up after a while and became more than one could really comprehend: at Tyne-Cot, 12,000 buried, 35,000 names of the missing on the wall; 20,000 known French buried at Notre Dame de Lorette, 22,000 unknown under the monument; 73,000 missing at Thiepval; on and on it went.

At the Vimy memorial, lambs grazed on the soft green grass covering the shell-pocked ground surrounding the entrances and exits of the now-preserved tunnels with their rusty relics. The day before the main ceremony a young Canadian guide took a group through the infamous Grange Tunnel, the longest of 11 built in the spring of 1917 for the attack on the ridge. Others wandered over the grounds.

"I'm trying to place the crater where I did duty. I can't place it. That's where I was so lousy I could crawl."

"There were no trees—nothing but mud. I've never been back in all those years."

"Sixty years makes a helluva difference, you know."

"I have a picture in my mind's eye of what it was then—and now to see the great change and absorb it."

The Saturday of the main ceremony was clear and cold; bright sunlight bathed the huge twin-pylonned memorial and sparkled off the instruments of the

French and Canadian bands. The mist rose from the plain below the ridge revealing small French villages nestled beside enormous heaps of coal. French veterans, each with a flag, lined the upper level of the monument base. The gold epaulettes, white puttees, black berets and khaki uniforms of a French unit led by officers in the traditional Kepi (French flat-topped hat with visor) contrasted with the Canadian green.

The prefect of Pas-de-Calais, almost seven feet tall, stepped elegantly from a black limousine in below-the-knee-length dark cape and joined the minister and the Canadian ambassador on the dais. The survivors were seated to one side.

The ceremony was an expanded version of the one held there annually on the Sunday preceding Nov. 11th and was carried off without a hitch. The survivors answered their roll call.

And there wasn't a dry eye on that field when those survivors (two on wooden legs and one on crutches) marched past the dais to the Col. Bogey march, 80 paces to the minute.

As the minister said:

"There are times, there are events, there are people in the life of every nation so splendid they illuminate the pages of its history and shed their light over all the generations that follow them."

And we were there, watching them. ॐ

HOW CAN YOU FORGET?
Kingsley Brown

November 11, Remembrance Day.

It's the day when we stand at attention and go through the formal ritual of "remembering them."

For those of us who knew them, some of it hardly seems necessary. How can you forget?

You can't forget a guy called MacLean, a fellow passenger on the boat in which you shipped overseas. He was an air force navigator. You didn't know too much about him, except that he was a married man with three small children and had volunteered for overseas service.

He seemed a smart, stoic young fellow, and you were quite surprised when you went below decks just as the ship was clearing Chebucto Head off Halifax and found him lying in his bunk, crying his eyes out.

You dried his eyes, straightened his tie and dragged him up to the bar, but you can never forget the way he had whispered that he was "sure he would never see them again."

You kept in touch with him in a careless sort of way when you got to England, and not long afterwards you had the news. He had done 10 or 12 "ops" over Germany and had disappeared one night in a burst of flak over the Ruhr.

Airmen prepare for a night mission in the Second World War.

Then there was Maxie McGowan, a pug-nosed professional boxer from Australia. We had taught him how to fly at a service training school in Western Canada.

Maxie broke every rule in the book. He was what you would call a "bad boy." He was late on parades, turned up for flying with a hangover (but was still the best formation flyer I ever knew!) and did several stretches in the "cooler" for going AWL on weekends.

When he shipped overseas they put him to work piloting a Stirling, our first four-engine bomber, and not a very good one. Maxie pushed his Stirling in to battle eight times and then never came back.

We can never forget his wicked grin and the way he always wiped his nose with his thumb.

Then there was Wilf Cameron, a happy bush pilot from Edmonton. Flying had been his whole life, but when he wasn't flying he was curled up somewhere with a book in hand.

Wilf had one ambition. He was an admirer of H.G. Wells, whose every book he had read. He yearned to meet the great author in person. Together we had planned to call on Mr. Wells during a weekend leave.

But Wilf was clobbered over Cologne in the first 1,000-bomber raid. He never did get to meet Mr. Wells.

Roger Bushell had studied law at the University of London, and became a pilot with the university's auxiliary fighter squadron of the RAF. He had fought with distinction in the Battle of Britain. After he was shot down and became a prisoner of war he swiftly moved in to the slot of Big X—our top escape organizer. He made several notable escape efforts himself, and masterminded the attempts of hundreds of others.

Roger had a sharp mind and a blue cold kind of courage. Eventually the Gestapo caught up with him. After burning him almost to death with a blowtorch in a fruitless attempt to make him talk, they shot him.

Then there were four or five nameless German boys. They were only teen-agers, high school students. Some fanatical Nazi gauleiter had put them in uniform and handed them rifles in the last awful days of the Battle of Berlin. They holed up in a clump of bushes a few hundred yards beyond the wire of our prison camp, and made a pitifully heroic stand against the endless stream of Russian tanks moving down the highway. They never had a chance. A few bursts of machine-gun fire and their little act was ended.

It was the end of April, and we could see the new grass springing up where their bodies lay. ⌒

An aircrew prepares to leave on a bombing over Berlin, May 1941.

Royal Canadian Air Force airmen examine their equipment, Second World War.

Aircrews are scrambled to their fighter aircraft in February 1941.

Trainees of the British Commonwealth Air Training Plan study a map before an exercise from RCAF Hagersville, Ontario, in May 1943.

BEYOND WORDS
James Hale

Driving across the fog-shrouded Lion's Gate Bridge to West Vancouver on Remembrance Day morning, I heard six high school radio debaters discuss the possibility of Canada ever having to fight another war. Their consensus that contemporary youth are too self-oriented to fight would have raised more than a few bitter-sweet smiles from the veterans of West Vancouver Branch.

Sprawled along the coast between the Pacific and the last mainland stretch of the Trans-Canada, West Vancouver is a small-town corner of the metropolis. Little shops line the main street, broken occasionally by compact shopping centres, and in keeping with this atmosphere the veterans' parade formed in the Safeway parking lot.

They began arriving singly on foot shortly before 10, warmly greeting those ahead of them, but soon tiny groups were filing down side streets to the plaza. There were handshakes, smiles and friendly jibes of "Closed the bar down last night, eh, Johnny" all around. Several proudly pinned on long bars of medals, and one 87-year-old WW I campaigner stood quietly embodying the term "ram rod straight."

The mid-morning sun had melted the last remnants of mist and the day was crisp and clear as the color party formed. From across the street the tentative first notes of the West Vancouver Boys and Girls Band brass section fluttered and fell. The band moved in front of the police barricade and came to a parade rest before the post office. Following commands learned by rote years ago, the legionnaires fell in behind and moved out.

Dogs and small children kept stride with the men down main street to the memorial park. Three hundred townsfolk crowded the front of the municipal library, waiting. The men moved into place smartly, many with proud eyes on loved ones in the crowd.

A rock cenotaph arched over the entrance to the park. The official party gathered under it to lead the men in worship. Somehow, in small groups, the remembrance ceremony becomes more meaningful. The nervous, faltering notes of a cadet's Last Post are more poignant, the children's hushed questions during the dead silence more real.

A shattering rifle salute echoed between the mountains and a ridge of concrete high rises, answered eerily by a bewildered child's cries. As the last of the shots sounded through the valley a lone girl began to pipe a Scottish lament, and Reveille broke the crowd's stark silence.

There is something beyond words in the faces of veterans as they watch wreaths placed to honor their comrades. In some you can trace the years and the memories—good and bad; in others the fear and pain of another era is all too clear. Others cannot be read at all. But one could not help but be moved by the pride and sorrow of these men. As they moved off in formation behind the band, the crowd broke into spontaneous applause. Not that type of applause that follows a performance, or a well-placed pause in a skilled politician's speech, but that type of applause that tightens your throat and averts your gaze. A young blond boy unselfconsciously saluted as the legionnaires passed.

Many in the audience paused after the ceremony to solemnly place their poppies on the grassy apron of the cenotaph. One man, too young to have fought but old enough to remember, placed the poppies of his many children one by one, pausing reverently after each as though reflecting on the spilled blood they represented.

Others stayed behind in the memorial library across the street to read the lists of those who left communities like this behind forever. Like many small Canadian towns, West Vancouver seemed to have given up far more than its share of young people.

The legionnaires, walking lighter now—some playfully razzing others who had fallen out of step—paraded back to the branch for their annual open house. Hot rum took the chill off the day and started the memories flowing.

West Vancouver Legion Branch officials conduct a Remembrance Day service in 1979.

As time passes I plunge deeper in to the mystery of war. Growing up in the sixties, I reflected the blind, youthful attitude that Remembrance Day and all other signs of war should be obliterated. As I met veterans, though, and began to think rather than react, I ceased my stereotyping and started to search for understanding. Perhaps it is most difficult for those who have never fought to comprehend how war for a young person could be both the best and worst time of their life.

For many, of course, particularly in the innocent early days of WW I, it was the first great life experience: "We'll go over and beat those Germans and be home for Christmas."

For others, it was a sense of duty: Not so much a conscious sense of patriotism (a term that has received much denigration), perhaps, but a feeling of common purpose with one's peers. The bonds of comradeship forged in war last forever. I still feel a touch of envy when I hear veterans speak of friendships struck in wartime that are solid through the years, and memories of fallen mates that remain fresh and alive.

The memories certainly seemed fresh for the 87-year-old veteran. He had proudly stated his intention to march to the cenotaph, sighed that there were few of his buddies remaining but declared that he was good for at least a few more ceremonies.

I stared hard after him, imagining him as a young man with hopes and goals, fighting in the deadly mud of France. It is far too easy to forget that our elders were once filled with dreams and the determination to live a good life, only to be thrust wholly into an uncompromising situation. No one wants to die, and very few want to kill. If the radio debaters could see the veterans reminisce with old friends or escape into song for a few brief moments by a piano with a glass of hot rum and the satisfaction that they faced a challenge and survived, they might not judge them harshly as a generation apart.

PHOTO CREDITS

Page i, Jack H. Smith, Library and Archives Canada—PA-166370

Page 2, Royal Canadian Air Force

Page 3, Library and Archives Canada

Page 15, Norflicks Productions

Page 21, Horace Brown, Library and Archives Canada—PA-107276

Page 25, Henry Edward Knobel, Library and Archives Canada—PA-000169

Page 29, National Film Board

Page 30, RCAF Photo

Page 31, Legion Magazine Archives

Page 32, Legion Magazine Archives

Page 33, Legion Magazine Archives

Page 42, Canadian Army Photo 1-282-6

Page 44, no photo credit

Page 46, Clifford M. Johnston, Library and Archives Canada—PA-056920

Page 48, Larouche

Page 50, Library and Archives Canada—PA-177242

Page 51, Legion Magazine Archives

Page 53, Library and Archives Canada, Clifford M. Johnston Collection—PA-056386

Page 58, Library and Archives Canada—PL-9838

Page 59, Library and Archives Canada—PL-42032

Page 60, National Defence Photo

Page 62 (bottom left), Legion Magazine Archives

Page 62 (top right), Library and Archives Canada—PA-204340

Page 62 (bottom right), Library and Archives Canada—PA-105302

Page 63 (top), National Defence

Page 63 (bottom right), Library and Archives Canada—PA-166878

Page 65, Library and Archives Canada—PA-133270

Page 67, Library and Archives Canada—N-502

Page 69, Library and Archives Canada—PA-176296

Page 70, Library and Archives Canada—N-336

Page 71, RCAF

Page 73, Library and Archives Canada—PA-803925

Page 74, Hart Massey, Library and Archives Canada—C-030795

Page 75 (bottom left), Legion Magazine Archives

Page 75 (top right), J. Rosettis, Calgary Herald

Page 76, A. Louis Jarche

Page 77, National Film Board

Page 78, no photo credit

Page 80, Associated Press

Page 81 (top), Agence L.A.P.I.

Page 81 (bottom left), Agence L.A.P.I.

Page 81 (bottom right), Agence L.A.P.I.

Page 82, Canadian Army Photo

Page 83, Hastings and St. Leonards Observer

Page 84, Legion Magazine Archives

Page 86, Library and Archives Canada—PA-128230

Page 87, Canadian Military Photo

Page 88, Stanley D. Wimble, Library and Archives Canada—PA-145679

Page 89, A. Louis Jarche

Page 90 (bottom left), A Louis Jarche

Page 90 (bottom right), A. Louis Jarche

Page 91, Library and Archives Canada—PA-108300

Page 92, no photo credit

Page 94, A. Louis Jarche

Page 95, Legion Magazine Archives

Page 96 (bottom left), Legion Magazine Archives

Page 96 (bottom right), Legion Magazine Archives

Page 97 (bottom left), A. Louis Jarche

Page 97 (bottom right), Agence L.A.P.I.

Page 98, Vancouver Public Archives, Photo 8516

Page 101, A Louis Jarche

Page 102, Flett's Studio, Moncton

Page 103, A. Louis Jarche

Page 105, Library and Archives Canada—C-049745

Page 106, Jack Hawes, Library and Archives Canada—PA-151738

Page 109, no photo credit

Page 110, Royal Canadian Navy

Page 112, Legion Magazine Archives

Page 117, Library and Archives Canada—C-014160

Page 119, Legion Magazine Archives

Page 123, Frederick G. Whitcombe, Library and Archives Canada—PA-174320

Page 125, Frank Royal, Library and Archives Canada—PA-166751

Page 127, Frederick G. Whitcombe, Library and Archives Canada—PA-163936

Page 128, Terry F. Rowe, Library and Archives Canada—PA-114040

Page 130 (bottom left), Jack H. Smith, Library and Archives Canada—PA-130217

Page 130 (bottom right), Frank Royal, Library and Archives Canada—PA-130249

Page 131, Jack H. Smith, Library and Archives Canada—PA-114509

Page 133, Frederick G. Whitcombe, Library and Archives Canada—PA-140560

Page 134, Library and Archives Canada—PA-129762

Page 137, Jack H. Smith, Library and Archives Canada—PA-129781

Page 138, Library and Archives Canada—PA-183278

Page 139 (bottom left), Terry F. Rowe, Library and Archives Canada—PA-114486

Page 139 (bottom right), W.H. Agnew, Library and Archives Canada—PA-151180

Page 140 (bottom left), Alex Stirton, Library and Archives Canada—PA-139891

Page 140 (top right), Alex Stirton, Library and Archives Canada—PA-144109

Page 140 (bottom right), C.E. Nye, Library and Archives Canada—PA-128986

Page 141, Library and Archives Canada—PA-174220

Page 142, Jack H. Smith, Library and Archives Canada—PA-166370

Page 145, Legion Magazine Archives

Page 149, DND, PL15382

Page 150, Library and Archives Canada—PA-065176

Page 152, Library and Archives Canada—PA-128144

Page 154, D.M. Smith, Library and Archives Canada—PA-125359

Page 159, Jennifer Morse

Page 161, Charles H. Richer, Library and Archives Canada—PA-169173

Page 167, Library and Archives Canada—C-014171

Page 168 (top), no photo credit

Page 168 (bottom right), Library and Archives Canada

Page 170, Legion Magazine Archives

Page 171, Legion Magazine Archives

Page 173, KY108669

Page 174, Canadian Army Photo

Page 175 (top), Canadian Army Photo

Page 175 (bottom right), Canadian Army Photo

Page 176, Canadian Army Photo

Page 177 (top), Canadian Army Photo

Page 177 (bottom left), Rapid Grip and Batten Limited, Montreal

Page 181, Paul Tomelin, Library and Archives Canada—PA-129739

Page 183, National Defence

Page 185, Bill Olson, Library and Archives Canada

Page 186, Bill Olson, Library and Archives Canada—PA-128877

Page 187, Sgt. Paul Tomelin, Library and Archives Canada—PA-128809

Page 189, National Defence Photo

Page 191, National Defence Photo

Page 195, Peter Magwood

Page 197, Library and Archives Canada—PL-7721

Page 198 (bottom left), British Air Ministry—CH.2672

Page 198 (bottom right), Library and Archives Canada—PL-41969

Page 199 (top), Library and Archives Canada—PL-3055

Page 199 (bottom), Library and Archives Canada—PL-16961

Page 201, Legion Magazine Archives